I HOPE YOU WILL ENJOY THE HISTORY OF JEWISH HEROES FROM PAPA DAVID

THE BIG BOOK OF JEWISH SPORTS HEROES

AN ILLUSTRATED COMPENDIUM OF SPORTS HISTORY AND THE 150 GREATEST JEWISH SPORTS STARS

by

Peter S. Horvitz

Picture Editor: Desiree Horvitz

SPECIALIST PRESS INTERNATIONAL

New York

THE BIG BOOK OF JEWISH SPORTS HEROES

For further information, contact:

S.P.I. Books
99 Spring Street, 3rd Floor
New York, NY 10012
Tel: (212) 431-5011
Fax: (212) 431-8646
E-mail: publicity@spibooks.com

10 9 8 7 6 5 4 3 2 1
First Edition
Library of Congress Cataloging-in-Publication Date available.
S.P.I. Books World Wide Web address: *www.spibooks.com*
ISBN: 1-56171-907-2

Photo Credits

Courtesy of The Topps Company, Inc.: p. 15, #8; p. 19, #15; p. 35, #46; p. 41, #58; p. 45, #66; p. 51, #77; p. 51, #78; p. 52, #79; p. 53, #81; p. 54, #84; p. 56, #87; p. 75, #126; p. 77, #129; p. 78, #131; p. 81, #138; p. 83, #142; p. 84, # 144; p. 86, #148; p. 100 (Lieberthal); p. 115 (Brown); p. 154 (Alexander); p. 165 (Friedman); p. 170 (Levy); p. 174 (Schneider); p. 177 (Zeidel); p. 230 (Rosenthal); p. 259 (Rosenberg); p. 276 (Rich); and p. 277 (Walk).

Courtesy of Fleer SkyBox: p. 18, #14; p. 19, #16; p. 21, #19; p. 23, #23; p. 32, #40; p. 37, #49; p. 38, # 51; p. 64, #104; p. 72, # 119; p. 79, #134; p. 82, # 140; p. 84 # 143; p. 85, # 145; p. 93 (Brown); p. 94 (Gilman); p. 117 (Larusso); p. 154 (Barton); p. 159 (Youngelman); p. 257 (Green); p. 266 (Reese); p. 269 (Schneider); and p. 271, (Mix).

Courtesy of Peter S. & Joachim Horvitz: p. 20, #18 and 111 (Berg).

Courtesy of Desiree Horvitz: p. 20, #17; p. 166 (Friedman); p. 167 (Friedman); p. 262 (Lieberthal); and p. 280 (Auerbach).

UPPER DECK and the Upper Deck Company, LLC. © 2004 The Upper Deck Company LLC. All rights reserved. Used with permission: p. 87, #149; p. 94 (Gilman); and p. 175 (Zeidel).

Donruss Playoff, LP: p. 87, #150; p. 93 (Melvin); and p. 141 (Fields).

Courtesy of the American Jewish Historical Society, Fleer/SkyBox, and Jewish Major Leaguers Inc.: p. 105 (Berkenstock); p. 106 (Pike); and p. 109 (Pike).

Courtesy of Harold "Bunny" Levitt: p. 131-133.

To the Memory of

David Berger, Zeev Friedman, Yossef Gutfreund, Elizer Halfin,
Yossef Romano, Amitzur Shapira, Kehat Shorr, Mark Slavin, Andre Spitzer,
Jacov Springer, and Moshe Weinberg, assassinated at Munich during the
Olympics of 1972.

Beyond the walls of the pale incarceration
I was driven by the wind
Over miles, of the dust and the heat, as they stretched of the land,
Among the clouds of the sun.

The town lay pale and distant as a light
One sees too far away,
And the wind blew hard out of the darkening sky
And set the sparks aflight.

And the night arose where the deep meets the edge of the slopes
And swept o'er the peaks of the waves
Across the wide valley where men fell down in their greaves
To the darkling walls of our hopes.

Seven days turned back along the way they had come
And at the last was the first.
Nothing at all of light was left in the blast,
The Universe was dumb.

I strained against sleep, but was chained to the edge of a star,
Useless I struggled to fly.
Ten times the thunder-claps broke at the edge of the sea
And reechoed the groans of Betar.

TABLE OF CONTENTS

PREFACE

In my previous book, *The Big Book of Jewish Baseball*, I explained my theory about who would be included as Jewish, someone with at least one Jewish parent or a convert, and my reasons for choosing that definition. In this book it will become clear that I have stretched my definition even further, including people with only a single Jewish grandparent. However, for anyone who may object to that definition, all entries have been clearly identified. Wherever in the text there is no further explanation, it is to be understood that the athlete in question has two Jewish parents.

My thanks for help in writing this book include the members of my own family. My daughter Desiree's help extended far beyond her work with the illustrations, which alone was a very arduous and complicated task. I particularly want to thank her for her help with the research in the sections on Larry Zeidel and Dara Torres. Similarly, my wife Michele helped me with the research on Georges Stern and Alex Bromberg. My son Joachim was too involved with other things to help much, but whenever an emergency arose, he was right there.

As with my previous book, my greatest debt is to the generosity and patience of David Spaner, who was always willing to share his research and his fund of ideas. His patience even extended to forgiving me for misspelling his name in my previous book. Let me also thank my other good Canadian friends Irwin Pinsky and Steve Berman.

My sincerest thanks to Harold "Bunny" Levitt for all of the help he gave me. The NBA Hall of Fame Library staff in Springfield, MA was most generous with their time and assistance. My hours spent in the Hall itself were also most fruitful. My research on the Sphas was also enriched with the help of the Philadelphia Jewish Archives Center.

Next, let me thank Shel Wallman, editor of *Jewish Sports Review*, the best and most dependable source of up-to-date information on the subject. The *Review* is a treasure trove of informantion and Shel has always been there to answer my e-mails.

My thanks to Katie Mullins-Hall for sharing her geneological research and family pictures. It was a great pleasure talking with her and discussing Rudolph Kalish. In regard to the same subject, the Cincinnati Public Library was most helpful. Also, my thanks go to the Bromberg and Zeidel families for their help. My thanks also goes to Howard Goldstein.

Since my earlier book serves as background for this book, I wish to thank once more everyone who was mentioned there, many of whom I was fortunate enough to reconnect with following the publication of that work.

My sincerest thanks are to Fleer Skybox International, the Topps Card Company, and the Upper Deck Company for allowing me to illustrate their cards. My thanks also go to Martin Abramowitz and the Jewish Historical Society for allowing me to use their recent series of Jewish Major Leaguers.

If I have forgotten to mention anyone, please accept my apologies. The opinions expressed in this book are strictly those of the author.

INTRODUCTION

In the days when the Maccabees dwelt in the ancient land of Judah, the gymnasiums and sporting events of the Greek invaders were considered heresy by the Jewish population. This was because the sports of the Greeks were viewed as a part of their pagan religion. Later, when the Romans had come to power, the conflicts of the gladiators were not only considered pagan rituals, but their lack of respect for the value of life was viewed by the Jews as an utter abomination.

Sports in the Middle Ages consisted of tournaments of the aristocracy, which precluded any Jewish involvement. So it was not really until the late eighteenth century that Jews had either the interest or opportunity to involve themselves in sporting competitions.

This work seeks to tell the story of nearly 225 years of sports and Jewish history between just two covers. To begin with, I have selected from among all the thousands of Jewish sports heroes, those who I consider to be the 150 greatest. For each of these I have given a brief summary of their achievements, provided portraits, and, wherever possible, reproduced their autographs.

I have been generous with lists. Here you will find lists of every Jewish player in each of the professional sports at their major league levels. Furthermore, you will find every Jewish winner of an Olympic medal, the greatest Jewish coaches and trainers, and the 100 Greatest Jewish Players of Games. But I have also found room for long discussions of individual players and teams. Sometimes the players listed are the same as those in the opening section of the 150 greatest, but often they are sports heroes whose achievements were of a different sort than would gain them entrance into a hall of fame, but achievements of the highest order, nevertheless.

Having covered all of the fields of sport, occasionally in a very selective way, the book concludes with a trivia section that serves as a summary, a review, and a supplement.

This book, like my first *The Big Book of Jewish Baseball*, has a structure. One could read each of these works from beginning to end without difficulty. But they were also designed as much for the casual browser as the careful reader. Just pick up this book and start anywhere and, if my design is successful, you have started the book in the place that's right for you. The index is there to lead you on, if you get lost, or are too busy to search through the pages for exactly what you want. But otherwise, it is for the wanderer through these pages that I have purposely designed it. Wherever you land, I hope you will find pleasure, knowledge and new paths for exploration.

THE 150 GREATEST JEWISH ATHLETES RATED ACCORDING TO THEIR ACHIEVEMENTS

[Except where noted, all of these athletes are sons and daughters of two Jewish parents.]

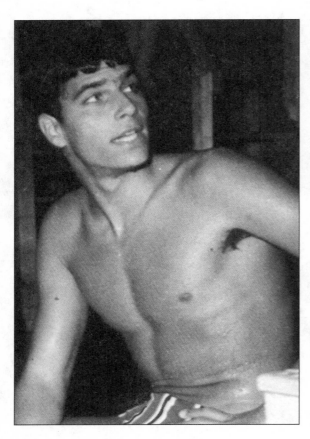

1. MARK SPITZ

(born 1950) Mark won 9 gold medals, 1 silver medal and 1 bronze medal in the 1968 and 1972 Olympics. He is one of the greatest swimmers of all time. He set 33 world records and won many other national and international titles and championships.

2. SANDY KOUFAX

(born 1935) Sandy was the most dominating and successful pitcher of early '60's baseball. He was a clutch pitcher, who was especially awesome in World Series play. Sandy's impressive life-time ERA of 2.76 is over-shadowed by his World Series ERA of .95. He is the youngest player ever elected to Baseball's Hall of Fame.

3. HENRY "HANK" GREENBERG

(1911-1986) In baseball, Hank was not only a great home run slugger, but a great run producer and outstanding defensive force. He was twice chosen as league's MVP. The original "Hammerin' Hank" was a self-made player who spent years perfecting and honing his baseball techniques. During his career he was a uniquely inspiring figure for America's Jews.

4. DANIEL MENDOZA

(1764-1836, England) Daniel was the first truly "scientific" boxer who used his skill to avoid the punches of his larger opponents and led them to tire themselves out. He was the first Jewish sports hero to win the respect of his fellow Jews and the citizens of the country where he lived. Daniel was the very first Jew to have an official audience with the British sovereign.

5. SID LUCKMAN

(1916-1998) Sid played on the Chicago Bears football team for 12 years (1939-1950) primarily as a quarter-back. He led his team to NFL championships in 1940, 1941, 1943, &1946. He was league's MVP in 1943, the same year he became the first NFL quarter back to throw 7 touchdown passes in one game.

6. AGNES KELETI (KLEIN)

(born 1921) Hungarian gymnast Agnes Keleti, despite the disadvantage of the cancellation of the 1940 Olympics, won more medals and has achieved greater success in the Olympics than any other Jewish woman. She won 10 Olympic medals during 3 Olympiads, including 5 gold. She also won, between 1947 and 1956, the All-Around Hungarian Gymnastics Championship ten times.

7. PETE SAMPRAS

[Jewish Paternal Grandmother] (born 1971) Over his remarkable tennis career Pete's record in singles competition is 762- 222. Pete won 64 singles titles and 2 double titles. The singles victories include 5 in the U.S. Open and 8 at Wimbledon. From 1988, when he turned pro, until his retirement in 2003, Pete earned $43,280,489 in prize money. He is universally recognized as one of the greatest tennis players of all time, being the all-time leader in Grand Slam titles, with 14.

8. ADOLPH "DOLPH" SCHAYES

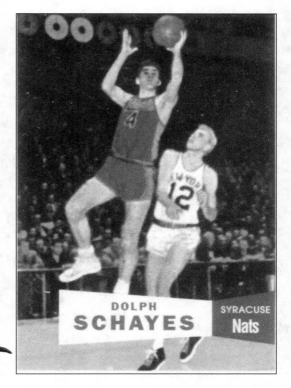

(born 1928) Dolph Schayes is one of the greatest figures in professional basketball during the period 1949-1964. At one time Dolph held the NBA regular season records for most games played, consecutive games played, most minutes played, most field goals made, most rebounds, and most points scored. During his years with Syracuse, Dolph was practically a one-man team. He even helped bring the NBA championship to the Nationals in 1955. Dolph was an NBA All-Star 12 years in a row, 1951-1962. Dolph didn't actually retire from playing, but segued himself into the job of coach. He was equally spectacular as a coach in the following years. Dolph's son, Danny, was the latest Jewish player to play in the NBA.

DOLPH SCHAYES   SYRACUSE Nats

Benny Leonard

9. BENNY LEONARD

(1896-1947) Benny, born Benjamin Leiner, was boxing's lightweight champion of the world from 1917 to 1925. He is often considered the greatest of Jewish boxers, as well as the greatest lightweight of all time. Benny often ended his fights as he began, with every hair in place. Benny never fought on a Jewish holiday. Of his 210 fights, he only lost 5.

10. NAT HOLMAN

(1896-1995) Nat, known as "Mr. Basketball," was a member of the original Celtics of New York, one of the greatest teams of all time, from 1920 to 1928. Nat helped the team to capture the national championship in 1927. He also had a great 41-year career as a coach at CCNY.

11. BARNEY ROSS

(1909-1967) Barney, born Beryl Rossofsky, held at one time three world boxing titles: lightweight champion and junior welter-weight champion from 1933 to 1935 and welterweight champion from 1934 to 1938. After hundreds of amateur matches, Barney won the Golden Gloves featherweight title in 1929, before turning pro. After his fighting career he joined the Marines. He was a hero at Guadalcanal, during WWII, but the injuries he suffered and careless medical treatment made him dependent on addictive drugs. He eventually overcame his problem and became a spokesman on drug addiction.

Barney Ross

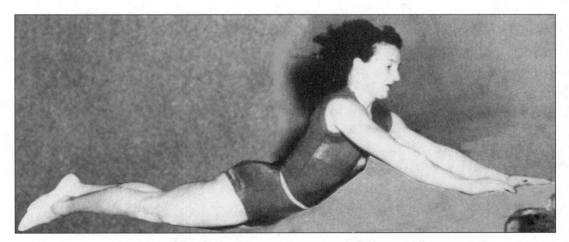

12. MARIA GOROKHOVSKAYA

(born 1921) A Russian Gymnast, Maria, won 7 medals at the 1952 Olympic Games held in Helsinki, including 2 gold and 5 silver. She was the top performer of the entire Olympiad, including both men and women. Maria emigrated to Israel in 1990 and only then was it learned that she was Jewish.

13. ABE ATTELL

(1884-1969) Abe, often referred to as "the Little Champ" or "the Little Hebrew," reigned as featherweight champion of the world from 1901 to 1912. Tex Rickard, the greatest fight promoter of all time said of him, "The greatest fighter of any weight and of any class… He had remarkable stamina and courage, hands and legs that moved so fast they were impossible to follow, and flawless coordination. But even more important was his uncanny shrewdness and ability to actually know what his opponent was thinking." It is a shame that the reputation of 168 hard fought matches should have been tarnished by his reputation as a gambler and his involvement in the Black Sox scandal.

14. LOU BOUDREAU

[Jewish Mother] (1917-2001) One of the finest short stops and one of the finest managers in the history of baseball. He played most of his career with the Cleveland Indians, but he also had a stint with the Boston Red Sox. He is given much of the credit for the Indians' 1948 World Series victory. He is also famous for popularizing the "Ted Williams shift."

LOU BOUDREAU
SHORTSTOP-CLEVELAND INDIANS

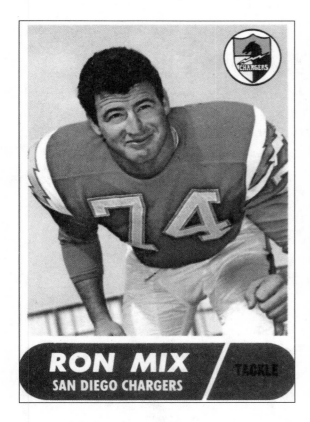

RON MIX
SAN DIEGO CHARGERS / TACKLE

15. RON MIX

(born 1938) Ron, known to the opposition as "the Intellectual Assassin," was one of football's most successful offensive tackles. His rare combination of good sportsmanship and fine tuned technique helped the 1963 San Diego Chargers to the AFL title. He was chosen AFL All-Pro every year from 1960-1968 except 1965.

16. AL ROSEN

(born 1925) Baseball's American League MVP for 1953 was elected unanimously, the first person ever so honored. All-Star 1952-1955. Al led the AL in RBI's in 1952 &1953; HR's in 1953. He was also an outstanding defensive player and had a fine career as a baseball executive. Al was noted during his playing years for his pride in his religion and his no nonsense attitude towards anti-Semitism.

HOME RUN CHAMPION

AL ROSEN

17. BENNY FRIEDMAN

(1905-1982) Benny was one of Football's greatest stars and the NFL's first great passing quarterback. He remains a legend at the University of Michigan and his NFL career over 8 years was 76 wins and 31 losses.

18. LIPMAN PIKE

(1845-1893) Lip was the first Jewish professional baseball player. He was also baseball's first important home run slugger, holding the one-year record for the National Association, baseball's first Major League. Lip's lifetime batting average was .321.

19. SHAWN GREEN

(born 1972) One of the finest baseball players of recent years. Shawn's new records of 7 home-runs in 3 days and 9 home runs in a week during late May of 2002 was just one of his amazing achievements. He is already recognized as one of the greatest Jewish batters of all time.

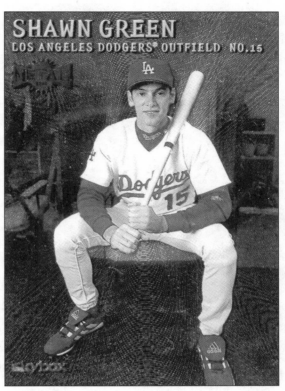

20. MAX BAER

[Jewish Paternal Grandfather] (1909-1959) Max, who boxed with a Star of David on his trunks, was the only heavyweight champion of the world in modern times of Jewish heritage. He maintained his title only from 1934 to 1935, but his fights against Primo Carnera, Braddock, and Joe Louis are considered classics of the ring. Max is remembered for his good-humored manner in the ring, almost as much as for his skill. After his retirement from boxing, he became an actor.

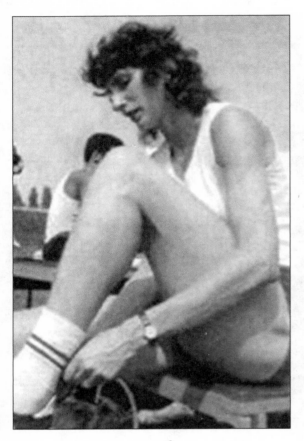

21. IRENA KIRSZENSTEIN-SZEWINSKA

(born 1946) Polish runner Irena Kirszenstein (the second family name added after her marriage) won medals in 4 consecutive Olympic Games from 1964 to 1976. No other runner has ever accomplished this, either male or female. Altogether, Irena won 3 gold, 2 silver, and 2 bronze Olympic medals. She was selected as Poland's Athlete of the Year for 1965 and Tass's 1965 Outstanding Woman Athlete in the World. She won 5 European gold medal championships, as well as 5 other European medals. From 1973 to 1975, she won 38 consecutive 200-meters titles; from 1973 to 1978, she won 36 consecutive 400-meters titles. (These streaks are the longest in these events in sport's history.)

22. BARNEY PELTY

(1880-1939) "The Yiddish Curver" was one of the finest control pitchers of all time. His lifetime ERA of 2.63 speaks for itself. Sadly, he spent the majority of his career with the luckless St. Louis Browns who could not provide even the modicum of offense needed to win games.

PELTY-ST.LOUIS-AMER.

23. DARA TORRES

[Jewish Father] (born 1967) Swimmer Dara won 9 Olympic medals in 4 different Olympics. Her 2 gold medals in the 2000 Olympics in Sydney, at age 33, made her the oldest woman ever to win a gold medal in swimming. Even though she was raised as a Jew, Dara, upon her marriage to an Israeli, went through the Jewish conversion ceremony.

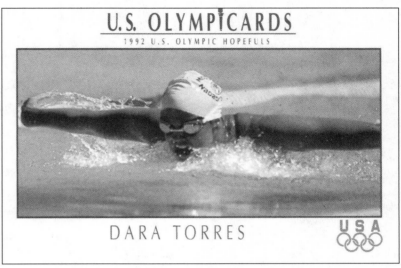

24. WALTER MILLER

(1890-1959) One of horse racing's greatest jockeys, Walter excelled for just a brief period, but during that time he was spectacular. Between 1905 and 1908 he rode in 4336 races and won 1094 of them, a 25% winning ratio. He was the National Riding Champion in both 1906 and 1907. His record of 388 victories in a season (1906) was not equaled until 1950 when bested by Willie Shoemaker.

25. JOE CHOYNSKI

(1886-1943) Joe was the earliest of the great Jewish-American boxers. During his career he fought many future world champions, all far heavier than himself. In every case he presented to his opponent one of the most difficult challenges of his career. After defeating the future champ Jack Johnson (the first African-American champ), Joe generously taught Jack the fine points of boxing. No non-champion has ever had the same impact on the sport or the public as Joe Choynski.

26. BARNEY SEDRAN

(1891-1969) Barney, half of the "Heavenly Twins," was one of the pioneers of professional basketball. At only 5'4", he proved that basketball was a game of intelligence and skill, not just height and brute force. Before his retirement from playing in 1926, he was the shortest yet highest paid player in professional basketball. Had a great second career as a basketball coach.

27. MAURI ROSE

(1906-1981) Automobile racer Mauri was three-time winner of the Indianapolis 500: 1941, 1947, and 1948. He participated in a total of 15 of the Memorial Day races. He also won the National Driving Championship in 1936.

28. MARTY FRIEDMAN

(1889-1986) Marty was a pioneer of early professional basketball, along with Barney Sedran they were known as the "Heavenly Twins." Their 1914 Utica, NY team won the world championship. During and just after WWI, Marty had a very important part in introducing basketball to Europe. He was captain of the Cleveland Rosenblums from 1925 to 1927. He later had a career in coaching.

29. "BATTLING" LEVINSKY

(1891-1949) Born Beryl Lebrowitz, "Battling" was boxing's light heavyweight champion of the world from 1916 to 1920. Known as an outstanding defensive boxer, he fought a great number of matches during his career. In one case, he fought three matches in a single day.

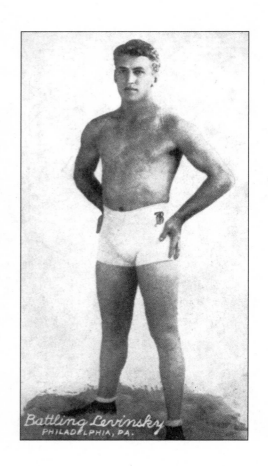

Battling Levinsky
PHILADELPHIA, PA.

30. FANNY "BOBBIE" ROSENFELD

(1903-1969) Gold medallist at the 1928 Olympics as part of Canada's 400-meter relay team that set a new world record, Fanny also took a silver medal in the 100 meter sprint. But Bobbie, as she was known for her bobbed hair, was also outstanding in basketball, softball, bowling, tennis, and ice hockey. She was a member of championship teams or held championships for all of these. She was also an outstanding coach and sports commentator in the Canadian press. In 1950, she was selected as Canada's Female Athlete of the Half-Century.

Bobbie Rosenfeld

L·E·MYERS
RUNNER
880 YDS, I MIN: 55 4/5 SEC·

31. LAURENCE "LON" E. MYERS

(1858-1899) The greatest runner of the nineteenth century, Lon, at one time held every American title between 50 yards and 1 mile. He won 15 US titles, 10 Canadian, and 3 British. Lon's popularity brought a higher level of interest to track events than had ever been shown before both in the U. S. and abroad. Lon's comparatively brief career can be seen as a major step towards the revival of the Olympic Games.

32. LILLIAN COPELAND

(1905-1964) Lillian, American Track and Field great achieved her greatest success in shot put and discus. In 1925, Lillian took her first of nine U.S. National Championships in 8 pound shot put. Between 1925 and 1932 she set 6 world records, each, in shot put, javelin, and discus. She won a silver medal in the 1928 Olympics in discus and a gold in the same event in 1932. She refused to participate in the 1936 Olympics as a protest against Hitler. She did participate in the 1935 Maccabiah Games, where she won three gold medals.

"Buddy" Myer

33. BUDDY MYER

[Jewish Father] (1904-1974) Baseball great Charles "Buddy" was an excellent second baseman for his defensive work and a great batter. In 1935 he won the American League batting title with .349 average. His team, the Washington Senators, won the pennant in 1933, largely due to Buddy's efforts. Buddy's lifetime batting average was .303 in a Major League career of 17 years, the longest for a Jewish ballplayer.

34. GEORGES STERN

(1882-1928) Georges was one of France's greatest contributions to horse racing and was known in his day as the "King of the Jockeys" and the "King of the Derbies." Georges rode from 1899 to 1926 and had thousands of victories all over Europe and Britain. In 1908, he won three derbies, the French, the Austrian, and the German. In 1911 he won at Epsom and he won the Grand Prix de Paris three times (1904, 1913, & 1914). He won the French Derby 6 times between 1901 and 1922.

35. ILONA SCHACHERER-ELEK

[Jewish Father] (1907-1988) Hungarian fencer Ilona is considered the greatest woman fencer of all time. She won Olympic gold medals in individual foils in 1936 and 1948. She barely missed a third gold medal in 1952, when she did take the silver. She was the women's world foil champion in 1934, 1935, and 1951.

36. LYLE ALZADO

[Jewish Mother] (1939-1992) Lyle was awesome in the exact sense of that word as an NFL defensive lineman, both when he was playing end and tackle. He inspired fear in the opposition in the most brutal of sports. The highlight of his career was probably SuperBowl 18, when Lyle and Al Davis's Los Angeles Raiders won it all. Near the end of his life, Lyle admitted to taking steroids throughout his career. "I started taking anabolic steroids in 1969 and never stopped. It was addicting, mentally addicting. Now I'm sick, and I'm scared. Ninety per cent of the athletes I know are on the stuff. We're not born to be 300 pounds or jump 30 feet. But all the time I was taking steroids, I knew they were making me play better. I became very violent on the field and off it. I did things only crazy people do. Now look at me. My hair's gone, I wobble when I walk and have to hold on to someone for support, and I have trouble remembering things. My last wish? That no one else ever dies this way." Lyle died at the age of 42 from brain cancer brought on by the use of steroids.

37. LENNY KRAYZELBURG

(born 1975) Lenny, who was born in Ukraine but settled along with his parents in the United States, is a swimming champion of the backstroke. In 1999, he set new world records in the 50-meter, 100-meter, and the 200-meter. During the Sydney Olympics of 2000, Lenny won gold medals in both the 100-meter and the 200-meter men's backstroke.

38. MYER PRINSTEIN

(1880-1928) An Olympic jumper, Myer was born in Russia, but represented his adopted home, the United States. Myer first participated in the 1900 Paris Olympics, where he won a gold medal in the triple jump and silver in the long jump. In the 1904 Olympics, Myer took gold in both of these events. He again won gold in the long jump in the unofficial Athens Olympics of 1906.

39. PETER REVSON

[Jewish Father] (1939-1974) Peter, heir to the Revlon Cosmetics fortune, dedicated his life to racing cars. After some success with Formula Three and Two (including a victory at Monaco) Peter was given the opportunity to race Formula One. On July 14, 1973 he won the Grand Prix of Great Britain. He followed this on September 23, 1973 with the Grand Prix of Canada. He was killed on March 22, 1974, while testing a car in South Africa.

40. NANCY LIEBERMAN CLINE

(born 1958) Nancy was one of the greatest women basketball players of all time. She played in the 1976 Olympics and became the youngest person to win an Olympic medal in basketball. She played for two national collegiate championship teams at Old Dominion. Twice she was named National Player of the Year. Nancy was even the first woman to play in a man's professional league, the USBL 1986-87. She was also the first woman to play for the Washington Generals, the team that constantly plays against the Harlem Globetrotters, as part of the Globetrotters 1988 World Tour. She came out of retirement to play in the WNBA for the inaugural year of that league, 1997. Since then she has served as general manager and head coach in that league.

41. MARK ROTH

(born 1951) One of the greatest bowlers of all time, Mark won 33 National Tour titles. During National tours, Mark bowled 23 perfect (300) games. His highest personal tour average was 221.66 in 1979. Mark shared double titles in 1977, 1984, and 1987 with fellow Jewish bowling great Marshall Holman. Mark was chosen PBA Player of the Year by Sporting News in 1977, 1979, and 1984.

42. "SLAPSIE" MAXIE ROSENBLOOM

(1904-1976) Slapsie's 289 bouts (210 victories, 35 losses) tell the story of this really tough light heavyweight. His later reputation as a comic actor belies his real abilities. After all, he was Light-heavyweight champion of the world from 1930-1934. His nickname did not come about because he was "slap-happy," but because of his slapping style of punching that would wear down his opponents.

Max Rosenbloom

43. SYDNEY FRANKLIN

(1903-1976) Not only the most successful Jewish bullfighter of all time, but the most successful bullfighter from the United States. Sydney first saw action in Mexico, but he soon established an outstanding reputation in Spain. Sidney, who was born Sidney Frumkin, displayed his skill during the 1939 World's Fair in New York in bloodless exhibitions. He continued to fight off and on until 1959, when he suffered a serious injury and retired from the ring.

44. BORIS BECKER

[Jewish Mother*] (born 1967) *(Becker's statement on this subject is somewhat confusing and it may be that his mother was not fully Jewish, herself, but only partly Jewish.) German tennis player Boris caught the world's attention by winning the Wimbledon singles title at age 17 in 1985. This was the youngest age ever for a male to win this title. He went on to win at Wimbledon again in 1986 and 1989 and making the final 4 every year between 1988 and 1991. Boris also won the U.S. Open in 1989 and the Australian Open in 1991. Boris had 49 tournament wins, the 7th all-time, as of 1998, and had won more than 24 million dollars.

45. RICHARD "DICK" SAVITT

(born 1927) Dick was the first Jewish tennis player to win a title at Wimbledon. In the same year, 1951, Dick also won the Australian title. His aggressive style and powerful serves left his opponents in awe. The next year, 1952 saw Dick win the U.S. Indoor Singles title. But then, in October of the same year, Dick announced his retirement to give his time over to business, his potential in tennis never fully explored.

46. SID GORDON

(1918-1975) An outstanding baseball player who, even though he lost 2 years of playing time during WWII, Sid had a 13 year Major League career, with a .283 BA. In 1949 he hit 2 home runs in he same inning (tying a ML record). In 1950 he hit 4 Grand Slams in one season, again tying a ML record. Sid died of a heart attack, after collapsing while playing a softball game in New York's Central Park.

47. HELENE MAYER

[Jewish Father] (1911-1953) Helene, a fencer, is best remembered as the only "Jew" to represent Germany in the 1936 "Hitler" Olympics. She won the silver medal in individual foils, loosing the gold to Ilona Schacherer-Elek. In the 1928 Olympics, Helene had won the gold medal in individual foils.

48. GEORGE COHEN

(born 1939) English soccer hero, George Cohen played his entire professional soccer career with Fulham FC—something almost unheard of in modern English football. George started with Fulham in 1956, when he was just 17, and retired in 1967, after a knee injury. During his time at Fulham, George was chosen as the team's captain. George was a member of England's 1966 World Cup team, which won the Cup in the final match against West Germany. This was the only time that England ever won the World Cup. For his contributions to the 1966 team, George was made an M.B.E. (Member of the British Empire) George's nephew Ben Cohen is a well-known rugby player.

49. RUDY LaRUSSO

[Jewish Mother] (born 1937) Rudy was an outstanding basketball player at Dartmouth, setting many records for his university and for the Ivy League. His rebound records at Dartmouth still stand. Rudy then spent 10 years in the NBA, first with the Lakers of Minneapolis and Los Angeles and then the San Francisco Warriors. From 1962 to 1966, Rudy and the Lakers went on to the NBA finals, each time being defeated by Red Auerbach's Boston Celtics. In the last game of the 1961-62 season, Rudy scored 50 points. In 1962, 1963, 1966, and 1969, Rudy was an NBA All-Star.

50. DR. JENO FUCHS

(1892-1954) Outstanding Hungarian fencer and winner of 4 Olympic Gold Medals. The official record of the 1912 Olympics said of him, "Although of slight build and rather low stature, he succeeded by means of well calculated sabre play, in repelling the attacks of and defeating the most powerfully built and vigorous opponents....Nothing was left to chance; determination and strength were not spared."

51. MIKE LIEBERTHAL

[Jewish Father] (born 1972) Mike was the third player picked overall in the 1990 Major League Baseball draft. He is the star catcher for the Philadelphia Phillies. He made his major league debut in 1994 and has been the Phillies first string catcher since 1997. During the 2003 season, Mike led his team in batting average for the entire year and served as a leader in the clubhouse and on the field.

52. WILLIE HARMATZ

(born 1931) Willie raced horses to victory in thousands of meets during some twenty years. In his very first year, 1953, he rode 169 winners. Willie won the Preakness in 1959. During 1954, he tied a 47-year-old record by riding six straight winners at the same meet.

53. LOUIS RUBENSTEIN

(1861-1931) Early world-champion figure skater (1890) from Canada and father of figure skating in North America. The 1890 championship was held in Russia and Louis won in the face of massive anti-Semitic feeling and despite being denied the prize when the results were first announced. Louis did much to spread the popularity of figure skating in the Western Hemisphere.

54. MATHIEU SCHNEIDER

(born 1969) Matt started his career with the National Hockey League as a defenseman in 1987 with the Montreal Canadiens. He has since played with the New York Islanders, Toronto Maple Leafs, New York Rangers, Los Angeles Kings, and Detroit Red Wings. Playing in 992 games, with 168 goals, he has played more and scored more than any other Jewish player in the NHL. He has also played in 86 postseason games, with 6 goals scored. He was chosen an NHL All-Star in 1996. Matt is considered particularly effective in the power play.

55. TAL BRODY

(born 1943) American born basketball player Tal became probably the greatest athlete to ever represent the State of Israel. Tal first came to Israeli attention when the American basketball team he led won the gold medal at the 1965 Maccabiah Games. By that time Tal had already established his reputation as an outstanding guard during his years playing at the University of Illinois. Tal captained and led Maccabi Tel Aviv to the 1977 European Champions' Cup, first defeating CSKA Moscow, the Russian Army team that had taken the 4 previous championships, and then Mobilgirgi of Varese, the Italian champion team, by a single point, 78 to 77.

Tom Okker with doubles partner Arthur Ashe.

56. TOM OKKER

[Jewish Father] (born 1944) Dutch tennis player Tom competed professionally between 1968 and 1981. During that time his win-loss record was 200-112. Tom won the singles title at Wimbledon in 1981; at Roland Garros in 1978; at the Australian Open in 1969; and the U.S. Open in 1969, 1978, 1979, and 1980. Tom holds the all-time doubles record with 78 wins. He also won singles titles in 1975 in Nottingham and 1979 in Tel Aviv. Tom continues to play on the senior's tour.

57. ENDRE KABOS

(1906-1944) Endre was another of the great Jewish-Hungarian fencers. He won 3 Olympic Gold Medals and 1 Bronze. He was also Individual Saber Champion of the World in 1933, 1934, and 1936. Endre died a victim of the Holocaust.

KEN HOLTZMAN

58. KEN HOLTZMAN

(born 1945) An outstanding left-handed pitcher who in his first season defeated Sandy Koufax in a 2-hitter. During 1972-1974, Ken was a key component in the Oakland A's three-peat World Series winning team.

59. WALTER BLUM

(born 1934) Walter was one of the outstanding jockeys of his day. He won 4,382 races, in a career that lasted from 1953 to 1975. Just 5'3" tall, Walter was national riding champion in 1963 & 1964. He was the recipient of the Woolf Award in 1965 and in 1987 he was elected to the National Racing Hall of Fame.

KID LEWIS.

60. TED "KID" LEWIS

(1894-1970) The Kid, an English boxer born Gershon Mendeloff, was welterweight champion of the world 1915-1916 and 1917-1919. He was also European middleweight champion 1921-1923; European welterweight champion 1920-1924; European featherweight champion 1913; British Empire middleweight champion 1922-1923; British Empire welterweight champion 1920-1924; British middleweight champion 1920-1923; British welterweight champion 1920-1924; and British featherweight champion 1913. Ted was known for his calm demeanor in the ring, which was matched with a killer instinct and an ability to bear pain that was phenomenal. From this and his birthplace in London he was known as the "Aldgate Sphinx."

61. IRVING JAFFEE

(1906-1981) Irving was one of America's greatest speed skating champions. He was denied an Olympic gold medal in 1928, at St. Moritz, even though his 10,000-meters race was the fastest, because of a sudden warming that ended the races early. But in 1930, Irving was back to the Winter Olympics, this time in Lake Placid, NY, and won gold medals in both the 5,000 and 10,000-meters races. In 1934, Irving set a new world record for the 25-mile ice skating marathon of 1 hour, 26 minutes, and one-tenth of a second. This replaced an old record that had stood for 30 years. Irving was responsible for training many younger skaters, including future Olympians.

62. ATTILA PETSCHAUER

(1904-1944) Like Endre Kabos, Attila died during the Holocaust. During his career, Attila won 2 Olympic Gold Medals and 1 silver medal. He also won the title of Hungary's Best Fencer. Attila was famous for his aggressive style of fencing, just as Fuch's was known for his great defense. Kabos showed more balance in his style.

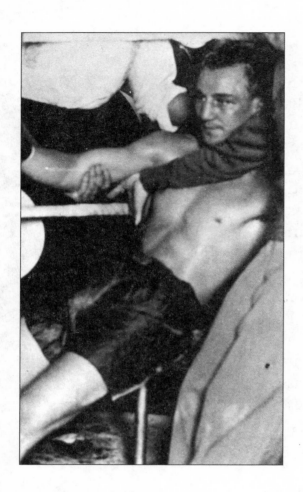

63. JACKIE FIELDS

(1907-1987) Boxer Jackie Fields, born Jacob Finkelstein, first caught the world's attention at the 1924 Olympics where he won the Gold Medal in the featherweight class when only 16 years old. He won this medal with the defeat of fellow American, Joe Salas. Fields and Salas would be matched again on two occasions. Jackie would win all of these fights. As he grew older he increased in weight and it was as a welterweight that he made his mark as a professional. He was welter-weight champion of the world 1929-1930 and 1932-1933.

64. KENNY BERNSTEIN

(born 1944) Kenny's interest in drag racing, driving at remarkable speeds over a short course, has seen him do the mile in 4.477 seconds, the quickest run in the history of the sport, and set the speed record of 332.18 miles per hour. Kenny has earned six NHRA World Championships. He is the first and only driver to win championships in both divisions of the sport, Funny Car (1985-1988) and Top Fuel (1996 and 2001).

65. ALFRED HAJOS-GUTTMAN

(1878-1955) Alfred was at the same time the first Jew, the first Hungarian, and the first swimmer to win an Olympic gold medal. He had been born simply Alfred Guttman, but he added the Hajos to his name, originally for sporting purposes, but eventually adopting it legally. His swimming notoriety dates back to 1885 and 1886 when he became the 100-meter European Swimming Champion. In the first modern Olympics of 1896 he won gold medals in the 100-meter freestyle and the 1200-meter freestyle. At a dinner given to honor the medalists, the king of Greece asked Alfred where he had learned to swim so well. Alfred replied, "In the water." In 1898, Alfred displayed his flexibility by becoming the 100-meter sprint champion of Hungary. In the same competition he also won the 400-meter hurdles and the discus titles. He later became an architect, specializing in sports facilities.

Among his other work, he designed the Hungarian Sports Swimming Pool in Budapest. At the 1924 Olympics, he was awarded a silver medal in architecture, the highest medal that was awarded for that competition. In 1953, he was awarded the Olympian Diploma of Merit. Alfred's younger brother, Henrik Hajos-Guttman, won a gold medal in the 1906 Olympic games as a member of the 1000-meter relay team.

66. JAY FIEDLER

(born 1971) Jay began his football career in 1994 with the Philadelphia Eagles. But it was not until 2000 and his joining the Miami Dolphins that he began to shine. In 2000, Jay led his team to the AFC east title. Jay became only the 2nd Dolphins quarterback, in 2001, to throw 3,000 yards in a season, after Dan Marino. Jay suffered some injuries that limited his production in 2002.

Jay Fiedler
 # 11

67. HARRY DANNING

(1911-2004) Baseball's Harry "The Horse" was an outstanding catcher and a major offensive force for the New York Giants from 1933 to 1942. Harry's .288 BA was a major factor in the Giant's 1937 NL Pennant. But in 1938 he hit .306; in 1939, .313; and in 1940, .300. Harry was an All-Star from 1938-1941. On June 15, 1940, he hit for "the cycle." His lifetime fielding average of .985 as a catcher is indicative of his defensive excellence.

Harry "The Horse" Danning

68. LEW TENDLER

(1898-1970) While Philadelphia-born boxer Lew never won a world championship, he is considered one of the greatest left-handed battlers of all time. It was Lew's misfortune to compete at the exact same time as the lightweight champion Benny Leonard and the welterweight champion Mickey Walker. Lew's 2 bouts with Benny in 1922 and 1923 are considered among the greatest boxing duels of all time. The first ended in a draw; the second in a decision for Benny, who retained his crown. When Lew grew into the welterweight category, he fought Mickey Walker in 1924. Mickey just managed to retain his title by a close decision in a very hard-fought battle.

Lew Tendler

69. PHIL KING

(1872-1938) Phil was the first Jewish college football player to be named as an All-American, which he was in 1891, 1892, and 1893. Sometimes as quarterback, sometimes as halfback, and sometimes as team captain, he turned Princeton during those years into the finest team in the nation. King was also outstanding as second baseman on Princeton's baseball team.

70. GOODY ROSEN

(1912-1994) A member of Canada's Baseball Hall of Fame, Goody spent only 6 years in the Majors due to the enmity of manager Leo Durocher. His lifetime BA was .291. Goody, born Goodwin George Rosen, was also an outstanding defensive player. On two occasions he ran into walls when going after fly balls. Both of these led to serious injuries that cost Goody precious playing time.

71. CHARLIE "PHIL" ROSENBERG

(1902-1975) Charlie Phil was boxing's batamweight champion of the world from 1925-1927. He had been born Charles Green but became Phil Rosenberg when a friend of his of that name, who had a boxing license, was too ill to fight a scheduled match and Charles fought for him under his name. After that he was always known as "Charlie Phil." In 65 professional fights, Charlie Phil was never once knocked down, much less knocked out. Charlie Phil was the only boxing champion to lose his crown because he came in over the weight limit at weigh-in time, even though he did win the scheduled match.

72. WILLIAM "RED" HOLZMAN

(1920-1998) Red was co-captain of the basketball team at CCNY from 1941-1943. He served with the Navy during WWII. He played with the Rochester Royals 1946-1953 and the Milwaukee Hawks 1953-1954. In 1951 the Royals won the NBA title. Red was coach of the New York Knicks from 1967 to 1977 and from 1979 to 1982. His team won championships in 1970 and 1973.

73. EVA SZEKELY

(born 1927) Eva, a swimmer from Hungary, set 10 world records and 5 Olympic records. She won a gold medal in the 1952 Olympics and a silver in 1956. Eva won 10 World University championships and 68 Hungarian national titles. She set 107 Hungarian national records. Her daughter, Andrea, also won 2 Olympic medals.

74. LOUIS "KID" KAPLAN

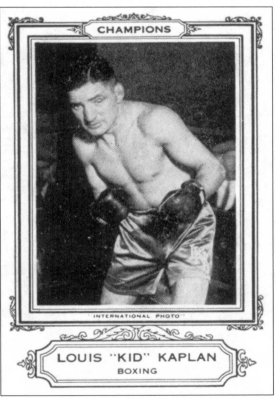

(1901-1970) Louis was boxing's featherweight champion of the world from 1925 to 1927. His career was marked with an epic series of bouts with Babe Herman. After a back and forth struggle between the two for 5 bouts, the Kid proved his superiority in their sixth and last match-up, with a decisive victory after a 15-round struggle. Louis retired from his championship when he could not make the weight.

75. DANIEL PRENN

(1904-1991) Dr. Prenn was a German tennis star, of Polish birth. Hitler felt it necessary to pass special laws to ban Daniel from representing Germany which would have greatly embarrassed the Third Reich. He escaped to England where he continued his tennis career.

76. ALPHONSE HALIMI

(born 1932) Alphonse, Algerian-born boxer and batamweight champion of the world 1957-1959 and 1960-1961, was the last Jewish champion in the "Golden Age of Jewish Boxers." He was born into terrible poverty and used boxing as his escape route. He is of Sephardic Jewish origins.

77. LARRY SHERRY

(born 1935) Larry, a relief pitcher, practically won the 1959 World Series for the Brooklyn Dodgers single-handedly. Out of the 4 Dodger's victories, Larry had 2 wins and 2 saves. Larry, who was first teamed with his brother, catcher Norm Sherry, in 1960, had overcome tremendous hurdles to become a professional athlete. He had been born with two club feet.

78. HARRIS BARTON

(born 1964) Offensive tackle for the San Francisco 49'ers football team for 10 years (1987-1996). San Francisco won the NFC championship in 1988, 1989, & 1994 and also won the Super Bowl in all 3 years.

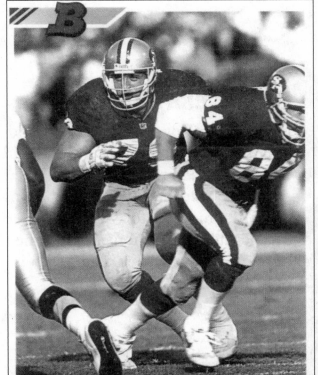

HARRIS BARTON

79. STEVE STONE

(born 1947) Steve, an average pitcher for most of his career, decided to risk his future by depending on his curve ball to give him a great year in 1980. Steve had a 14-game winning streak, a 3.23 ERA, and won the AL Cy Young award. But injury followed and Steve had to retire in 1981.

STEVE
STONE
SAN FRANCISCO GIANTS   PITCHER

R. COHEN

80. ROBERT COHEN

(born 1930) Robert was a boxer and batamweight champion of the world from 1954-1956. He was born in terrible poverty and used the boxing ring, like many before him, to escape these conditions. He is one of few noted Jewish athletes who is of Sephardic origin.

81. JOEL HORLEN

[Convert to Judaism] (born 1937) Joel spent 12 years in Major League Baseball as a right-handed pitcher. His lifetime ERA is 3.11. On September 10, 1967, he pitched a no-hitter for the White Sox against the Tigers. In that same year he was on the All-Star team and came in second in the balloting for the Cy Young Award. Joel's wife is Jewish and he converted at the time of his marriage. However, Joel insists that he had always "been interested in the history of the Jews and Judaism."

JOEL HORLEN PITCHER

WHITE SOX

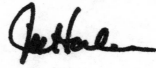

82. RONNIE ROSENTHAL

(born 1963) Ronnie was the first Israeli ever to join a Major League sport in another country. Ronnie was an outstanding striker with a number of European and British soccer teams. On March 31, 1990, Ronnie scored a hat-trick (3 goals) for Liverpool in a 4-0 victory over Charlton Athletic.

83. MIKE EPSTEIN

(born 1943) "SuperJew" Mike was an outstanding offensive force for 9 seasons in the Major Leagues, with 130 home runs. Mike wears a World Series ring from the 1972 Oakland Athletics. Mike contributed to that victory with a homerun, 4 walks, and a stolen base in the playoffs and with 5 walks in the series itself. The 1972 A's also included Ken Holtzman and Joel Horlen.

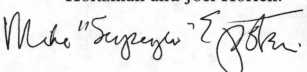

84. BRAD AUSMUS

[Jewish Mother] (born 1969) Brad has been a catcher with San Diego, Detroit, and Houston. He is an outstanding defensive catcher with decent offensive skill. He has been playing in the Major Leagues since 1993.

85. JACK "KID" BERG

(1909-1991) Jackie was boxing's Junior World Welterweight Champion 1930-1931 and British Lightweight Professional Champion 1934-1936. English-born Jackie, during his 197-bout career defeated such greats as Tony Canzoneri, Harry Mizler, Mushy Callahan, and Kid Chocolate. Jackie's professional career stretched from 1924 to 1945 (with time out to serve with the RAF during WWII.)

86. ALEX "MINE BOY" LEVINSKY

(1910-1990) Alex played with the National Hockey League from 1930 to 1939, the first substantial career for a Jewish player in the league. He played with the Toronto Maple Leafs, New York Rangers, and Chicago Black Hawks. He was an NHL All-Star in 1934. He played with Stanley Cup Champions in 1931-1932 and 1932-33 [Toronto] and again in 1937-38 [Chicago]. He played one additional season with the Philadelphia Ramblers of the AHL.

ALEXANDER LEVINSKY

87. RANDY GROSSMAN

(born 1952) Randy played as a tight end for the Pittsburgh Steelers football team for 8 years (1974-1981). Pittsburgh won, during Randy's career, the Super Bowl in 1974, 1975, 1978, & 1979. In the 1975 game (played on January 18, 1976) Randy scored a touchdown on a 7-yard pass from Terry Bradshaw.

88. BOB OLIN

(1908-1956) Light-heavyweight champion of the world 1934-1935. Bob won the title on a 15 round decision in his November 16, 1934 match with Maxie Rosenbloom. This was the last time a Jewish contender captured a world boxing title from a reigning Jewish champion.

89. JODY SHECKTER

(born 1950) South African Formula One racecar driver. Jody won the Monaco Grand Prix twice (1977 & 1979) and the 1979 World Championship. His son, Tomas, is also a Formula One driver.

90. HAROLD ABRAHAMS

(1899-1978) Harold is best known for winning the gold medal in the 1924 100-meters foot race for Great Britain. Harold was the first non-American to win this Olympic event. His achievements were immortalized in the motion picture *Chariots of Fire* (1981). Harold also won a silver medal in the 1924 Olympics, in the relay. In his later years, Harold held many executive positions in English sporting associations. He was also a pioneer in sports broadcasting in Britain. His track career was cut short when he broke a leg while long jumping in 1925.

91. MARSHALL "BIGGIE" GOLDBERG

(born 1917) "Biggie" was an All-American running back with the University of Pittsburgh's football team in 1937 & 1938. Marshall joined the Chicago Cardinals in 1939 and played until 1943, when he joined the Navy as a lieutenant. He was back with the Cardinals from 1946 to 1948. He led the NFL with 7 interceptions in 1941. The 1947 Cardinals won the NFL title with a record of 9 wins and 3 losses.

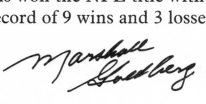

92. LEACH CROSS

(1886-1957) Leach, who was born Louis Charles Wallach, was called the "Fighting Dentist" and boxed as a lightweight. Leach, who really was a dentist, was known to knock out an opponent's teeth at night and replace them the next morning. He was one of the most colorful boxers of his day and a great favorite of the Jewish community. In 154 bouts, Leach lost only 10 times. His right hand was legendary for its power. While never a champ, Leach was a constant contender.

93. HARRY NEWMAN

(1909-2000) Harry, as the team's quarterback, lost only one game and brought the University of Michigan's football team 3 national championships (1930-1932). In his senior year he scored 57 of the team's 83 points against Big 10 opponents. In the team's last three games, Harry scored all of the team's points. He was voted the 1932 Douglas Fairbanks Trophy, the forerunner of the Heisman Trophy. On graduation, Harry played for the New York Giants from 1933 to 1935. In 1933, Harry led the NFL in passing and, despite Harry's two touchdown passes, Harry's Giants lost the very first NFL championship game 23-21. Harry also played in the AFL, with the Brooklyn Tigers, retiring in 1937.

94. AARON KRICKSTEIN

(born 1967, USA) At the age of 16 years, 2 months, Aaron was the youngest tennis player to ever win a Grand Prix title, when he won the Tel Aviv Grand Prix in 1983. Between 1983 and 1996, Aaron won 5 Grand Slam singles events: at Wimbledon in 1985; at Roland Garros (France) in 1988 and 1995; at the U.S. Open in 1994; and at the Australian Open in 1996. He won an additional 9 singles titles, including Tel Aviv.

95. JOSEPH ALEXANDER

(1898-1975) Joe served as both a guard and a center on Syracuse University's football team. He was chosen All-American 1918-1920. Joe played professional football from 1921 to 1927, including a period with the Giants alongside Jim Thorpe. He also had a long career in coaching football, as well as being a physician (he was a noted lung specialist.) Joe was considered one of the finest linemen of his day.

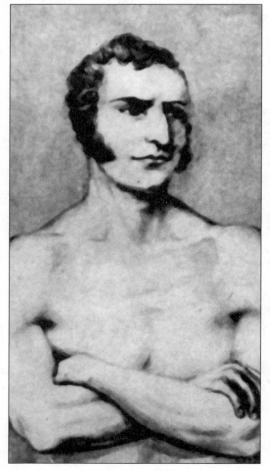

96. "DUTCH" SAMUEL ELIAS

(1775-1816, England) Dutch Sam fought around 100 boxing matches and only lost 2, even though many of Sam's matches were against fighters far heavier than himself. He is credited with introducing the uppercut to the sport. Sam's son, "Young Dutch" Sam Evans, whose mother was not Jewish, also achieved renown as a boxer, with a record of 12-0. "Dutch" and his son are the earliest known father-son combination in professional sports.

97. AARON ROSENBERG

(1912-1979) Aaron's football career was strictly collegiate, but this does not keep him from being considered one of the greatest running guards of all time. During his time with the University of Southern California, 1931-1933, Aaron's team won 27 straight games, 2 Rose Bowl victories, and 2 national championships. In 1932, USC allowed only 13 points. Aaron was an All-American in 1932 & 1933. He went on to become a noted Hollywood producer.

98. HARRY LEWIS

(1886-1956) Boxer Harry Lewis was a legitimate claimant to the world welterweight title from 1908 to 1911. Harry, who was born Harry Besterman, was a tough fighter who would allow his opponents to wear themselves out hitting him, before he would finish them off. This worked well until his last fight in 1913, when he suffered a blood clot to the brain that almost killed him.
He remained partially paralyzed for the rest of his life.

Harry Lewis

99. FRED SINGTON

(1910-1998) Fred had two outstanding athletic careers, as a collegiate football tackle with the University of Alabama (1928-1930) and as a Major League baseball player with the Washington Senators and the Brooklyn Dodgers (1934-1939). With "Bama" Fred was an All-American in both 1929 and 1930. His 1930 team was undefeated and triumphed in the Rose Bowl.

Fred Sington

100. MAX ZASLOFSKY

(1925-1985) When basketball player Max retired from the NBA in 1956, he left with 7990 points scored, the league's third highest of all-time. Max began his pro career, following a brief time with St. Johns, with the Chicago Stags, for the 4 seasons from 1946 to 1950. Max was the star of the team and led it to the lead of the Western Division in 1947. In the 1947-48 season, Max led the league in scoring and in 1949-50 in free throw percentage. Max also played with New York, 1950-1953; Baltimore, 1953-54; and Ft. Wayne, 1954-1956. Max was famous for his one-handed push-shot and he was the sports idol of young Sandy Koufax.

Max Zaslofsky.

101. MITCHELL "MITCH" GAYLORD

(born 1961) Gymnast Mitch was the first American to score a perfect 10 in an Olympic event. In the 1984 Los Angeles Olympics, Mitch won a gold medal in team event, a silver medal in vaulting, and bronze medals in rings and parallel bars. In the 1981 Maccabiah Games, Mitch had won 6 gold medals and one silver. Mitch has achieved popularity as an actor, a Hollywood stuntman, a broadcaster, and a motivational speaker.

102. SARAH HUGHES

[Jewish Mother] (born 1985) Sarah won the hotly contested gold medal for figure skating for the U.S. in the 2002 Winter Olympics. Sarah has followed up her Olympic victory by attending Yale and appearing in Stars on Ice.

103. SYLVIA WENE MARTIN

(born 1928) Sylvia was one of the greatest women bowlers of all time. She was the first woman to bowl three sanctioned perfect (300) games. Sylvia won the BPAA All-Star Match Game title in 1955 and 1960. She was named "Woman Bowler of the Year" in 1955 and 1960. She held the record breaking season average for the WIBC of 206 in 1953 and then repeated at the same average in 1954 and 1955.

104. NEAL WALK

(born 1948) Neil has had two sports careers, one as a college and NBA basketball star and one as a disabled player, playing basketball from a wheel chair. As a player with the University of Florida, Neal was an All-American and, as a senior, the only player in the U.S. to rank in the Top 10 in both scoring and rebounding. He was named the MVP of the 1969 College All-Star Game. A flip of a coin sent him to the Phoenix Suns and Lew Alcindor to the Milwaukee Bucks. Neal played for Phoenix from 1969 to 1974 and, after a brief stopover in New Orleans, for the New York Knicks from 1975 to 1976. Following his NBA career, Neal played in Israel, for Ramat Gan Hapoel, from 1979 to 1980. One day, during the 1980's, he awoke with a backache. He had developed a tumor on his spinal cord. In 1987, after treatment and surgery the tumor was controlled but Neal had lost the use of his legs. But Neal did not let this stop him. He joined the Samaritan Wheelchair Suns in the Southern California League of the National Wheelchair Basketball Association. He played with the Suns for a number of years. He now works for the Phoenix Suns in its community relations department. Furthermore, he travels the country as a motivational speaker.

SID YOUNGELMAN
DEFENSIVE TACKLE   NEW YORK TITANS

105. SID YOUNGELMAN

(1931-1991) Sid, as a football player for the University of Alabama, took part in his team's overwhelming victory in the 1953 Orange Bowl, 61-6, over Syracuse. Sid was a tackle with the Crimson Tide from 1952 to 1954 and in 1954 he was captain of the team. In 1955, Sid joined the San Francisco 49ers. He soon became one of the league's most feared players, both as an end and as a tackle. He also played with the Philadelphia Eagles (1956-1958), the Cleveland Browns (1959), the New York Titans (1960-1961), and the Buffalo Bills (1962-1963). During his off-seasons, Sid was a professional wrestler.

106. RICHARD "RICHIE" SCHEINBLUM

(born 1942) Richie was the baseball hero of three continents. During the 1966-67 season, Richie led the Nicaraguan League in batting with a .331 average. On July 20, 1969, Richie got his first Major League home run the day astronauts first landed on the moon. During the 1969-70 and 1970-71 Venezuelan seasons he starred with the Leones of Caracas. His 1971 .388 batting average (with .726 slugging · percentage) for the then minor league Denver team is the highest season batting average ever for a Denver player. Richie was the starting right fielder for the American League in the 1972 All-Star Game. In 1975 and 1976, Richie played in Japan for Hiroshima. His team won the pennant in 1975 and in 1976 he batted .308, a very difficult achievement in the pitcher friendly Central League of Japan.

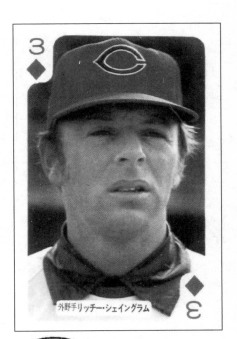

外野手リッチー・シェイングラム

107. KERRI STRUG

(born 1977) Kerri vaulted to fame in the 1996 Olympics as part of the Women's Gymnastics team. The team won for the United States its first ever gold medal in the event when gutsy Kerri refused to allow a broken ankle from keeping her from doing her part for the team. As a child of just four, Kerri, inspired by her heroine Nadia Comaneci, began her career in gymnastics. Though only 4'9" and 88 pounds, Kerri is a giant in her field.

108. DANA ROSENBLATT

(born 1972, USA) "Dangerous" Dana is the first Jewish boxer to attract a large following since the "Golden Age" of Jewish boxers. Dana is the former IBA and WBU middleweight champion. He also held the IBO super middleweight championship, which title he won from Vinny Pazienza in 1999. Vinny had previously handed Dana his only defeat in a fight in 1996. Dana fought professionally from 1992 to 2002 and he fought 40 bouts. Dana's career was cut short by injuries, particularly cuts around his eyes, which would reopen during matches.

109. IRINA SLUTSKAYA

[Jewish Father] (born 1979) The 1996 and 1997 European Champion, Irina is the first Russian or former Soviet woman to have won a major figure skating title. She also won the hotly contested silver medal for figure skating in the 2002 Winter Olympics.

110. ABEL KIVIAT

(1892-1991) Abel was a middle distance runner who won a silver medal for the U.S. in the 1912 Olympics in the 1,500 meters race. During the trials for this Olympics, Abel had set a new world record for the 1,500 meters of 3:55.8. This record stood as the world standard until 1917 and as the U.S. mark until 1928. Abel was also part of the U.S. baseball team at the 1912 Olympics, the first to include baseball, if only as a demonstration sport. During the later years of his life, Abel received numerous honors as the oldest living Olympian. He passed away at the age of 99.

ABEL R. KIVIAT

111. HENRY WITTENBERG

(born 1918) U.S. wrestler Henry won some 400 consecutive matches between 1939 and 1952, including a gold medal in the Light Heavyweight Freestyle division in the 1948 Olympics. He received his first defeat in 13 years at the 1952 Helsinki Olympics, but still won the silver medal. He served as captain of the 1952 U.S. wrestling team. Henry won 8 U.S. Freestyle titles between 1940 and 1952 and two Maccabiah gold medals in 1950 and 1953. Between 1959 and 1979 Henry served as a wrestling coach at Yeshivah University and then CCNY.

112. ANDY COHEN

(1904-1988) Andy was the first baseball player embraced by the Jewish population as a community hero. He was the fourth Jewish player featured by Giant's coach John McGraw and, by far and away, the most successful. Andy's triumphant play during the Giant's opener for the 1928 season led to a near riot at the Polo Grounds by Cohen's Jewish fans. Andy also had a great career in the minors and as a coach and manager. El Paso's Cohen Stadium is named in honor of Andy and his brother Syd.

113. CHARLES "BUCKETS" GOLDENBERG

(1911-1986) Charlie had an outstanding career as a college football player for the University of Wisconsin before his 13-year career in the NFL, with the Green Bay Packers. Charlie began with the Packers as a fullback, but soon found his true place as a lineman. Charlie was part of NFL champion teams with the Packers in 1936, 1939, and 1944. In 1938, they also took the Western Division title.

"Buckets" Goldenberg

114. AMY ALCOTT

(born 1956) From 1973, when as a girl of 17 she won the USGA Junior Girls championship, to the early 1990's, Amy dominated the world of Women's golf. In 1975, she was the LPGA Rookie of the Year and won the Orange Blossom Classic. She took the U.S. Women's Open in 1980. Altogether she had 24 LPGA Tour victories and 5 major victories, including the Dinah Shore Invitational in 1983, 1988, and 1991. Despite her success in the super serious world of professional golf, Amy has always been known for her sense of humor, her cheerful attitude, and her numerous works of charity.

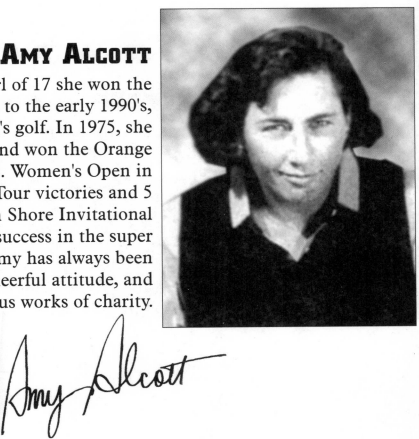

Amy Alcott

115. DR. ARON "ALI" BACHER

(born 1942) Ali was an outstanding South African cricket player, who represented his country in 12 Test Matches. During 1970 he captained South Africa in its triumphal romp over Australia, 4-0. From 1981 to 2001, Ali, who is also a physician, headed the United Cricket Board of South Africa, including overseeing the full racial integration of the game in 1991. Ali is currently the CEO of the Cricket World Cup. In 1998, Ali's nephew, Adam Bacher, made news in the English newspapers when he delayed playing for his South African cricket team to observe the Jewish New Year, reminiscent of Greenberg and Koufax.

116. HARRY "COON" ROSEN

"COON" ROSEN

(1908-1997) Great softball pitcher and pioneer of the game, Harry pitched some 300 no-hit games, including 195 perfect games. Harry won more than 3,000 games in a pitching career that stretched over 50 years. Harry's outstanding success at the first Softball World Series of 1933 did much to popularize the game. Harry's nickname was awarded to him for his curly, black hair during a period innocent of political correctness.

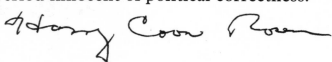

117. COREY PAVIN

(Born 1959) Golfer Corey Pavin has 14 PGA tour victories. He was a member of the U.S. Ryder Cup teams in 1991, 1993, and 1995 and was chosen 1991 PGA Player of the Year. Corey's most important win was the 1995 U.S. Open.

118. HARRY BOYKOFF

(1922-2001) At 6'9", Harry was one of the first really big stars of high school, college, and professional basketball. He led St. John's University to the NIT championship in 1943. Harry was an All-American in 1943, 1946, and 1947. (The gap in his achievements was caused by Harry's voluntary service during WWII.) Harry's professional career was brief, but spectacular and by the time of his retirement he was the highest paid player in the NBA. Harry is credited with inspiring the goaltending rule, which was created to thwart Harry's style of play.

119. JAMILA WIDEMAN

[Jewish Mother] (born 1975) Jamila is the daughter of Pulitzer Prize winning novelist John Edgar Wideman. She led her Stanford University basketball team, as its captain, to three consecutive Final Four appearances. She started with the WNBA in 1997 with the Los Angeles Sparks. The league's expansion draft brought her to the Portland Fire in 1999. During the 1999-2000 season, she played in Israel on the Ramla team. This did not interfere with her WNBA season, which is during a different part of the year. She is presently a point guard.

120. MORRIS "MOE" BERG

"MOE" BERG

(1902-1972) Though often kidded for his weak hitting, Moe's catching skills and defensive know-how made him an invaluable member of any of the teams he belonged to. These included the Dodgers, the Red Sox, the White Sox, and the "Manhattan Project". The last refers to Moe's position during WWII as America's top espionage agent in the field of atomic energy. Moe's off field accomplishments were amazing (summa cum laude graduate from Princeton, law degree from Columbia, speaker of a dozen or so languages, expert in espionage, and so on), but his skills behind the plate made him the favorite of practically every pitcher he worked with. Hall-of-Famer Ted Lyons claimed that in all the games that Moe caught for him, he never once shook off one of Moe's signs.

121. JACOB "BUDDY" BAER

[Jewish Paternal Grandfather] (1915-1986) Heavyweight boxer Buddy never achieved the success of elder brother Max, during his 1934-1942 career, but he did KO such fighters as Abe Simon and Tony Galento. He was at this time ranked the number one contender for the heavyweight title. In his first title bout he knocked Joe Louis out of the ring in the first round. He lost the fight, however, on a disqualification. In the rematch, Joe knocked Buddy out in the first round. Buddy then retired and followed brother Max into a career in acting.

122. MARSHALL HOLMAN

(born 1954) Bowler Marshall was PBA player of the year in 1987. He won PBA doubles titles with Mark Roth in 1977, 1979, and 1984. He also has won 21 national tour titles. He has had twenty-four 300 games while on the national tour. Marshall was the first PBA player to surpass 1.5 million dollars in prize money. He was elected to the PBA Hall of Fame in 1990.

J. ERSKINE MAYER
P.—Philadelphia Nationals
112

123. ERSKINE MAYER

[Jewish Father] (1889-1957) Erskine was an excellent pitcher who worked alongside the legendary Grover Cleveland Alexander. The two men led the Phillies to their first pennant in 1915. Erskine had won 21 games that season with an ERA of 2.58. Erskine's lifetime ERA is 2.96, including his stint with the 1919 "Black Sox" Chicago White Sox. Erskine was not involved with the corruption scandal on that team.

124. HYMAN "HY" BULLER

(1926-1958) Hockey player Hy had a comparatively short career in the NHL, but the elegance and quality of his play left a lasting impression on all who had the opportunity to see him. Hy played in just 9 games for the Detroit Red Wings during 1943-45 and 179 games for the New York Rangers during 1951-54. During this time he had 22 goals and 58 assists. He played in the 1952 All-Star game. His career in minor league hockey was also notable.

"Hy" Buller

125. AUGUST BELMONT II

[Jewish Father] (1852-1924) August II was a pioneer in polo in this country both in organizing it and in playing in matches. Like his famous father, August I, who founded the Belmont Stakes, the oldest of the Triple Crown races, he was a giant in the field of horse racing. It was Jr. who built Belmont Park, in 1905, and whose stables bred the legendary horse known as Man O' War.

126. DANNY SCHAYES

(born 1959) Danny, a center, played in 1138 career NBA games, the most among all Jewish players in NBA history. Danny is the son of Dolph Schayes. During his years in the NBA, Danny played for Utah, Denver, Milwaukee, the LA Lakers, Phoenix, Miami, and Orlando."

127. MARCHMONT "MARCHY" SCHWARTZ

[Jewish Father] (1909-1991) Marchy was a halfback at Notre Dame and helped the Irish to their 1930 national title and was a unanimous All-America pick as a senior in 1931. He was ranked second behind George Gipp on Notre Dame's career rushing list when he finished his career. He led the team in rushing, passing, and scoring during the 1930 and 1931 seasons. He still holds the record for most punts in a game, with 15 vs. Army in 1931. He rushed for 1,945 career yards on 355 carries for 16 touchdowns and still stands 10th on Notre Dame's career rushing list. After graduation, he became an assistant coach at Notre Dame and then the backfield coach at the University of Chicago. Later he became head coach at Creighton University and then Stanford University. In 1974, he was inducted into the College Football Hall of Fame.

128. SARA DeCOSTA

[Jewish Mother] (born 1977) Sara served as the goalie on the U.S. Olympic Women's Hockey teams in 1998, when it won gold, and 2002, when it won silver, with the Canadian team taking the gold. Sara played collegiate hockey with Providence College. In college she led the nation with her .943 save percentage. Sara was also the first girl to play in Rhode Island's top high school ice hockey division.

BARRY LATMAN   pitcher

129. BARRY LATMAN

(born 1936) Barry was a right-handed pitcher for 5 different baseball teams. While Barry's career as a starter is only mediocre, his time spent as a reliever was outstanding. He pitched 28 complete games, including 10 shutouts. His lifetime ERA was 3.91 over an 11-year career.

130. MIKE ROSSMAN

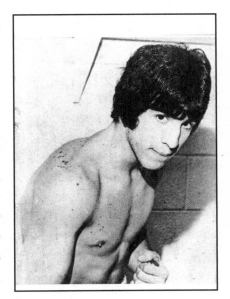

[Jewish Mother] (born 1956) Mike was born Michael Albert DePiano, but chose to box under him mother's maiden name. He also was known in his fighting days (1973-83) as the "Jewish Bomber." Mike won the light heavyweight title from Victor Galindez, on a knockout in the 13th round on September 15, 1978. During the same program, Muhammad Ali recaptured the heavyweight title from Leon Spinks for an unprecedented third time. The audience was the largest ever to see a bout indoors. Mike lost his title in 1979, back to Galindez.

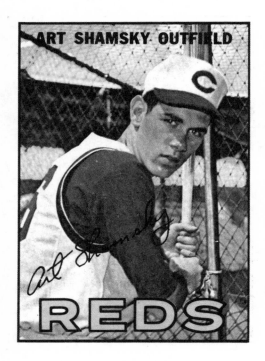

131. ART SHAMSKY

(born 1941) Member of the great 1969 "Miracle Mets" baseball team. In that season, Art's batting average was .300. Also played with Cincinatti, Chicago Cubs, and Oakland.

132. ISAAC "IKE" BERGER

(born 1936) Jerusalem-born weightlifter, Ike won the world featherweight weightlifting championship three times. Between 1956 and 1960, he won three Olympic medals (1 gold, 2 silver) in three different Olympics, while representing the United States. Twelve times, he was the national US champion. Over the years he has set 23 world records. Ike is the son of a rabbi and is himself a cantor. He is the first featherweight to ever lift more than 800 pounds. From 1964, with his 336 pound jerk at 130 pounds, he was considered the strongest man in the world, pound for pound, a title which he would hold for 9 years.

133. HENRY LASKAU

(1916-2000) In 1951, race-walking expert Henry set a record for the mile of 6 minutes, 19.2 seconds, a record which stood for 12 years. Born in Germany, Henry escaped from a concentration camp (where his family perished) and made his way to the United States. After service in the U.S. Army, during which he uncovered an infamous SS officer hiding in a POW compound, he became an American citizen. He won 42 national championships in race-walking and represented the U.S. in the Olympics and in the Maccabiah games. He was so associated with his sport that he became known as "Mr. Walking".

134. BO BELINSKY

[Jewish Mother] (1936-2001) Bo pitched the first no-hit, no-run game in West Coast, Major League history on May 5, 1962. Bo's great natural pitching abilities may have developed better if he had not been so busy pursuing beautiful women and hustling pool games. Nevertheless, Bo was always a fan favorite, whether with the Angels, Phillies, Houston, Pittsburgh, or Cincinatti. In 1968, Bo pitched a second no-hit game, in the minors, while playing for Hawaii.

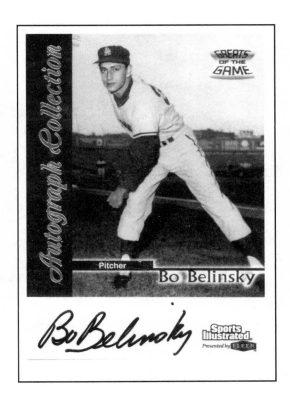

135. KAROLY KARPATI

(1906-1996) Karoly, a wrestler from Hungary, performed in three Olympics from 1928 to 1936, taking the silver medal in the Lightweight Freestyle class in 1932 and the gold in 1936. Karoly was a national champion in Hungary ten times and he took the European crown in 1927, 1929, 1930, and 1935. After his years of competition he became a wrestling coach and wrote 6 books on the subject.

136. MORRIE ARNOVICH

(1910-1959) In a 7-year career, baseball outfielder, Morrie had a .287 lifetime batting average. His best year was 1939, when he batted .324. Morrie played for the Phillies (1936-40), Cincinnati (1940), and the NY Giants (1941, 1946).

137. HAROLD SOLOMON

(born 1952) Harold was recognized during his tennis career as a great defensive player who often wore out his opponents rather than overwhelmed them. Harold won the South African Open in 1975 and 1976. In 1977, he won the Tournament of Champions. He was ranked No. 5 in 1980, a year which saw him win tournaments in Hamburg, Cincinnati, Baltimore, and Tel Aviv.

138. RON BLOMBERG

(born 1948) Ron shall always be remembered as baseball's very first designated hitter. He also is the most successful Jewish player to have played with the New York Yankees. Ron also played for the Chicago White Sox. Unfortunately, Ron's career was shortened by injuries.

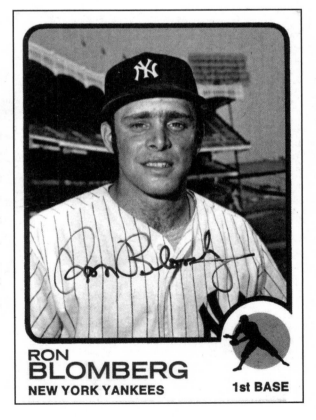

RON BLOMBERG
NEW YORK YANKEES

1st BASE

JIMMIE REESE

139. JIMMIE REESE

(1905-1994) Jimmie's 77-year career in professional baseball (including stints as batboy, minor league player, Major League player alongside Babe Ruth, coach, and scout) was the longest in the history of the sport. He was a major star of the Pacific Coast League for many years. His ability to use his fungo bat during batting practice and to exercise the outfielders was legendary.

140. SCOTT RADINSKY

[Jewish Mother] (born 1968) With a lifetime ERA of 3.34 and many seasons with his ERA below 3, Scott spent some 10 seasons in the majors as a master relief pitcher. But his time there was not uninterrupted. In 1994, Scott was diagnosed with Hodgkin's disease. He fought back against this life threatening disease and returned to the lineup more effective than ever. He had a second career as a rock singer with Ten Foot Pole and Pulley

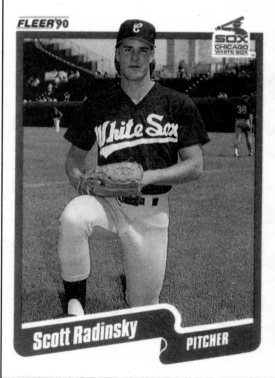

Scott Radinsky   PITCHER

141. JULIE HELDMAN

(born 1945) Julie was one of the top ranked women tennis players during the late 1960's and early 1970's. She was one of the founding players of the Virginia Slims Tour, the first women's professional tour. Julie won 25 singles titles over her career, she also represented the U.S. in the Davis Cup competition for women in 1966, 1969, and 1974. During 1969, her best year, she was ranked as the 2nd best player in the U.S. and the 5th best in the world.

142. JEFF HALPERN

(born 1976) Jeff played ice hockey with Princeton University between 1997 and 1999, where he accumulated an excellent record and served as the team's captain. He was drafted by the Washington Capitals and debuted as a center with the club for the 1999-2000 season. In his 368 games over 4 seasons, Jeff has scored 76 goals and has 94 assists. In postseason play he has appeared in 17 games, with 4 goals and 5 assists.

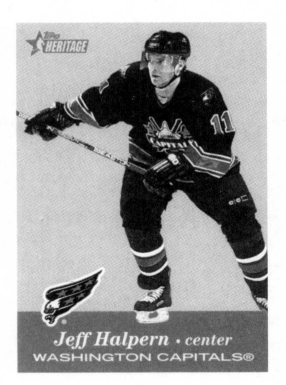

Jeff Halpern • center
WASHINGTON CAPITALS®

143. MIKE LACOSS

[Jewish Father] (born 1956) Mike spent 14 years as a Major League Baseball pitcher. Mike's best pitch was his split-finger fastball. Mike played for Cincinnati (1978-81), Houston (1982-84), Kansas City (1985), and San Francisco (1986-89).

144. NORM SHERRY

(born 1931) One of baseball's great defensive catchers and the inspirer of Koufax's rise to greatness. His younger brother, Larry, also owed much to Norm.

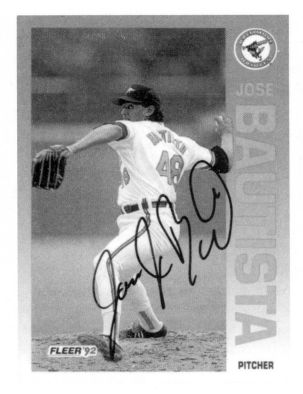

PITCHER

145. Jose Bautista

[Jewish Mother] (born 1964) Jose was born and raised in the Dominican Republic. He spent 9 years in the Majors, mostly as a relief pitcher. His lifetime ERA is 4.62. He is married to a Jewish woman and is very serious about his Judaism. Between 1988 and 1997, Jose played for Baltimore, the Chicago Cubs, San Francisco, Detroit, and St. Louis.

146. Monte Attell

(1885-1960) While Monte, "the Nob Hill Terror," never achieved the notoriety of his brother and fellow boxer, Abe Attell, his career was by no means insignificant. Monte, a bantamweight, fought 99 matches in his career and he was recognized as the legitimate clamaint to the world championship from 1909 to 1910. An eye infection blinded him in 1913 and forced his retirement from the ring. He spent the remainder of his life selling newspapers in San Francisco. Other boxers in the family included his brother Caesar and his nephews Jack and Gilbert.

MONTE ATTELL

147. HERMAN BARRON

(1909-1978) Golfer Herman was one of the top professional golfers of the 1930's and 1940's. He played at a time when the professional circuit was limited to just a handful of pro golfers. Herman won his first tournament in 1934 and he continued collecting victories until 1947, when failing health forced him to retire. But during the early 1960's he staged a dramatic comeback on the Senior Circuit, taking the World Senior's Championship in 1963. In 1964, Herman hit the eleventh hole in one of his career.

148. BOB PLAGER

[Convert to Judaism] (born 1943) Bob played ice hockey for the New York Rangers and the St. Louis Blues from 1964 to 1978.
His tough defensive style during his long career marked him as a good, solid player. He converted in 1977, prior to his marriage.

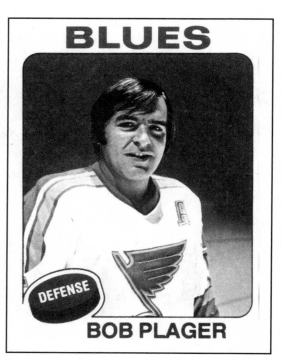

Jeff Agoos   USA

149. JEFF AGOOS

(born 1968) U.S. soccer star Jeff was born in Geneva, Switzerland. Jeff plays with the San Jose Earthquakes in the MLS, with the U.S. National team, and with the U.S. Olympic team. He is a top notch defensive player who is recognized for his steady play. He served as the captain of the U.S. Cup team in 1997, playing every minute of every game of that series.

150. RUBEN AMARO, JR.

[Jewish Mother] (born 1965) Ruben, of an old baseball family on his father's side, had 8 years in the Major Leagues to his credit. Much of his best work was done as a pinch hitter. Ruben is currently the Assistant General Manager of the Phillies.

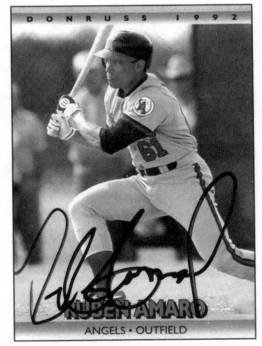

THE 100 GREATEST JEWISH GAME PLAYERS

CHESS - (the first 8 are World Champions arranged chronologically; the remainder are arranged alphabetically)

1. **WILHELM STEINITZ** 1866-1894 (Czech Republic)
2. **EMANUEL LASKER** 1894-1921 (Germany)
3. **MIKHAIL BOTVINNIK** 1948-57, 1958-60, 1961-63 (Russia)
4. **VASILY SMYSLOV** (Jewish Mother) 1957-1958 (Russia)
5. **MIKHAIL TAL** 1960-1961 (Latvia)
6. **BORIS SPASSKY** (Jewish Mother) 1969-1972 (Russia)
7. **ROBERT "BOBBY" FISCHER** 1972-1975 (USA)
8. **GARY KASPAROV** (Jewish Father) 1985-2000 (Azerbaijan)
9. **ARTHUR BISGUIER** (USA)
10. **DAVID BRONSTEIN** (Ukraine)
11. **LARRY EVANS** (USA)
12. **REUBEN FINE** (USA)
13. **SALOMON FLOHR** (Ukraine)
14. **EFIM GELLER** (Ukraine)
15. **HARRY GOLOMBEK** (Great Britain)
16. **ISADOR GUNSBERG** (Hungary)
17. **ISRAEL HOROWITZ** (USA)
18. **BERNARD HORWITZ** (Germany)
19. **DAVID JANOWSKY** (Poland)
20. **MAX JUDD** (USA)
21. **MONA MAY KARFF** (USA)
22. **ISAAC I. KASHDAN** (USA)
23. **IGNATZ KOLISCH** (Hungary)
24. **GEORGES KOLTANOWSKY** (Belgium)
25. **VICTOR KORCHNOI** (Jewish Mother) (Russia)
26. **ABRAHAM KUPCHIK** (USA)
27. **ALLA KUSHNIR** (Russia)
28. **IRINA LEVITINA** (Russia, USA)
29. **ANDREAS LILIENTHAL** (Hungary)
30. **JOHANN JACOB LOWENTHAL** (Austria)

EMANUEL LASKER

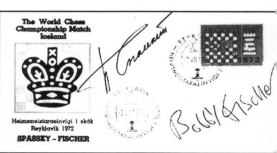

SOUVENIRS OF THE 1972 FISCHER-SPASSKY MATCH

MIKHAIL BOTVINNIK, WORLD CHESS CHAMPION

31. **JACQUES MIESES** (Germany)
32. **MIGUEL NAJDORF** (Poland, Argentina)
33. **AARON NIMZOVICH** (Latvia)
34. **JUDIT POLGAR** (Hungary)
35. **SOFIA POLGAR** (Hungary)
36. **ZUZSA POLGAR** (Hungary)
37. **VYACHESLEV RAGOSIN** (Russia)
38. **SAMUEL RESHEVSKY** (Poland, USA)
39. **RICHARD RETI** (Slovakia)
40. **ISAAC RICE** (Germany, USA)
41. **AKIBA RUBINSTEIN** (Poland)
42. **SIEGBERT TARRASCH** (Germany)
43. **SEVILIJ TARTAKOWER** (Russia, France)
44. **MAX WEISS** (Hungary)
45. **S. WINAWER** (Poland)
46. **JOHANN ZUKERTORT** (Poland)

POKER

47. **JUDAH P. BENJAMIN** (USA)
48. **JOE BERNSTEIN** (USA)

BILLIARDS

49. **HARRY P. CLINE** (USA)
50. **SYDNEY LEE** (Great Britain)
51. **LEON MAGNUS** (USA)
52. **ARTHUR B. RUBIN** (USA)
53. **MAX SHIMON** (USA)
54. **SIMON "CY" YELLIN** (USA)

JUDAH P. BENJAMIN, Sec. of War
C.S.A.

Chas. Magnus, 12 Frankfort St. N.Y.

BRIDGE

55. **LARRY COHEN** (USA)

56. **CHARLES H. GOREN** (USA)
—the most familiar name in the world of bridge. Goren wrote numerous and definitive books on the subject.

57. **JAMES JACOBY** (USA)

58. **OSWALD JACOBY** (USA)

59. **EDGAR KAPLAN** (USA)

60. **ALVIN L. ROTH** (USA)

61. **BORIS SCHAPIRO** (Great Britain)

62. **HOWARD WEINSTEIN** (USA)

—Other great bridge players include:

63. **DAVID BERKOWITZ** (USA)

64. **LISA BERKOWITZ** (USA)

65. **BILLY COHEN** (USA)

66. **BILLY EIZENBERG** (USA)

67. **FRED GITELMAN** (USA)

68. **CONNIE GOLDBERG** (USA)

69. **ROBERT GOLDMAN** (USA)

70. **GEORGE JACOBS** (USA)

71. **AMOS KAMINSKI** (USA)

72. **RALF KATZ** (USA)

73. **BOBBY LEVIN** (USA)

74. **SHAYA LEVIT** (USA)

75. **ALAIN LEVY** (USA)

76. **RUTH LIEBERMAN** (USA)

77. **BILL POLLACK** (USA)

78. **LEE RAUTENBERG** (USA)

79. **MICHAEL ROSENBERG** (USA)

80. **JAMES ROSENBLOOM** (USA)

81. **RICHARD SCHWARTZ** (USA)

82. **JOE TAUSSIG** (USA)

83. **STEVE WEINSTEIN** (USA)

84. **DORON YADLIN** (Israel)

85. **ISRAEL YADLIN** (Israel)

CHECKERS

86. **SAM COHEN** (Great Britain)
87. **LOUIS C. GINSBERG** (USA)
88. **MORRIS KRANTZ** (USA)
89. **SAM LEVY** (Great Britain)
90. **HARRY LIBERMAN** (USA)

PING PONG OR TABLE TENNIS★

91. **VIKTOR BARNA** (Hungary)
92. **RICHARD BERGMANN** (Austria, Great Britain)
93. **MICHEL HAGUENAUER** (France)
94. **DR. ROLAND JACOBI** (Hungary)
95. **RICHARD MILES** (USA)
96. **LEAH THALL NEUBERGER** (USA)
97. **ANGELICA ADELSTEIN ROSEANU** (Romania)
98. **A. SIPOS** (Hungary)
99. **MIKLOS SZABADOS** (Hungary)
100. **ELLA ZELLER** (Romania)

★Many would argue that table tennis is more sport than game. I will stick to the distinction that it, like other games, is played on a table.

TABLE TENNIS - G. V. BARNA

JEWISH MANAGERS, COACHES AND TRAINERS

BASEBALL

JAKE ATZ
STANLEY "SKIP" BERTMAN
GORDON "JACK" BLOOMFIELD
LOU BOUDREAU
ANDY COHEN
SYD COHEN
STEVE HERTZ
BOB MELVIN
HAROLD "LEFTY" PHILLIPS
LIPMAN PIKE
LARRY ROTHSCHILD
NORM SHERRY
JERRY WEINSTEIN

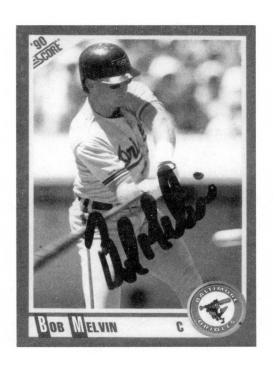

BASKETBALL

ARNOLD "RED" AUERBACH
LARRY BROWN
ALEXSANDR GOMOLSKY
EDDIE GOTTLIEB
LES HARRISON
NAT HOLMAN
WILLIAM "RED" HOLZMAN
RALPH KLEIN
HARRY LITWACK
SHMUEL MAHROUSKI
FANNY ROSENFELD
RON ROTHSTEIN
LEONARD SACHS
ABE SAPERSTEIN
ADOLPH "DOLPH" SCHAYES

BOXING

RAY ARCEL
JIMMY AUGUST
HEINIE BLAUSTEIN
FREDDIE BROWN
HYMIE CANTOR
MOE FLEISCHER
CHARLEY GOLDMAN
HARRY "SPITZEL" GOODMAN
LOU GROSS
IZZY KLINE
MIKE MULLIGAN
"DOC" LIPPMANN ROBB
MANNY SEAMON
J. J. "MOOSE" TAUSSIG

FOOTBALL

AL DAVIS
SID GILLMAN
PHIL "MOTSY" HANDLER
LOUIS E. HAYMAN
PHILIP "PHIL" KING
MARV LEVY
LUCIUS NATHAN LITTAUER
MARCHMONT "MARCHY" SCHWARTZ
ALEXANDER "ALLIE" SHERMAN

HOCKEY

CECIL HART
NIKOLAY EPSHSTEIN
BOB PLAGER

HORSES

"UNCLE" MOSE GOLDBLATT
MARY HIRSCH
MAXIMILLION JUSTICE HIRSCH
MAXIMILLION HIRSCH JR. (Died 1950)
W. J. "BUDDY" HIRSCH
EUGENE JACOBS
HIRSCH JACOBS
SIDNEY JACOBS
HOWARD "BUDDY" JACOBSON
ROBERT MERRITT
JACOB PINCUS
SOL RUTCHICK
ARNOLD N. WINICK

CECIL HART,
Gérant du Canadien.

OLYMPICS

MEL ROSEN (Track)
ALLEN ROSENBERG (Crew)
WILLIAM "BACH" BACHRACH (Swimming)

SOCCER

YOSEF "YOSSI" MIRMOVITCH

SWIMMING

JABEZ "JAPPY" WOLFF
CHARLOTTE "EPPIE" EPSTEIN

TENNIS

BRAD GILBERT

Jewish Players In Major League Baseball

- **Calvin "Cal" Abrams** 1949-52 First base/Outfield (567 games)
- **Lloyd Allen** 1969-75 RHPitcher (159 games)—Convert to Judaism
- **Ruben Amaro Jr.** 1991-98 Outfield (485 games)—Jewish Mother
- **Morris "Morrie" Arnovich** 1936-41, 1946 Outfield (590 games)
- **Jacob "Jake" Atz** (aka John Jacob Zimmerman?) 1902, 1907-9 Infield (209 games)—Jewish Father
- **Bradley "Brad" Ausmus** 1993-2005 Catcher (1577 games)—Jewish Mother
- **Jesse Baker** (aka Michael Silverman) 1919 Infield (1 game)
- **Brian Bark** 1995 LHPitcher (3 games)
- **Ross Baumgarten** 1978-82 LHPitcher (90 games)
- **Jose Bautista** 1988-92, 1993-97 RHPitcher (312 games)—Jewish Mother
- **Robert "Bo" Belinsky** 1962-67, 1969-70 LHPitcher (146 games)—Jewish Mother
- **Joseph "Joe" Bennett** 1923 Infield (1 game)
- **Morris "Moe" Berg** 1923, 1926-39 Catcher (663 games)
- **Nathan "Nate" Berkenstock** 1871 Outfield (1 game)
- **Robert "Bob" Berman** 1918 Catcher (2 games)
- **Seymour "Cy" Block** 1942, 1945-46 Infield (17 games)
- **Ronald "Ron" Blomberg** 1969, 1971-76, 1978 Outfield/DH (461 games)
- **Samuel "Sam" Bohne** (aka Samuel Cohen) Infield 1916, 1921-26 (663 games)
- **Henry Bostick** (aka Henry Lipschitz) 1915 Infield (2 games)
- **Louis "Lou" Boudreau** 1938-52 Shortstop (1646 games)—Jewish Mother
- **Craig Breslow** 2005 RH Pitcher (14 Games)
- **Louis "Lou" Brower** 1931 Shortstop (21 games)
- **Conrad "Randy" Cardinal** 1963 RHPitcher (6 games)

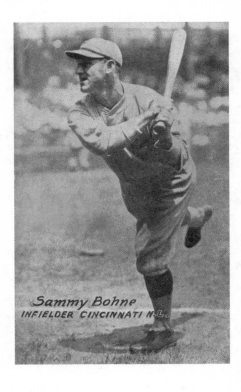

Sammy Bohne
INFIELDER CINCINNATI N.L.

- **FRANK CHARLES** 2000 Catcher (4 games)—Jewish Mother
- **HARRY CHOZEN** 1937 Catcher (1 game)
- **ANTHONY "TONY" COGAN** 2001 LHPitcher (39 games)
- **ALTA "SCHOOLBOY" COHEN** 1931-33 Outfield (29 games)
- **ANDREW "ANDY" COHEN** 1926, 1928-29 Infield (262 games)
- **HYMAN "HY" COHEN** 1955 RHPitcher (7 games)
- **SYDNEY "SYD" COHEN** (aka Pablo García) 1934, 1936-37 LHPitcher (55 games)
- **RICHARD "DICK" CONGER** 1940-43 RHPitcher (19 games)—Jewish Mother
- **PHILIP "PHIL" COONEY** (aka Philip Cohen) 1905 Infield (1 game)
- **EDWARD "ED" COREY** (aka Abraham Cohen) 1918 RHPitcher (1 game)
- **WILLIAM "BILL" CRISTALL** 1901 LHPitcher (6 games)
- **HARRY "THE HORSE" DANNING** 1933-42 Catcher (890 games)
- **IKE DANNING** 1928 Catcher (2 games)
- **ROBERT E. DAVIS** 1958, 1960 RHPitcher (29 games)
- **HARRY EISENSTAT** 1935-42 LHPitcher (165 games)
- **MICHAEL "MIKE" EPSTEIN** 1966-74 (907 games)
- **REUBEN EWING** (aka Reuben Cohen) 1921 Infield (3 games)
- **ALFRED "AL" FEDEROFF** 1951-52 Second Base (76 games)
- **EDWARD "EDDIE" FEINBERG** 1938-39 Infield (16 games)
- **HARRY FELDMAN** 1941-46 RHPitcher (143 games)
- **SCOTT FELDMAN** 2005 RH Pitcher (8 Games)—Jewish Father
- **SAMUEL "SAM" FISHBURN** 1919 Infield (9 games)
- **LEOPOLD "LEO" FISHEL** 1899 Pitcher (1 game)
- **MATHEW "MATT" FORD** LHPitcher 2003 (25 games)
- **AUGUST "HAPPY" FOREMAN** 1924, 1926 LHPitcher (6 games)
- **MICAH FRANKLIN** 1997 Infield (17 games)—Jewish Mother
- **MURRAY "MOE" FRANKLIN** 1941-42 Infield (61 games)
- **MILTON "MILT" GALATZER** 1933-36, 1939 Outfield (251 games)
- **JAMES "JIM" GAUDET** 1978-79 Catcher (2 games)—Convert to Judaism
- **MARK GILBERT** 1985 Outfield (7 games)
- **MYRON "JOE" GINSBERG** 1948, 1950-54, 1956-62 Catcher (695 games)
- **KEITH GLAUBER** 1998, 2000 RHPitcher (7 games)
- **JONAH GOLDMAN** 1928, 1930-31 Infield (148 games)

- **ISADORE "IZZY" GOLDSTEIN** 1932 RHPitcher (16 games)
- **JACOB "JAKE" GOODMAN** 1878, 1882 First Base (70 games)
- **GREGORY "GREG" GOOSEN** 1965-70 Catcher (193 games)—Jewish Father
- **SID GORDON** 1941-43, 1946-55 Infield/Outfield (1475 games)
- **HERBERT "HERB" GORMAN** 1925 Infield/Outfield (1 game)
- **JOHN GRABOW** 2003-05 LHPitcher (136 games)—Jewish Mother
- **SHAWN GREEN** 1993-2005 Outfield (1672 games)
- **ADAM GREENBERG** 2005 Outfield (1 game)
- **HENRY "HANK" GREENBERG** 1930, 1933-41, 1945-47 First Base and
    Outfield (1394 games)
- **ERIC HELFAND** 1993-95 Catcher (53 games)
- **STEPHEN "STEVE" HERTZ** 1964 Third Base (5 games)
- **KENNETH "KEN" HOLTZMAN** 1965-79
    LHPitcher (451 games)
- **JOEL "JOE" HORLEN** 1961-72 RHPitcher (361 games)
    —Convert to Judaism
- **DOUGLAS "DOUG" JOHNS** 1995-96, 1998-99
    LHPitcher (114 games)—Jewish Mother
- **ALFRED "SKIP" JUTZE** 1972-77 Catcher (264 games)
    —Convert to Judaism
- **HARRY "KLONDIKE" KANE** (aka Harry Cohen)
    1902-03, 1905-06 LHPitcher (15 games)
- **GABE KAPLER** 1998-2005 Outfield (778 games)
- **RYAN KARP** 1995, 1997 LHPitcher (16 games)—
    Adopted by Jewish parents and raised as a Jew
- **HERB "LEFTY" KARPEL** 1946 LHPitcher
    (2 games)
- **ALAN KOCH** 1963-64 RHPitcher (42 games)
- **MIKE KOPLOVE** 2001-05 RHPitcher (215 games)
    —Jewish Father
- **SANDY KOUFAX** (aka Sandford Braun) 1955-66
LHPitcher (397 games)
- **BRIAN KOWITZ** 1995 Outfielder (10 games)
- **MICHAEL "MIKE" LACOSS** 1978-1991 RHPitcher (415 games)—Jewish Father

SANDY KOUFAX

- **(ARNOLD) BARRY LATMAN** 1957-67 RHPitcher (344 games)
- **JAMES "JIM" LEVEY** 1930-33 Shortstop (440 games)
- **ALAN "AL" LEVINE** 1996-2005 RHPitcher (416 games)
- **JESSE LEVIS** 1992-1999 Catcher (30 games)
- **MICHAEL "MIKE" LEIBERTHAL** 1994-2005 Catcher (1107 games)— Jewish Father
- **LOUIS "LOU" LIMMER** 1951, 1954 First Base (209 games)
- **ANDREW LORRAINE** LHPitcher 1996-2000, 2002 (59 games)
- **ELLIOTT MADDOX** 1970-80 Outfielder (1029 games)—Convert to Judaism
- **CYRUS "CY" MALIS** 1934 RHPitcher (1 game)

MICHAEL "MIKE" LEIBERTHAL

- **MARK "MOXIE" MANUEL** 1905, 1908 RHPitcher (21 games)
- **HARRY "DUKE" MARKELL** (aka Harry Makowsky) 1951 RHPitcher (5 games)
- **JASON MARQUIS** 2000-05 RHPitcher (161 games)
- **EDWIN "ED" MAYER** 1957-58 LHPitcher (22 games)
- **ERSKINE MAYER** (aka James Mayer) 1912-19 RHPitcher (245 games)
- **SAMUEL "SAM" MAYER** 1915 Outfield (11 games)
- **ROBERT "BOB" MELVIN** 1985-94 Catcher (692 games)—Jewish Mother
- **EDWARD "ED THE MIDGET" MENSOR** 1912-14 Outfield/Infield (127 games)
- **MICHAEL "MIKE" MILCHIN** 1996 LHPitcher (39 games)—Jewish Father
- **NORMAN "NORM" MILLER** 1965-74 Outfield (540 games)
- **CHARLES "BUDDY" MYER** 1925-41 Infield (1923 games)—Jewish Father
- **SAMUEL "SAM" NAHEM** 1938, 1941-42, 1948 RHPitcher (90 games)
- **DAVID NEWHAN** 1999-2001, 2004-05 Right Field/Second base (254 games)
- **JEFFREY "JEFF" NEWMAN** 1976-84 Catcher/All other pos. (735 games) —Convert to Judaism

- **Barney Pelty** 1903-12 RHPitcher (266 games)
- **Jonathan "Jon" Perlman** 1985, 1987-88 RHPitcher (26 games)—Jewish Father
- **Jacob Pike** 1877 Right Field (1 game)
- **Lipman "Lip" Pike** 1871-1878, 1881, 1887 Infield/Outfield (425 games)
- **Jacob "Jake" Pitler** 1917-18 Infield (111 games)
- **Scott Radinsky** 1990-93, 1995-2001 LHPitcher (557 games)— Jewish Mother
- **Steven "Steve" Ratzer** 1980-81 RHPitcher (13 games)
- **Jimmie Reese** (aka Hymie Solomon) 1930-32 Infield (232 games)
- **Allen "Al" Richter** 1951, 1953 Shortstop (6 games)
- **David A. Roberts** 1969-81 LHPitcher (445 games) —Jewish father
- **Saul Rogovin** 1949-53, 1955-57 RHPitcher (150 games)

Barney Pelty

- **Albert "Al" "Flip" Rosen** 1947-56 Third base (1044 games)
- **Goodwin "Goody" Rosen** 1937-39, 1944-46 Outfield (551games)
- **Harry Rosenberg** 1930 Outfield (9 games)
- **Louis "Lou" Rosenberg** 1923 Second base (3 games)
- **Steven "Steve" Rosenberg** 1988-91 LHPitcher (87 games)
- **Max Rosenfeld** 1931-33 RHPitcher (42 games)
- **Simon "Sy" Rosenthal** 1925-26 Outfield (123 games)
- **Wayne Rosenthal** 1991-92 RHPitcher (42 games)
- **Marvin "Marv" Rotblatt** 1948, 1950-51 LHPitcher (35 games)
- **Lawrence "Larry" Rothschild** 1981-82 RHPitcher (7 games)— Jewish Father
- **Milton "Mickey" Rutner** 1947 Infield (12 games)
- **Michael "Mike" Saipe** 1998 RHPitcher (2 games)
- **Roger Samuels** 1988-89 LHPitcher (20 games)
- **Samuel "Ike" Samuls** 1895 Infield (24 games)
- **Morris "Moe" Savransky** 1954 LHPitcher (16 games)

- **ALEXANDER "AL" SCHACHT** 1919-21 RHPitcher (53 games)
- **SIDNEY "SID" SCHACHT** 1950-51 RHPitcher (19 games)
- **HAROLD "HAL" SCHACKER** 1945 RHPitcher (6 games)
- **HENRY "HEINIE" SCHEER** 1922-23 Infield (120 games)
- **RICHARD "RICHIE" SCHEINBLUM** 1965, 1967-69, 1971-74 Outfield (462 games)
- **MICHAEL "LEFTY" SCHEMER** 1945-46 First base (32 games)
- **SCOTT SCHOENEWEIS** 1999-2005 LHPitcher (303 games)—Jewish Mother
- **WILLIAM "BILL" SCHWARZ** 1914 Catcher (1 game)
- **ARTHUR "ART" SHAMSKY** 1965-72 Outfield (665 games)
- **RICHARD "DICK" SHARON** 1973-75 Outfield (242 games)—Jewish Father
- **LAWRENCE "LARRY" SHERRY** 1958-68 RHPitcher (416 games)
- **NORMAN "NORM" SHERRY** 1959-63 Catcher (194 games)
- **HARRY "HANDSOME HARRY" SHUMAN** 1942-44 RHPitcher (30 games)
- **AARON "AL" SILVERA** 1955-56 Outfield (14 games)
- **FREDERIC "FRED" SINGTON** 1934-39 Outfield (181 games)
- **MOSE SOLOMON** 1923 Outfield (2 games)
- **WILLIAM "CHICK" STARR** 1935-36 Catcher (13 games)
- **JEFFREY "JEFF" STEMBER** 1980 RHPitcher (1 game)
- **ADAM STERN** 2005 Outfield (36 games)
- **STEVEN "STEVE" STONE** 1971-81 RHPitcher (320 games)
- **SHERWIN "BUD" SWARTZ** 1947 LHPitcher (5 games)
- **DONALD "DON" TAUSSIG** 1958, 1961-62 Outfield (153 games)
- **ROBERT "BOB" TUFTS** 1981-83 LHPitcher (27 games)—Convert to Judaism
- **EDWARD "EDDIE" TURCHIN** 1943 Infield (11 games)
- **STEVEN "STEVE" WAPNICK** 1990-91 RHPitcher (10 games)
- **JUSTIN WAYNE** 2002-04 RHPitcher (26 games)
- **PHILLIP "LEFTY" WEINERT** 1919-24, 1927-28 LHPitcher (131 games)
- **PHILIP "PHIL" WEINTRAUB** 1933-35, 1937-38, 1944-45 Infield (444 games)
- **ED "LEFTY" WINEAPPLE** 1929 LHPitcher (1 game)
- **STEPHEN "STEVE" YEAGER** 1972-86 Catcher (1269 games)—Convert to Judaism
- **LAWRENCE "LARRY" YELLEN** 1963-64 RHPitcher (14 games)
- **KEVIN YOUKILIS** 2004-05 Infield (116 games)
- **GUY ZINN** 1911-15 Outfield (314 games)
- **EDWARD "EDDIE" ZOSKY** 1991-92, 1995, 1999-2000 Shortstop (44 games)—Jewish Mother

JEWISH BASEBALL PLAYERS BEFORE THE MAJOR LEAGUE

On June 19, 1846, the first organized baseball game was played on the Elysian Fields of Hoboken, NJ by two New York teams. The rules those teams followed would be the ancestors of the modern rules of the game.

From very early on, the new, highly organized version of the ancient game of rounders, now "base ball," attracted Jewish players. In 1859, for instance, the Gotham Club had an outfielder named Cohen and the Empire Club had a player named Levy. Both of these clubs were from New York and important competitors in the baseball world of that time.

The first important association of baseball clubs was the National Association of Base Ball Players, formed in 1857. Already in that first year, the Empire Club of New York had a first basemen named Thomas Leavy. Leavy played in all the team's ten games that year and scored 12 runs. Empire won 8 games that year, with 1 loss and 1 tie. Leavy would play with the same team again in 1860, when he would play outfield and third base. He would play in six of the team's seven games but score only 3 runs, the lowest figure of the team's starting nine. The team would finish the season with 3 wins and 4 losses. Leavy would be one of three players to represent Empire at the January 22, 1857 meeting at Smith's Hotel on Broome Street, New York, NY that would see the formation of the National Association of Baseball Players. He became a member of the "Committee to Draft a Code of Laws on the Game of Base Ball." Leavy was also mentioned in the lyrics of a song composed in 1858 to celebrate New York's baseball teams. This song is one of the earliest known concerning baseball and one of the earliest sources known advocating baseball as our national sport. Here is the verse in question, number 12, along with the chorus of "Ball Days' in the Year A.D. 1858":

> But we'll cross to the westward, where Empire takes its way,
> At our home, the Elysian Fields, this club enjoys its play;
> They've Benson, Hoyt, and Miller, Leavy, Thorne, and Fay,
> And are noted for their even play on every practice day.
>
> Then shout, shout for joy, and let the welkin ring,
> In praises of our noble game, for health 'tis sure to bring;
> Come, my brave Yankee boys, there's room enough for all,
> So join in Uncle Samuel's sport-the pastime of base ball.

During the 1858 season, the Osceola team of Brooklyn had an outfielder with the family name of Solomon. Solomon scored 4 runs in 2 games, though he may have played in more games than just 2 as records have been recovered for only 3 of the team's games. Osceola finished the season 3-2. Another player of that year whose name may indicate a Jewish background is Salsman of the Gothic team of New York. Salsman was a 2nd and 3rd baseman and seemed to play in all the team's games. In the 3 games with records he scored 6 runs. The team finished 1-6.

As already noted, Levy played for Empire in 1859, as a bench player. He appeared in only 3 of the team's eight games, but did score 6 runs, more than any other bench player did. Empire finished the season 4-4. It seems quite likely that this name was misspelled and that this is the same Thomas Leavy who had played with the team in 1857 and would do so again in 1860. Cohen, also mentioned above, played this season with Gotham. He was one of the team's starting nine and played the outfield. He scored 11 runs in 4 games, the second highest run total of the team, which finished 4-5. Cohen played with Gotham again in 1860, now playing both outfield and catching. He scored 15 runs for the season, during which Gotham had an 8-1-4 record. In 1861, Cohen was strictly a catcher. He scored 6 runs in the team's 1-2 season. In 1862, Cohen had been moved out of the team's starting nine and his position was changed to 2nd base. He scored 2 runs in the team's 6-3 season. The records for Gotham for 1863 are not complete and Cohen's name does not appear. But the team was enriched that year with the membership of the great Harry Wright (1835-1895). His brother George (1847-1937), like himself one of the earliest of Hall of Famers, joined the team in 1864, when Cohen returned to the team's starting nine, playing 2nd, 3rd, and the outfield. That season Cohen scored 18 runs, four more than Harry Wright did and just one less than George. The Gothams had a 3-7-1 year. Cohen played his last year with Gotham in 1865. Harry Wright was again with the team. George Wright does not seem to have played baseball in 1865. Cohen, again one of the starting nine, played all the infield positions, except 1st, as well as catching. Cohen again scored 18 runs, four below Harry Wright. The team ended the season 5-7.

1861 marked the first appearance in the records of the Association of one of the Pike brothers, the eldest brother, Boaz Pike. Lipman and Jacob Pike were the first Jewish brothers to play in the Major Leagues. Boaz was a bench player for Exercise of Brooklyn. He appeared in 3 of the team's 8 games and scored 6 runs. His position was outfield. Exercise finished the year with a 4-4 record.

The year 1863 saw the first appearance in the National Association of Nathan Berkenstock (1831-1900), a player who would go on to play in the National Association of Professional Base Ball Players, a new group for salary players in 1871, its first year. Nate played for the Athletics of Philadelphia, appearing on 1st base and in the outfield. He scored 19 runs during the season, which the Athletics finished 7-5. The Athletic team was even better in 1864,

Jewish Major Leaguers

Nate Berkenstock

during which Nate played only the 1st base position, with an 8-1 record. Nate scored 28 runs during this season. In 1865, Nate again played 1st base, scoring 59 runs in 15 games. The team was joined that year by Al Reach (1840-1928), later the founder of both Reach Sporting Goods and the Philadelphia Phillies. Reach, who played 2nd base and had a reputation as an excellent hitter scored 57 runs in 15 games. The Athletics finished the year 15-3. Nate's last year with the amateur Athletics was in 1866, when he became a bench player, rather than one of the starting nine, though still covering 1st. Reach was still on 2nd and the team added to its roster Lipman Emanuel Pike (1845-1893) for his first appearance in the association. Thus the 1866 Philadelphia Athletics, which is famed for being the first team to pay some of its players, including Pike and Reach, was also the first team with two Jewish players. Nate scored 66 runs in his 13 games. The team had a 23-2 season. Perhaps in memory of his fine services for the team between 1863 and 1866, and perhaps at the suggestion of Al Reach who was still with the team, Nate Berkenstock was called back to the now all-professional Philadelphia Athletics to play one last game on October 30, 1871. This was the final game of the season and the league's championship game. The Athletics won the game and the title of Base Ball World Champions, the very first such title and a title that Philadelphia teams would rarely hold over the next 130 some years.

Lip Pike, as I mentioned, started his career in 1866, with the Philadelphia Athletics, a team that was the ancestor of the present day Oakland Athletics only in name. Lip played that year mostly on 3rd, but occasionally on 2nd and in the outfield. He scored 100 runs in his 16 games played, to earn his $20 a week salary. During a game on July 16 against another Philadelphia team, the Alerts, Lip hit six homeruns, five of them in consecutive at bats. The game ended with the Athletics outscoring the Alerts 67 to 25.

In 1867, Lip played for two different teams, the Irvington team of Irvington, NJ and the Mutuals of New York. Lip started the year with Irvington and played 6 games at 3rd base and scored 19 runs. There were no contracts or reserve clauses in those days, so Lip accepted a better offer from Boss Tweed's Mutuals. Even without Lip, Irvington had a good year, ending 16-7. Lip appeared in 21 of the Mute's 30 games, appearing in the outfield and at all three bases. He scored 82 runs in the team's 23-6-1 season.

Lip was back with the Mutuals for the 1868 season, this time strictly as an outfielder. He appeared in 25 of the team's 41 games, scoring 109 runs. The Mutes finished the year 31-10. In 1869, Lip joined the Atlantic team of Brooklyn, playing strictly as a 2nd baseman. Atlantic had a season of 40-6-2. Lip played in all 48 games the team played and scored 193 runs on 175 hits. This was the first season when hits were counted. Lip's teammate on 1st base during this season and 1870 was Joe "Old Reliable" Start (1842-1927), one of the great stars of early baseball. It was an 11th inning triple by Start on June 14, 1870 that ended the Cincinnati Red Stockings' 88 game win streak of 1869-70. In 1870, Lip's second season with Atlantic covering 2nd base, he had 144 hits in 58 games, again not missing a single game. During his career Lip earned for himself the sobriquet of "the Iron Batter."

Jewish Major Leaguers

"Lip" Pike

Atlantic finished 41-17. Starting with 1871, Lip would go on to play ten years in the Major Leagues.

In 1866, the Liberty team of New Brunswick, New Jersey had a player named A. Solomon. He played in all six games of Liberty's 4-2 season. It is not known what position he played, but he did score 17 runs. In the same season, A. Oppenheimer played for his first year with the Oriental team of Greenpoint, New York. Oppenheimer scored 9 runs in the team's 1-6 season. Oppenheimer was back in 1867, scoring 30 runs in just 8 games of the team's 15-3 year. For neither season is Oppenheimer's position listed.

The year of 1867 saw a new player named Silberman for the Geary team of Philadelphia. Silberman played in 16 of the teams 25 games (19-6) and scored 60 runs. Levi Meyerle (1845-1921), a great early player who was long believed, mistakenly, to have been Jewish was also a member of this team. Levi, like Al Reach and Nate Berkenstock, played for the Athletics in the 1871 championship game. Silberman's field position is not known. That is true of another 1867 player, C. Leavitt of the Excelsior team of Elmira, NY. Leavitt appeared in 3 of the team's 12 games, with 7 runs scored. Excelsior had a 6-6 season.

In 1868, the Cincinnati club Great Western secured the services of a Jewish catcher and outfielder named Rudolph Kalish. This was the first year the team appeared in the records of the National Association of Base Ball Players, the amateur predecessor of the National Association of Professional Base Ball Players (1871-1875), the first Major League and antecedent of the present National League. The Braves and Cubs of that second National Association are still with us. The Great Western would continue through the start of the 1869 season, the great year of the appearance of the first all-professional baseball team, the Cincinnati Red Stockings. In 1868, Great Western would play the Red Stockings twice, before the latter had become an all-professional team.

Rudolph does have the rather strange statistics that were recorded for players in 1868, under the influence of cricket record keeping. He appeared in 11 of the team's 20 games that season. He had 31 hands lost (outs), which averaged 2 per game, with 9 left over. Of the team's starting 9, only two players had higher hands lost figures. (High, in this case, being bad.) Rudolph scored 31 runs, which averaged 2 per game, with 9 over. Only one of the starting 9 had a lower figure, (with low being bad.) Still, it must be remembered that Rudolph was primarily a catcher, which has always has been a low scoring position. In any case, the 1868 Great Western had a winning season of 11-9, including 4 games against the Live Oak team of Cincinnati, two wins and two losses. They lost both of their games against the Red Stockings, mentioned above.

Rudolph Kalish was the son of Philip Kalish. Philip had been born as Fabische Mendel Kalischer in Leszno, Poland (then Lissa, Prussia) around 1810. He came to the United States around 1836. He had made the trip with his brother David. Soon after their arrival, Fabische Kalischer became Philip Kalish and followed the trade of a furrier on Grant Street, Brooklyn. Philip had married an English woman, Charity Roberts. It seems unlikely that Charity was Jewish, but Philip saw to it that his children were raised in the Jewish faith. Rudolph was born in January 1848 in Brooklyn. During the

1860's, Philip with his wife and their five children, three boys and two girls, moved west and settled in downtown Cincinnati, having sold his New York business to his brother David. Philip soon established himself in his new home as a furrier, traveling further west in search of pelts, including at least one expedition to Denver. Philip belonged to a synagogue in Cincinnati.

In 1870, Rudolph joined the Live Oak team of Cincinnati. This team, the earliest baseball team in the city, had been in existence since 1860 as a town ball club and had been reorganized in 1866 as a base ball club. It would continue to play through 1868, but suspended operations for 1869, coming back in 1870. In that year it played at least 17 games, but scores for only 10 of these have survived. According to those results, Rudolph was now a bench player, no longer one of the starting nine, and playing third base. He appeared in six games. In those 6 games he had 13 hits, giving him a hits average of 2.17. This is a new system of statistics adopted since Rudolph's 1868 stats. Only two other players on his team had a higher (or better) average than this. However, with the exception of a single double, all of Rudolph's hits were singles. Therefore his total bases were only 14, giving him a total base average of 2.33, just the eighth best on his team. Of the 10 recorded games for the team, they won 6 and lost 4, including its two games against the Red Stockings.

RUDOLPH KALISH

After this season, Rudolph Kalish turned for his living to the furrier trade, working with his father. Around 1875, he married Lucy Thorpe (1854-1892), a local Ohio girl whose father had come from England and whose mother was from Missouri. The Rudolph Kalish's had six children, four boys and two girls. In 1895, Philip, Rudolph's father, died. On his death, he was buried in a Jewish cemetery in Cincinnati. In his latter years, Rudolph became a house painter. He died in 1921 in Cincinnati, where he was buried in the Wesleyan Cemetery. He has numerous descendants alive today, including a great, great granddaughter who recently won a university scholarship for her abilities in track and field. A number of other descendants through the years have displayed athletic abilities.

In 1869, a player name J. Holtzman played 1st base and outfield for the

Southern club of New Orleans. He scored 59 runs in 14 games. Southern had a 13-7 season. The following year, Holtzman played on the same team on 3rd and in the outfield. In 14 games, Holtzman scored 62 runs, the most by any player on the team, which completed 1870 with a 13-8 record. New Orleans produced another Jewish player in 1869, J. Levy of the R. E. Lee club. Levy was a short stop and played in 5 of the team's 8 games, scoring 10 runs. R. E. Lee, which played Southern in four of its eight games in 1869, split the series with 2 victories each. R. E. Lee had a 7-3 year. It seems likely that J. Holtzman and J. Levy, as probably the only Jews playing baseball in New Orleans at that time, must have known each other quite well.

Jewish Major Leaguers

Jacob Pike (?)

It should be clear to the reader that this chapter is based both on research and speculation. I have tried to be as conservative as possible as far as the speculation is concerned. There may very well have been far more Jewish players in the records than I have discussed. Where names alone have been the determinate, I have tried to stick to the most "Jewish" sounding I could find. But among the Marks, Schwartz's, Abrams, Freemans, Myers, Steiners, Hambergers, Goldsmiths and so on there are very likely other Jewish players. But even of those players that I have discussed, it should be understood that only in those cases where both first and last names are known is the situation definite beyond any doubt, except in the case of Thomas Leavy, where again I have based my analysis on speculation.

The result of this investigation shows that as far back as records can be examined, there has always been a consistent Jewish presence in baseball. Jewish athletes have been especially drawn to baseball long before it was our national game, long before Berg, or Greenberg, or Koufax, from its very beginnings. Perhaps it has something to do with the game's apparent simplicity combined with the subtlety of its strategies that makes it a rare combination of physical effort and mental challenge. Most sports consist of dull repetitions of the same actions. But in baseball there is enough variety of activities for the most sophisticated palate, yet the game remains fascinating to the complete amateur.

LIFE IMITATING ART IMITATING LIFE

On August 19, 1951, the outlook wasn't brilliant for the St. Louis Browns. They were floundering at the bottom of their league and their harassed owner, Bill Veeck (pronounced to rhyme with "wreck") was struggling to get customers into the stadium. Veeck had already broken many of the old, unwritten rules of baseball etiquette by putting entertainment before sportsmanship in his plans. The baseball "purists" could never tire of blasting the daring owner.

Veeck may not have started the tradition of giveaways, but he brought it to new heights. He hired the great Jewish baseball comedian Max Patkin to coach at first base. Max would not coach all through the game, but in the early innings, during which he pulled all kind of antics, including mocking the players and umpires as well as his famous water spitting trick. On one occasion, a newspaper published a scathing editorial by one of the "purists" denouncing Patkin's act. Max went to see Bill Veeck to apologize, for the editorial had really upset him. When Max was through with his apology, Veeck asked him if the editorial had spelled his name right. When Max told him they had, Veeck asked him then what in the world could he possibly be sorry about. Then he told Max to go back to work and keep up the clowning.

Photo: UPI

EDDIE GAEDEL

Nevertheless, despite Max, the giveaways, a "you manage the team contest," and many other types of promotional come-ons, the Browns were not filling their stands, or anywhere close to it. By August, the only mystery left in the Browns' season was whether they would loose more than 100 games before the year was out. (They would.)

On that famous date and year, August 19, 1951, a special celebration was being held at Sportsman's Park. It was the 50th anniversary of the American League and St. Louis was celebrating in royal style. A large cake was rolled out and a midget popped our, wearing a St. Louis Brown's uniform cut just for him, with the number 1/8 on the back, and carrying a diminutive bat. It was a double header against the Detroit Tigers and nothing important took place during the first game.

But during the second game something very historical took place. It was the bottom of the first and the home team was batting. A pinch hitter was announced for Brown's batter Frank Saucier, "Number 1/8, Eddie Gaedel." The fans gasped, they had seen the midget. The photographers (the few who were there to cover the Brown's games) clicked their shutters. Eddie Gaedel, the first midget to ever get an official at-bat in a Major League game, came to the plate.

MOE BERG & DONALD DAVIDSON

Detroit Tigers' pitcher Bob Cain threw the first pitch well over Gaedel's head and Detroit's catcher Bob Swift received it in his glove. Home plate umpire Ed Hurley crouched down as low as he could to keep the strike zone in view. The second pitch was also too high, as the strike zone for the tiny man was too small an area for the pitcher to hit. Cain ended up walking the 3'7" tall midget on just four pitches. The Browns' first base coach waiting to greet Bill Veeck's latest sensation was Max Patkin. Eddie was quickly replaced with a pinch runner, Jim Delsing, and the St. Louis fans gave him a standing ovation as he trotted off to the dugout.

Commissioner Albert "Happy" Chandler found the incident amusing and took no action, but the president of the American League, William

Harridge was outraged. He immediately banned the use of midgets and ordered Gaedel's at-bat and walk removed from the record books. That final indignity has since been reversed, but, presumably, midgets remain banned from American League play. Apparently midgets are legal to use in the National League, although no manager has ever taken advantage of this loophole. Veeck had expressed his intention of using Gaedel again, but this time with the bases loaded, a good way to win a tied game in the bottom of the ninth.

This incident has another Jewish connections, besides Max Patkin. The story "You Could Look It Up" by James Thurber, which presumably inspired Veeck and which first appeared in *The Saturday Evening Post* in 1941, has the following passage, concerning the pitcher who pitched to the midget (in Thurber's fictional story, by a strange twist, it is St. Louis who is pitching to the midget, rather than putting the midget in): "I wisht [sic] I could call the pitcher's name--it wasn't old Barney Pelty." Barney Pelty was one of the greatest of Jewish pitchers. His lifetime ERA was lower than that of Sandy Koufax. During his playing years he was known as the "Yiddish Curver." The team that the midget was playing for was not identified. The story is written in a kind of baseball lingo that is more typical of Ring Lardner than it is of Thurber.

In Thurber's story the midget has the strange name of Pearl du Monville and measures only 2'11" or 2'10". Unlike the Polish-Lithuanian Gaedel, he is of French-Hungarian origin. And unlike Gaedel, he didn't keep the bat on his shoulder and walk, as he was supposed to, but lightly hit the ball, which resulted in his being tagged out.

And where did Thurber get his idea for the

MOE BERG & DAVIDSON'S PARENTS

story? As Veeck chose to draw his inspiration from Thurber's story (although he denied it), Thurber himself probably drew his inspiration from a series of real incidents that took place around Boston in 1938. These events involved the mysterious Moe Berg, the Jewish catcher, a graduate of Princeton, who later became one of the nation's most important spies during WW II.

In 1938, Joe Cronin was the player-manager of the Boston Red Sox, the first manager in the American League to win pennants for two different teams. Cronin would be inducted into the Baseball Hall of Fame in 1956. (Only Hank Greenberg would accompany him into the Hall that year.) The batboy for the team was young Donald Davidson, a dwarf who would later rise through the ranks of the Boston  Braves (including its reincarnations as the Milwaukee Braves and the Atlanta Braves). For many years he was the team's travelling secretary and then assistant to the team's president. Later he would serve in similar capacities with the Houston Astros. He was probably the only man besides Hank Aaron to be present for every one of Aaron's homeruns. In 1970, at that year's All Star Game, Donald received special recognition for his accomplishments in baseball.

Donald was a good student in high school. But Donald's grades were vastly improved when Moe Berg, the team's second string catcher, took over tutoring Donald in Latin and French. Berg himself was extraordinarily gifted in languages and could speak at least a dozen. Donald's parents were amazed when Donald brought home A's in both languages. Joe Cronin would kid Berg that the team would do better if the catcher spent more time warming up the pitchers and less time on Don Davidson's lessons.

During an exhibition game in Brockton, Massachusetts, Cronin put Donald in as a pinch hitter. Donald was only 3'6" at that time, but he estimated that he crouched down another two inches at the plate. A kid's bat was on his shoulder. Donald was walked on four straight pitches. Donald's name appeared next day in the box scores.

Some time passed and it was almost the end of the season. The Yankees had assured themselves another pennant and the Red Sox were out of the running. Cronin decided to do something he had been thinking about for some time. Moe Berg was due to bat. Cronin handed Donald a fungo bat and aimed him towards home plate. A message was sent off to the public address announcer. But then fate stepped in in the shape of Bill Summers, the home plate umpire. Summers was furious. He ordered Donald back to the dugout and called Cronin over. He told the player-manager that no one was going to turn the game into a farce while he was umpiring. Thus ended the on-field Major League baseball career of Donald Davidson, with one at-bat in an exhibition game, a walk, and one approach towards the plate. And thus began the legend of the small person batting in a Major League game that would inspire a great humorist and finally become full-blown reality in the figure of Eddie Gaedel.

As the year's passed, Davidson continued his friendship with Moe Berg. Moe visited Donald some years after his heroic spying feats in WWII and Donald snapped Polaroid pictures of him in a restaurant along with Don's parents and wife. There is another color Polaroid picture of Moe relaxing in Donald's house, a bit older Moe than in the other pictures. In 1960, Donald was having a party in his hometown of Milwaukee. Moe had promised to attend, but couldn't make it. He sent a telegram, "Only an act of God last moment kept me away from there. Get off my lap. Love to Patty. Regards, Moe Berg."

The "Get off my lap" was a joke referring to a photo from the time when Donald was a batboy, taken sitting on Berg's lap. Patty was Donald's wife. Donald collected clippings concerning Berg, including a number of obituaries from the New York papers. He also corresponded with Charles Owen, an admirer of Moe, many years after the catcher's death.

Since his death, Moe Berg has also become a legendary figure. He was the subject of a folksinger's ballad, a novel, and an exhibition at the headquarters of the CIA. A number of documentary films have been produced about his life and the rights to a biography of him were purchased by actor George Clooney, who planned to play Berg in a full scale Hollywood production. So not just one, but two legends were being created in the dugout of the 1938 Boston Red Sox.

Jewish Players In The National Basketball Association*

(*including the ABA and the NBL)

- **Morris "Moe" Becker** 1945-47 Guard (73 games)
- **Irving Bemoras** 1953-54, 1956-57 Guard/Forward (131 games + 3 playoff games)
- **Meyer "Mike" Bloom** 1947-49 Forward/Center (93 games + 4 playoff games)
- **Nelson Bobb** 1949-1953 Guard (227 games + 6 playoff games)
- **Harry Boykoff** 1947-1951 Center (229 games)
- **Lawrence "Larry" Brown** 1967-1972 Guard (376 games + 47 playoff games + 3 All-Star games)
- **Stanley Brown** 1947-48, 1951-52 Forward (34 games)
- **Howard Carl** 1961-62 Guard (31 games)
- **Stephen Chubin** 1967-1970 Guard (226 games + 11 playoff games)
- **William Evans** 1969-70 Guard (53 games + 6 playoff games)
- **Philip Farbman** 1948-49 Guard/Center (48 games)
- **George Feigenbaum** 1940-50, 1952-53 Guard (17 games)
- **Jerome "Jerry" Fleishman** 1946-50, 1952-53 Guard/Forward (262 games + 22 playoff games)
- **Donald Forman** 1948-49 Guard (44 games + 9 playoff games)
- **Nathan Frankel** 1939-40, 1946-47 Guard/Forward (33 games)

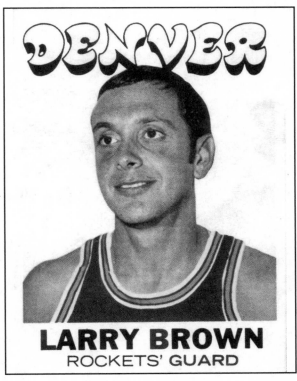

LARRY BROWN
ROCKETS' GUARD

- **LAWRENCE "LARRY" FRIEND** 1957-58
  Forward (44 games)
- **JACK "DUTCH" GARFINKEL** 1945-49
  Guard (120 games +
  3 playoff games)
- **NORMAN "NORMIE" GLICK**
  1949-50 Forward (1 game)
- **BENJAMIN GOLDFADDEN** 1946-47
  Forward (2 games)
- **LEO "ACE" GOTTLIEB** 1946-48
  Guard (84 games + 4 playoff
  games)
- **GERALD "JERRY" GREENSPAN**
  1963-65 Center (25 games)
- **NORMAN GREKIN** 1953-54
  Forward (1 game)

"LARRY" FRIEND

- **ROBERT "BOBBY" GROSS** 1975-83
  Forward (513 games + 25 playoff games)—Jewish Father
- **ERNEST GRUNFELD** 1977-1986 Forward (693 games + 42 playoff
  games)
- **SIDNEY "SONNY" HERTZBERG** 1946-1951 Guard (293 games +
  18 games)
- **ARTHUR HEYMAN** 1963-1970 Forward (310 games + 22 playoff games)
- **MELVIN HIRSCH** 1946-47 Guard (13 games)
- **WILLIAM "RED" HOLZMAN** 1945-1954 Guard (496 games +
  28 playoff games)
- **RALPH "KAPPY" KAPLOWITZ** 1946-48 Guard/Forward (105 games +
  23 playoff games)
- **LOUIS HERMAN "RED" KLOTZ** 1947-48 Guard (11 games + 6 playoff games)
- **BARRY KRAMER** 1964-65, 1969-70 Forward (59 games)
- **JOEL KRAMER** 1978-83 Forward (328 games + 28 playoff games)
- **HERBERT KRAUTBLATT** 1948-49 Guard/Forward (10 games)

- **RUDOLPH "RUDY" LaRUSSO** 1959-69 Forward/Center (737 games + 93 playoff games + 4 All-Star games)—Jewish Mother
- **HENRY "HANK" LEFKOWITZ** 1946-47 Forward (24 games + 3 playoff games)
- **BARRY LIEBOWITZ** 1967-68 Guard (82 games)
- **NORMAN MAGER** 1950-51 Forward (24 games)
- **LIONEL MALAMED** 1948-49 Guard (44 games)
- **SAUL MARIASCHIN** 1947-48 Guard (43 games + 3 playoff games)
- **NATHAN MILITZOK** 1946-47 Forward (56 games)
- **EDWIN MILLER** 1952-54 Forward/Center (142 games + 2 playoff games)
- **JACOB "JACK" MOLINAS** 1953-54 Forward (29 games)

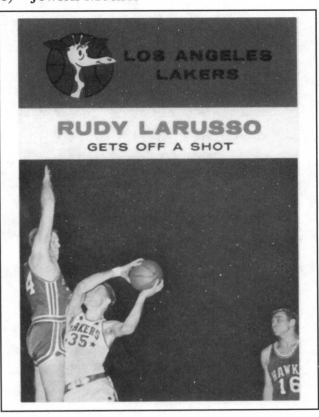

- **BORIS NACHAMKIN** 1954-55 Forward/Center (6 games)
- **DAVID NEWMARK** 1968-71 Center (176 games + 6 playoff games)
- **HOWARD RADER** 1946-49 Guard/Forward (99 games)
- **SHERWIN RAIKEN** 1952-53 Guard (6 games + 4 playoff games)
- **ALEXANDER "PETEY" ROSENBERG** 1946-47 Center (51 games + 9 playoff games)
- **LEONARD ROSENBLUTH** 1957-59 Forward (82 games + 4 playoff games)
- **HENRY "HANK" ROSENSTEIN** 1946-47 Forward (60 games)
- **IRWIN "IRV" ROTHENBERG** 1946-49 Center (131 games + 11 games)
- **MARVIN "MICKEY" ROTTNER** 1945-48 Guard (105 games + 14 playoff games)
- **MARVIN SCHATZMAN** 1949-50 Forward (34 games)

- **Adolph "Dolph" Schayes** 1948-64 Forward/Center (1059 games + 97 playoff games + 11 All-Star games)
- **Daniel "Danny" Schayes** 1981-99 Center (1138 games + 69 playoff games)
- **Oscar "Ossie" Schectman** 1946-47 Guard (54 games)
- **Arthur "Speed" Spector** 1946-50 Forward (169 games + 3 playoff games)
- **Sidney Tanenbaum** 1947-49 Guard (70 games + 6 playoff games)
- **Irving Torgoff** 1939-40, 1946-49 Forward (173 games + 8 playoff games)
- **Neal Walk** 1969-77 Center (568 games + 8 playoff games)
- **Ronald Watts** 1965-67 Forward (28 games + 1 playoff game)
- **Richard "Rick" Weitzman** 1967-68 Guard (25 games + 3 playoff games)
- **Max Zaslofsky** 1946-56 Guard/Forward (540 games + 63 playoff games + 1 All-Star game)

LENNIE ROSENBLUTH

THE SPHAS

The word Sphas is an anagram for South Philadelphia Hebrew Association (pronounced like "spas"). Often it is written either SPHAS or SPHAs, but I have adopted the style that appears in the team's own publications. However capitalized the name stands for one of the finest professional basketball teams of the first half of the twentieth century. Around 1918, certain Jewish former members of the South Philadelphia High School basketball team sought a way to continue their association. They approached a Jewish social club in the neighborhood, at Fourth and Reed Streets, and offered to perform exhibition basketball games for the club in exchange for free membership. The deal was struck. The players involved were Edwin I. "Hughie" Black, who had been captain of the high school team, Eddie Gottlieb, Mark "Mockie" Bunnin, Charlie Newman, and the brothers Herman "Chickie" and Harry Passon. The exhibition games, which were first held at a church hall at Sixth and Reed Streets, became a remarkable success and soon moved

PHILA. SPHAS — AMERICAN PRO LEAGUE AND WORLD'S BASKETBALL CHAMPIONS
Season 1939-40

Left to Right—Manager Eddie Gottlieb, Petey Rosenberg, Leo Gottlieb, Howard Rosan, Si Boardman, Moe Goldman, Inky Lautman, Shikey Gotthofer, Cy Kaselman and George Wolfe.

to the Philadelphia Athletic Club at Broad and Wood Streets.

In a short time, the Sphas were performing on a regular basis each Saturday night. When the game was over, the floor would be cleared and a dance band would come out and the dancing would start. The Sphas games became the central social event of the Jewish community in Philadelphia. Many a Jewish couple in Philadelphia can trace their initial meeting back to a Sphas game.

In 1926 the Sphas went into a temporary hiatus, but in 1929 they came back better than ever. Their driving force now was Eddie Gottlieb alone, as owner, coach, and manager.

The Sphas were soon recognized as not only the finest Jewish team in Philadelphia, but also the finest basketball team of any kind in the area. Soon they were traveling across the country bringing with them their brand of hard fought, but skillful playing.

But despite their nationwide notoriety, the Sphas did not find basketball in the period between the World Wars a remunerative career. Players often had to go without salaries; the money the team earned often went to pay their expenses, including their room and board, travel, and even their uniforms.

At first, the Sphas played in the Philadelphia League, but their skill was too great for this local organization, so they moved up to the Eastern League. Here too, they quickly outmatched the competition, and they eventually joined the American League, which is now recognized historically as the

Sphas Sparks

Edited by
DAVID ZINKOFF

VOLUME 2—NUMBER 15   FEBRUARY 3, 1940   Philadelphia, Pa.

Confucius Say - Next Sat. Troy Celtics Play Game Great - Sphas Careful - Order Tickets Now!

Confucius Say —

That wise old sage Confucius is giving you the correct dope on next Saturday's attraction.

The Troy Celtics with five of the players yet to meet defeat on the Broadwood floor this season, will be here next Saturday, in an attempt to keep their slate clean. The Kingston Club featuring Pete Berenson, Bernie Fliegel, Charlie Johnson, Sam Kaplan and Chick Reiser decisioned the SPHAS 41-39, and the same 5 representing Troy and augmented by Joe Polcha, Moe Frankel and Mickey Kupperberg also won on their last appearance, 38-36.

Heeding Confucius, the SPHAS will be rarin' to go, determined to avenge these setbacks!

Another thrill in store for you. Bitter player and team rivalry predominates when these clubs meet!

TORRID PLAY!

CLOCKWISE:
Mike Bloom, Shikey Gotthofer, Cy Kaselman, Red Wolfe, Moe Goldman, Red Rosan, Inky Lautman, Petey Rosenberg, Eddie Gottlieb.

Tonight's Attractions

N. Y. JEWELS

•

Mac Kinsbrunner
Playing Leader

Moe Spahn
Cagey Cogwheel

Ace Goldstein
Spades High

Georgie Slott
Trouble Shooter

Stretch Pelkington
Southpaw Sizzler

Hagen Anderson
Comeback Kid

Al Benson
Merger Pivot

Willie Rubenstein
Sparkplug

Red Paris
City College Sensation

predecessor of today's National Basketball Association.

Through the late teens, the twenties, the thirties, and the forties, the rosters of the Sphas continually developed and changed. The team, at first, were all alums of South Philly High. But they were soon joined by Lou Schneiderman, of the city's Central High. After that, the team attracted Jewish players from New York, like Red Wolfe, Moe Goldman, Shikey Gotthofer, and Dutch Garfinkel.

The games would earn for the young players about $5 each. This was not a profession to make a living. Most of the players pursued further education or other careers while devoting their Saturday nights to the Sphas.

One such player was Gil Fitch, who played with the team between 1932 and 1940. Gil was a music student who formed his own band. It was often Gil's band, which would play for the audience after the games were over. The singer for Gil's band was a beautiful Jewish girl named Kitty Kallen. Kitty would later go on to sing with bands led by Jack Teagarden, Jimmy Dorsey, Harry James, and others. Her hit songs would include "Besame Mucho," "I'm Beginning to See the Light," "It's Been a Long, Long Time," and "Little Things Mean a Lot."

In their early years, the Sphas often had their home games in local churches. At first the team's opponents were largely made up of local Philadelphia Catholic clubs. Later they would play Protestant clubs as well. As one member explained it, the gentiles came to see the Jews get killed and the Jews came to see the Jews kill the gentiles. In later years, however, the Sphas played their games at the Broadwood Hotel on Broad Street. Here the audiences were mostly Jewish and decidedly friendly.

While they were with the Philadelphia League, the Sphas won three championships. With the larger and more prestigious Eastern League they won another three. When they joined the (basketball) American League, it was the top league in the country. When the Basketball Association of America was formed in 1946, it was not as yet clear that it was the future of basketball. The position of that league was not really secure until it absorbed the Midwestern National Basketball League in 1950, when the union was renamed the National Basketball Association. At that time the American League became clearly established as a minor league. But up to that time it was the leading professional basketball venue in the country. The Sphas won seven American League championships.

When Eddie Gottlieb formed his team for the new NBA, the Philadelphia Warriors, he used many players from his own old team, the Sphas. In 1950, he sold the rights to the team, but apparently none of the

Sphas Sparks

| Vol. 8 — No. 6 | SATURDAY, DECEMBER 1, 1945 | PHILA., PA. |

Baltimore Bullets Make Their First Appearance Here At The Broadwood Next Saturday Night Against Sphas

LOUIS "Inky" LAUTMAN

The Sphas will continue their American League schedule here next Saturday night by playing the team that they opposed in the final playoff series last season, with the Baltimore Bullets.

The Maryland quintet, coached by a former popular Sphas star, Red Rosan, will present a line-up studded with former college stars, including Moe Dubilier, NYU; Art Spector, Villanova; Ben Goldfadden, George Washington University; Ben Scharnus, Seton Hall; Hagan Anderson, NYU; Stutz Modzilewski, Rhode Island All-American; Walt Osiewalski, Michigan, and Price Brookfield, All-American at West Texas State.

This is quite a different array from the team that lost the championship to the Sphas, but is considered much stronger than last season's aggregation, and only needs more games together to make them a formidable pennant contender. In Brookfield, the Bullets have one of the coming stars of pro basketball. His sensational one-hand shots were the talk of Madison Square Garden and Convention Hall several years ago. He was ranked by the New York writers as one of the best basketball players ever to appear in the Garden.

Bill Dyer, former popular Philadelphia sportscaster, and present general manager of the Baltimore Bullets, is scouring the country for outstanding players who will put Baltimore on the basketball map.

The Marylanders have gone to considerable expense to renovate the 104th Regiment Armory, located at Fayette and Paca sts., Baltimore, Md., and opening night attendance proved that their investment was sound, over one thousand fans being turned away.

ORDER and PICK UP your tickets NOW!

players, to "Red" Klotz, an old member. The new Philadelphia Sphas, now practically denuded of Jewish players, aside from Klotz himself, who acted at first as player-manager, became the constant companions and foils of the Harlem Globetrotters. The team subsequently changed its name to the Washington Generals and, then, to the New York Nationals.

The idea of an all-Jewish basketball team is probably now politically incorrect and such a team will probably never happen again, at least outside of Israel. But for the entire period when Adolf Hitler was bamboozling the German people about their racial superiority, the Philadelphia Sphas were quietly proving the absurdity of the Nazi theories by being simply the greatest basketball team in the world.

MEMBERS OF THE SPHAS

The Sphas (South Philadelphia Hebrew Association) basketball team was the greatest all-Jewish sports team in American history. It won Eastern League championships three times (1931, 1932, and 1933) and basketball American League championships seven times (1934, 1936, 1937, 1940, 1940, 1941, 1943, and 1945.) The American League title, at that time, was the national championship. The Sphas was a breeding ground of great figures in basketball history, such as Eddie Gottlieb, one of the founders of the NBA, and Harry Litwack, Hall of Fame coach of Temple University. I list here, alphabetically, as complete a list as I have been able to create of Sphas (pronounced "spas") members. Non-playing associates of the organization are indicated with brackets. Some of the dates represent my best educated guesswork and some names must be missing. In addition, some of the members, other than those I have mentioned, may not have been Jewish. Alas, there is no authoritative history of the Sphas and published material of the time, like copies of *Sphas Sparks*, the team's program and newsletter, are very hard to find:

Dave Banks 1923-26

Thomas Barlow 1925-32

Moe Becker 1943-44

Ed Beron 1933-34

Solly Bertman 1931-32

Edwin I. "Hughie" Black 1918-25
    (Team Captain 1918-21)

Mike Bloom 1937-40

Si Boardman 1939-41

Stanley Brown 1946-50

Mark "Mockie" Bunnin 1918-22

Jim Cascia 1946-47

Joe Corman 1921

David Dabrow c. 1930

STANLEY BROWN

Manny Davidson 1920

Irv "Hy" Davis 1942-43

Lou Dubin 1937-38

Gil Fitch 1932-40

Jerry Fleishman 1943-46

Heshie Forman 1930-31

Lou Forman 1929-34

Jim Fox 1936-37

Jack "Dutch" Garfinkel 1940-46

Moe Goldman 1933-43

Dave Gordon 1930-31

Joel "Shikey" Gothoffer 1934-43

Edward "Eddie" Gottlieb 1918-24, 1930, 1941
    (Team Captain 1921-24), [Coach 1929-39,
    Manager 1939-46]

Leo "Ace" Gottlieb 1939-41

["Iz" Heller, Business Manager c.1921]

Arthur Hillhouse 1944-46

Leonard Kaplan 1946-47

Ralph Kaplowitz 1945-47

David "Cy" Kaselman 1929-41

Jules Kassner 1945-46

"Babe" Klotz 1918-25

Louis Herman "Red" Klotz 1940-50 (Player-coach 1949-50)

Harry Knorr 1923-24

Herb Knuppel 1943-44

Louis "Inky" Lautman 1933-47

Harry Litwack 1929-37 [Coach 1946-50]

LEONARD KAPLAN

RED KLOTZ

"Babe" Lyman 1929-32

Bill McCann (non-Jewish pitcher with Philadelphia A's) 1949-50

Meehan 1925-26

Sol Miehoff 1938-39

"Chink" Morganstein 1941-43

Elmore Morganthaler 1949-50 (In 1946, 7'1" Morganthaler was NBA's 1st
      7 footer.)

Charlie Newman 1918-22

Harry "Doc" Newman 1923-24

Paul Nowak 1943-44

Bernard "Bernie" Opper 1942-46

Harry Passon 1918-25

Herman "Chick" Passon 1918-26, 1929-31, 1932-33 (Team Captain 1925-26)

Max Patkin 1949-50

Max Posnack 1931-32

Lou Possner 1940-41

Hessie Pressman 1949-50

Phil Rabin 1939-40

[Abe Radel—official scorer & timekeeper]

Howie Rader 1944-45

Lenny Rader 1944-45 (twin brother of above)

Beno Resnick 1937-38

Howard "Red" Rosan 1934-43

Harry "Red" Rosen 1932-3

Alexander "Petey" Rosenberg 1939-44

Irwin "Irv" Rothenberg 1944-46

Jerry Rullo 1947-48 (not Jewish)

[Mike Saxe, Coach 1921-26]

Oscar "Ossie" Schectman 1942-46

Lou Schneiderman 1918-22

Schwartz 1925-26

Solomon "Butch" Schwartz 1942-43

[Bobby Seitchick, Manager 1918-21]

George Sensky 1945-46

"Red" Sheier 1930-33

Art "the Great" Shires 1929 (non-Jewish baseball player, played 1 game
    with Sphas)

Charley Tettemer 1923-24 (non-Jewish player)

Irv Torgoff 1940-46

Paul "Hook" Wallace c. 1944

Lenny Weiner 1949-50

Butch Weintraub 1940-41

Jack "Yock" Welsh 1929-33

Lou Wisner 1937-38

George "Red" Wolfe 1922-26, 1929-44

[David Zinkoff—Public Address Announcer & editor of programs 1935-50]

HARRY LITWACK

Harry Litwack was born in Galicia, Austria on September 20, 1907. His parents found asylum in the United States and Harry found his lifetime home in Philadelphia. Harry attended Philadelphia's Temple University and graduated in 1930, after serving three years on Temple's varsity basketball team, two of those years as captain of the team. And this was despite the fact that Harry was only 5'5" tall and weighed 160 pounds. On graduation he took two jobs, coaching basketball at Simon Gratz High School in Philadelphia and playing for the famous Sphas. In both positions he was outstanding. Gratz High School, under his leadership for 1930-1 had a record of 15-2. The Sphas during his career with them (1930-36) won two league championships, in the Eastern Basketball League and in the American Basketball League. The latter of these was the 1930's equivalent of the NBA.

Coach Harry Litwack

In 1931, after just one year of high school coaching, Harry was offered the job as head coach of Temple's freshman basketball team. He accepted and held this post until 1947. His record as freshman coach during those sixteen years was the amazing 181-32.

During the period 1948 to 1951, Harry was active in the Basketball Association of America and the NBA as assistant coach to the Philadelphia Warriors. The team's coach and owner during those years was Harry's old pal from the Sphas, Eddie Gottlieb.

In 1952, Harry, known as "The Chief," became head coach of Temple's varsity team, a position he would hold until 1973. In this position he would earn recognition across the nation as one of the most successful college basketball coaches in the history of the game. His overall record for his varsity career at Temple was 373-193. In all his 21 years in that position he suffered only a single losing season. Many experts of basketball have pointed out that Litwack's success was not due to the vast pool of talent with which Temple was endowed, but quite the opposite. No coach in history did so much with so little talent on the part of his players. Harry succeeded because he saw his mission to build educated, full-rounded students who could play basketball, rather than basketball players who attended a university.

At Temple, Harry took the Owls to 13 postseason tournaments and won the NIT championship in 1969. Twice Harry's team finished in third place in the NCAA tournament, in 1956 and 1958. In that latter year, Harry was chosen as the New York Basketball Writers Association Coach of the Year. In 1957, Harry coached the United States basketball team in that year's Maccabiah Games. His team took the gold medal.

In 1976, Harry was recognized for his achievements by being elected to the national Basketball Hall of Fame in Springfield, Massachusetts. Harry was also inducted into the Temple University Hall of Fame, the Pennsylvania Sports Hall of Fame, and the International Sports Hall of Fame in Netanya, Israel.

Harry died at his home in Huntington Valley, in the Philadelphia suburbs, on August 7, 1999.

BUNNY LEVITT

Records come and records go: Pete Rose got more hits than Ty Cobb; Hank Aaron hit more homers than Babe Ruth; Barry Bonds hit more homers in one year than Mark McGuire. But there is one record in the world of sports, particularly in basketball, that seems like it will never fall, the number of consecutive free throws at 499. This record was set on April 6, 1935 by 28-year

old Harold Levitt at a contest sponsored by the Chicago Sun-Times newspaper. Harold stood at only 5'4", but he was fast, so fast that he had earned the nickname "Bunny." But that evening it would not be Bunny's speed that would be tested but his eye and the steadiness of his hands. Bunny made basket after basket. The second best shooter, Wilfred Hetzel, had hit a remarkable 86 free throws. But Bunny soon surpassed that figure. Now he was approaching number 500 but, at last, Bunny missed. His figure stood at 499. But after the miss, Bunny insisted on going on. He continued shooting for a total of more than seven and a half hours. He had hit 871 free throws out of 872. He wanted to continue, but at 3:00am the Judge declared the end of the contest, with Levitt the winner.

Bunny was born in Chicago in 1920 and grew up in its teeming streets. There he learned to play baseball, handball, and basketball. As a child he played on the Chicago Cubs Junior baseball team. When he was older, he played on an all left-handed softball team, which was undefeated.

With his victory in the Sun-Times contest, Bunny became famous. Even though Bunny was white, stood only 5'4" in his tennis shoes, and weighed just 140 pounds, Abe Saperstein recruited him for the Harlem Globetrotters. Bunny would not play with the other members of the team in the competitive portion of the show, but between quarters he would stand at the free throw line and hit shot after shot. The Globetrotters would offer anyone in the audience who thought they could outshoot Bunny to come down and try his luck. If he won, they promised him $1,000. But the Globetrotters never had to pay. Bunny always won.

The first time that Bunny appeared with this challenge, William Hetzel, the runner-up for the Sun-Times contest challenged Bunny. He lost again. Then at the team's next stop, there was Hetzel. Again he lost. Hetzel followed the team wherever they went, still refusing to accept his defeat at the hands of Bunny. Finally, Saperstein got tired of it and barred Hetzel from attending the team's games.

Bunny recollects, "As the Globetrotters traveled from town to town, sometimes two games on Sundays—the team members usually slept on the bus. During my freshman year, however, I was wide awake just to take in the sights. My second year was different. I slept like everyone else."

Life on the road was rough and the Globetrotters were far from the wealthy celebrities they have become today. The whole team received just $100 per game, plus one half of the gate receipts. The comic genius of their show, which has held up so well all this time, was developed during those hard Depression years, when it was necessary to guarantee a full house to insure a full belly—even if that belly was only to be filled with hard salami, tins of sardines, and saltines eaten on the team bus. Particularly in the Deep South, the bus was often the only place that Abe Saperstein, Bunny Levitt, and the otherwise Black team could find to eat. Restaurants were not an alternative for the Harlem Globetrotters, even in those very same years that they traveled around Europe, including special appearances for the King and Queen of England and the Pope.

After appearing with the Globetrotters for four and a half years, Bunny accepted an offer from Converse Rubber Company to serve as a salesman. At that time U.S. Rubber was the nation's leading manufacturer of basketball shoes, with its Keds brand. Converse was just beginning to compete in what would eventually become a very competitive field.

Bunny worked only a few days as a salesman when he was assigned by Converse to conduct basketball clinics all across the country. These proved extremely successful for Bunny, Converse, and the sport of basketball. Bunny would appear at about 64 camps and clinics each season, travelling some 150,000 miles every year by car and air. He worked at this 363 days a year, only taking two vacation days.

During the Second World War, Bunny served with the Army Air Corps. The majority of his four years in the service was spent as a physical fitness instructor at Mitchell Field on Long Island. Bunny's responsibilities included supervising one of the New York Major League teams, each Monday, at Mitchell Field in order to play the service team. Near the end of the War, he was also was assigned to give physical therapy to wounded service men on the base. It was during this time that Bunny met his wife, Edith, who was a WAC serving at Mitchell. The couple met on the Field's handball court.

After the War, Bunny returned to his job for Converse, often appearing on television as a representative of the company and to display his amazing

athletic abilities. Among the shows he appeared on were *I've Got a Secret*, *What's My Line*, and *To Tell the Truth*. He also became a consultant to certain NBA stars to help them with their free throwing technique. These included Rick Barry of the Golden State Warriors and the Houston Rockets and Bill Sharman of the Boston Celtics.

After 37 years with Converse, Bunny is retired and living in Ocala, Florida. He rides a bike eight miles every day and still offers basketball clinics in the local high school. His record of 499 consecutive free throws remains the record after almost 70 years. His achievement has been noted in *The Guiness Book of Records* and *Ripley's Believe It or Not*.

Furthermore, he is remembered in the Basketball Hall of Fame in Springfield, Massachusetts, which displays his Harlem Globetrotter uniform.

Bunny Levitt's most famous quote is, "The best thing in life are free throws." This has certainly proved true for Bunny.

HARRY BOYKOFF

Harry Boykoff has left permanent marks on the history of basketball. Some of his pioneering efforts were minor. He was one of the first basketball players of modern times to play with a mustache. But some of his achievements were of the utmost importance. The rule against goaltending was created as a direct result of his style of play. Harry, with his great height, was able to jump up and use his fingertips to push out balls about to fall into the basket.

Harry Boykoff was born on July 24, 1922. He was not given a middle name, Harry used to kid, because his parents couldn't afford one. Harry's parents were Russian immigrants of average height and below average income. Life in America was not easy for them and their three children, two daughters and 6'9" Harry. Even today this sounds like a very tall young man, but in the late 1930's, this height was far more unusual.

When Harry entered Thomas Jefferson High School of Brooklyn, New York, the basketball coach, Max Hodesblatt, a former player for CCNY, saw great potential in the gangling young man. Not in his natural athletic ability, for Harry was more of a klutz than an athlete, but in that one quality one can never teach, height. So Hodesblatt set out to teach all the other things a great basketball player would need to know, dribbling, passing, shooting, and defending the basket. The process took time. Harry scored only a single point in his first 20 games for Thomas Jefferson. But by the time he graduated he was selected for the New York City All-Scholastic Team. He also won a scholarship to St. John's University.

At that time, St. John's University of Brooklyn, a Catholic institution, was famous all over the country for the fine quality of its basketball teams. But strangely, it was mostly famous for the number of great Jewish players that it attracted. Of five starters for its 1931 team, for instance, four were Jewish. These included two All-Americans, Max Posnack and Max Kinsbrunner. Posnack was the captain of the St. John's team during the 1930-31 season. That team is considered one of the best collegiate teams in the early history of basketball, with a 68-4 record over three years. Other outstanding Jewish players at St. John's include Reuben Kaplinsky, the team's captain in 1936; Alan Seiden, an All-American and captain of the team in 1958-59; and All-Americans Nathan Lazar and Jack Garfinkel. Another great St. John's player was Hy Gotkin, who was a member of Harry's class at Thomas Jefferson, as well as a fellow member of the basketball team there under Hodesblatt. The 5'8" Gotkin was a close friend of Harry and both were outstanding members of St. John's team and All-Americans.

At the time that he entered St. John's, Harry was the tallest player to ever have appeared for a New York school. But what Harry had learned at Thomas Jefferson was to prove just the basics of his trade. Under the hands of St. John's coach, Joe Lapchick, Harry would grow into a true master. Lapchick was himself a Hall of Fame player with the reputation as the first big player to master the sport. His reputation as a coach was equally high both at the college and professional levels.

In his sophomore year at St. John's, 1943, Harry led the team to victory in the NIT, at that time the most prestigious tournament in the country. That year, Harry averaged 16.6 points per game and the team finished with a 21-3 record. Harry was named an All-American that season. During a game played in Madison Square Garden against St. Joseph's, on February 8, 1943, Harry scored 45 points, setting a record for points scored in the Garden.

After his first season, the Second World War still raging, Harry enlisted in the Army. At 6'9", he was far taller than the services' 6'5" maximum. But when it came time to be measured, during his physical exam, he stepped off the scale and straddled it, while stooping, so the examiner, who wasn't paying close attention, passed him. Harry's first assignment in the Army was to serve in the president's honor guard at Hyde Park, NY. After six months, he was transferred to West Point, where he served as a field artillery instructor. A few months later, the War over, he was discharged, and he returned to St. John's to complete his degree in accounting and to continue his basketball career.

Some critics claim that Harry's stay in the Army robbed him of some of his skills. Before leaving Harry played 40 minutes a game, after he could only manage about half of that, but Harry still made the most of the time he was in there. In 1945-46, Harry led his team in scoring, with 16.5 points a game. The

THE BIG BOOK OF JEWISH SPORT HEROES

following year this mark improved to 16.7. In that last year at St. John's, Harry became the first player at the University to score 1000 points. During a game on March 11, 1947, Harry scored 54 points against St. Francis. Harry was again chosen as an All-American for both of his post service years.

Following graduation, Harry turned professional and joined the Toledo Jeeps of the NBL (1947-48). The next season (1948-49) he played with the same league's Waterloo (Iowa) Hawks. During his two years with the NBL, Harry scored 1351 points in 120 games. After the end of the 1948-49 season, there was a fusion of the NBL with the rival BAA, to form the NBA. Harry continued with the now NBA Waterloo Hawks for the 1949-50 season. The following year, with Waterloo folding, Harry joined the Boston Celtics, one of the worst teams in the league, still years away from the glory that "Red" Auerbach would bring it. In midseason, Harry was sent to the Tri-Cities (Moline & Rock Island, Illinois and Davenport, Iowa) Blackhawks.

Following this season, Harry retired, while receiving, at that time, the highest salary in the NBA, $15,000. While in the NBA, Harry scored 1105 points in 109 games.

Harry took up a career in advertising. He lived for awhile in Tennessee, then in Jamaica, New York. He was married and had three children. Eventually Harry also retired from business.

Following his second retirement, Harry found a new career, as an actor. Harry made brief appearances in a number of popular television series, including *Frasier* and *The Nanny*. As a film actor, he had parts in the Richard Dreyfuss, Burt Reynolds comedy *The Crew* (2000), where he played Louie the Lip, and the Warren Beatty, Diane Keaton comedy *Town and Country* (2001), where he played Henry.

Harry was elected to St. John's Athletics Hall of Fame and the New York City Basketball Hall of Fame. Harry died on February 20, 2001 in Santa Monica, California. He was 78 years old.

MACCABI TEL AVIV

One of the outstanding collegiate basketball players of the period 1993 to 1996 was Doron Sheffer of the University of Connecticut. Doron was the first player in his university's history to score at least 1,000 points and have more than 400 assists during three seasons. Doron is a native of Israel, from the town of Ramat Hasharon, and, in a land where watching tapes of American games is practically a national sport unto itself, he is comsidered a national hero. Doron was the first sabra to be drafted by a National Basketball Association team, when, during the second round of the 1996 NBA draft, he was selected by the Los Angeles Clippers. However, the 24-year-old guard, feeling that his chances of actually making the Clippers team that year were "close to zero," signed a three-year contract with a team in Israel, Maccabi Tel Aviv.

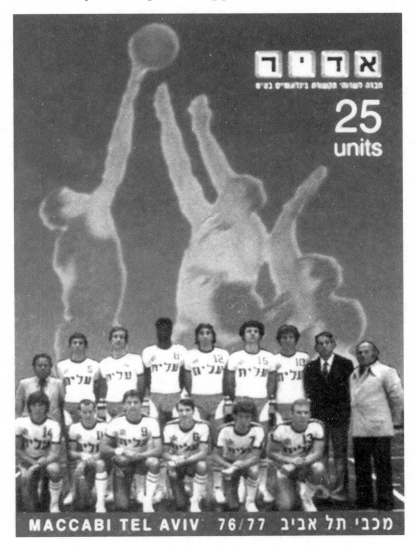

Sheffer's contract contained an escape clause, in case Sheffer was offered a contract by a team in the NBA, which, alas, never happened. But the NBA is not the only game in town in Israel and professional basketball has, for many years, been a major activity in Israel. Of all the professional basketball teams in Israel, the national favorites and the greatest team in the Israeli league is the team that represents Tel Aviv.

TAL BRODY

Two millennia ago, when faced with seemingly unbeatable odds, the Jewish people rose in revolt against the Syrian Greeks, under the leadership of the Maccabees. In 1977, faced with seemingly unbeatable odds, the basketball fans of Israel faced down the forces of all of Europe, under the leadership of Maccabi Tel Aviv.

Maccabi Tel Aviv is a member of the eleven team Israeli Basketball Association. The Association is not an amateur league, but professional. Some of its players are sabras, like Sheffer, but others are American born. By 1991, the team had won the league championship twenty-one times in a row. As the winners of the league championship, Maccabi Tel Aviv represented the nation in the annual European Champion Clubs Cup competition.

The European Championship was established in 1958 and Israel was represented in that very first competition by Maccabi. But it was not until 1968 that the team had its first major success, when it reached the semi-final round. Maccabi was defeated by the team that represented Spain, but only by 2 points. In 1975, Maccabi again reached the semifinals, but again they were defeated. In 1976, Maccabi had to settle for third place. But then came the magic year of 1977.

The captain of the 1977 team was Tal Brody, an all-American, University of Illinois basketball star and a member of the team since 1967. Tal was born in Trenton, NJ and emigrated to Israel in 1966. Other American college stars on the team included Lou Silver, Jim Boatwright, Eric Minkin, and Aulsie Perry. The coach of the team was Shmuel Mahrouski, the manager was Ralph Klein, and the assistant manager was Arieh Davidesov. Other members of the team included Bob Fleisher, Dan Shabi, Shuki Shwartz, Hanan Keren, Mickey Berkowitz, Motti Aroesti, and Bob Griffin. The team's first victory in the play-offs came against Madrid, whom they defeated 94 to 85. Then they faced Brno, Czechoslovakia, which fell to Tel Aviv,

קליין רלף
RALPH KLEIN

91 to 76. The semifinal game was held in Vitron, Belgium, against the Red Army team, representing Moscow. The Russian team was favored, but Israel won 91 to 79. Despite Maccabi's upset victory against the Russians, the team from Varese, Italy was highly favored to win the ultimate victory. The championship game was held at Belgrade on April 7, 1977. The game was hard fought, but Maccabi Tel Aviv triumphed by just a single point, 78 to 77.

Following their 1977 victory, the team of Maccabi Tel Aviv were again semi-finalists in 1978. In 1981, Maccabi once again captured the European title. As in 1977, Mickey Berkowitz played a major role.

In 1991, during the Gulf War, when Maccabi was again in contention for the European championship, the dangers of the conflict forced the Federation Internationals de Basketball to cancel all European Champions Cup games that were scheduled to be played in Israel. This placed a terrific burden on the team, which would have to fly to all of its competitions. It was suggested that the team withdraw from the tournament for that year. But the team voted to continue and complete its part, greatly to the approval of the Israeli public.

In 2000, Maccabi Tel Aviv again had an outstanding club. As he had done since joining the team, Doron Sheffer lead it in rebounds. On May 13, 2001, Israel had made it to the final stage of the playoffs for the European Championship. They were pitted against Greece, the game taking place in Paris. Some 8,000 Israelis came to France to be present at the big game. Maccabi Tel Aviv, representing Israel, for their third time captured the European championship. The team would go on to capture the European title again in 2004 and 2005.

MICKEY BERKOWITZ

JEWISH WORLD BOXING CHAMPIONS
(*Including* ★Legitimate Title Claimants)

HEAVYWEIGHTS

- **DANIEL MENDOZA** 1792-95 (1784-1820) 35 bouts, 31-4 W-L
- **MAX BAER** [Jewish Paternal Grandfather] 1934-35 (1929-41) 79 bouts, 65-13 W-L, 43 KO's

LIGHT-HEAVYWEIGHTS

- **"BATTLING" LEVINSKY** 1916-20 (1910-30) 172 bouts, 76-19 W-L, 34 KO's
- **"SLAPSIE" MAXIE ROSENBLOOM** 1930-34 (1923-39) 289 bouts, 210-35 W-L, 18 KO's

MAX ROSENBLOOM

- **BOB OLIN** 1934-35 (1929-39) 85 bouts, 54-27 W-L, 25 KO's
- **MIKE ROSSMAN** [Jewish Mother] 1978-79 (1973-83) 54 bouts, 44-74 W-L, 27 KO's

MIDDLEWEIGHTS

- **AL McCoy** 1914-17 (1908-19) 157 bouts, 44-6 W-L, 26 KO's
- **★DAVE ROSENBERG** 1922 (1919-25) 57 bouts, 39-9 W-L, 9 KO's
- **BEN JEBY** 1933 (1928-36) 73 bouts, 54-14 W-L, 22 KO's
- **SOLLY KRIEGER** 1938-39 (1928-42) 111 bouts, 80-24 W-L, 53 KO's

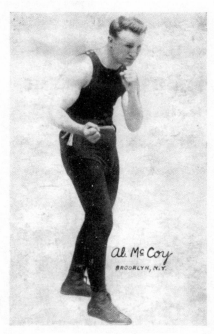

AL McCoy

WELTERWEIGHTS

- **★HARRY LEWIS** 1908-11 (1903-13) 171 bouts, 163-15 W-L, 47 KO's
- **WALDEMAR HOLBERG** 1914 (1908-21) 58 bouts, 31-23 W-L, 20 KO's
- **★MATT WELLS** 1914-15 (1909-22) 77 bouts, 28-18 W-L, 6 KO's
- **TED "KID" LEWIS** 1915-16, 1917-19 (1909-29) 250 bouts, 155-24 W-L, 65 KO's
- **JACKIE FIELDS** 1929-30, 1932-33 (1924-33) 87 bouts, 73-9 W-L, 30 KO's
- **BARNEY ROSS** 1934, 1935-38 (1931-38) 82 bouts, 74-4 W-L, 24 KO's

JUNIOR WELTERWEIGHTS

- **MUSHY CALLAHAN** 1926-30 (1924-32) 77 bouts, 59-13 W-L, 19 KO's
- **JAKIE "KID" BERG** 1930-31 (1924-45) 192 bouts, 157-26 W-L, 57 KO's

- **BARNEY ROSS** 1933-35
- **SAOUL MAMBY** [Convert to Judaism] 1980-82 (1969-84, 1998-2000) 83 bouts, 45-32 W-L, 19 KO's

LIGHTWEIGHTS

- **BENNY LEONARD** 1917-25 (1911-32) 210 bouts, 89-5 W-L, 71 KO's
- **AL SINGER** 1930 (1927-31) 70 bouts, 60-8 W-L, 24 KO's
- **BARNEY ROSS** 1933, 1935

JUNIOR LIGHTWEIGHTS

- **"YOUNG" ARTIE O'LEARY** 1917-19 (1910's) 67 bouts, 19-2 W-L, 5 KO's
- **JACK BERNSTEIN** 1923 (1914-1931) 107 bouts, 65-23 W-L, 17 KO's
- **BENNY BASS** 1929-31 (1923-40) 197 bouts, 140-28 W-L, 59 KO's

FEATHERWEIGHTS

- **ABE ATTELL** 1901-12 (1900-17) 168 bouts, 91-10 W-L, 47 KO's
- **LOUIS "KID" KAPLAN** 1925-27 (1921-33) 131 bouts, 101-13 W-L, 17 KO's
- **BENNY BASS** 1927-28

ABE ATTELL

JUNIOUR FEATHERWEIGHTS

- **FABRICE BENICHOU** (IBF) 1989-90 (1986-1995)

BATAMWEIGHTS

- **HARRY HARRIS** 1901 (1895-1904) 54 bouts, 40-2 W-L, 15 KO's
- **★MONTE ATTELL** 1909-10 (1902-17) 106 bouts, 38-26 W-L, 27 KO's
- **ABE GOLDSTEIN** 1924 (1916-27) 128 bouts, 67-16 W-L, 34 KO's
- **CHARLIE "PHIL" ROSENBERG** 1925-27 (1921-29) 65 bouts, 35-16 W-L, 7 KO's
- **ROBERT COHEN** 1954-56 (1951-58) 43 bouts, 36-4 W-L, 14 KO's
- **ALPHONSE HALIMI** 1957-59, 1960-61 (1955-64) 50 bouts, 41-8 W-L, 21 KO's

FLYWEIGHTS

- **PINCUS "PINKY" SILVERBERG** 1927 (1920-34, 1937) 78 bouts, 29-30 W-L, 4 KO's
- **"CORPORAL" IZZY SCHWARTZ** 1927-29 (1922-31) 124 bouts, 69-33 W-L, 10 KO's
- **VICTOR "YOUNG" PEREZ** 1931-32 (1926-38) 131 bouts, 89-26 W-L, 26 KO's

THE MEMOIRS OF DANIEL MENDOZA

Daniel Mendoza, one of England's greatest boxers during the period of the late eighteenth century and the recognized heavyweight champion from 1792 to 1795, was the subject for a series of handsome tokens that were struck in his honor in 1790 by the well known medallist Thomas Spence. The obverse on all these tokens is the same portrait of the boxer. The varieties consist of different backs, only one of which depicts Mendoza. Another issue, a medal, was struck in 1791, to mark the match between Mendoza and William Ward. This piece shows facing portraits of the two boxers on the obverse.

Mendoza was a popular figure at this time and his likeness also decorated pottery, paintings, and numerous engravings. When, in 1787, Mendoza published his first book, a discussion of the art of boxing, it was the lead story in the newspapers of the day. Mendoza is considered the father of scientific boxing and his book was snapped up by all who wished to learn the secrets of his success.

Mendoza's second book is, however, the more interesting of his literary works. The title of the book tells us a great deal about it: *Memoirs of the Life of Daniel Mendoza; Containing a Faithful Narrative of the Various Vicissitudes of His Life and an Account of the Numerous Contests in Which He Has Been Engaged, with Observations of Each; Comprising also Genuine Anecdotes of Many Distinguished Characters, to Which Are Added, Observations on the Art of Pugilism; Rules to be Observed with Regard to Training, Etc.*

The memoirs of Daniel Mendoza are a unique document in Jewish history and the history of sports. Never before had any boxer, much less a Jewish boxer, written his memoirs. Not only have boxers rarely been of contemplative enough natures to tell of their own careers, but Mendoza also holds a unique position in Jewish history. He was honored in his lifetime beyond any other English Jew. For instance, he was the first Jew to hold a conversation with a king of England. With his fists, he won a degree of respect for his people that they had never held before in the English capital, both in its boulevards and in its back alleys.

In these memoirs, there appear two passages of special interest. The first of these passages deals with Mendoza's tour of Scotland:

> Before my return to London, I went accompanied by Mr. Fewterell, to Edinburgh, and had there the honour of being introduced to the Gymnastic Society, and of sparring with several of the members, who possessed considerable knowledge of the theory and practice of the pugilistic art....

While in Edinburgh, Mendoza, having outboxed the president of the club, was made the honorary president of the Gymnastic Society. "This was an honour I by no means aspired to, and endeavoured to decline; but this gentleman, as well as the other members of the society, so strenuously urged my acceptance of it, that I was obliged to yield to their solicitations.

"I had afterwards the honour of being presented with a gold medal, by these gentlemen, as a testimonial of the opinion they unanimously held of me."

This incident took place sometime late in the year 1790, or possibly very early in the year 1791. Mendoza makes no further reference to this gold medal in his memoirs. Later in his life, he faced a number of periods of grave financial difficulties and it is quite possible that this unique medal may have found its way to the smelters.

The second passage relates to just such a period in his life of financial embarrassment, in late 1799 or early in 1800: "I was reduced to great inconvenience and distress for want of money, when I fortunately discovered another expedient for ameliorating my condition.

"The Bank of England had, some short time previous to this, stopped payment in specie, and were consequently obliged to issue notes for the small sums of one and two pounds. The measure was regarded by many as a very disgraceful one, and to ridicule and burlesque such conduct, notes were issued by some persons for twopence. It occurred to me that, being a very public character, I had a fair chance of disposing of a quantity of such; I therefore caused a plate to be engraved, and had a number of impressions taken, which were quickly disposed of. So great was the demand for them, that two persons besides myself were constantly employed in filling them up, and signing them. I sometimes jocosely told my customers, these notes would pass for their value at all public houses and chandler shops in the neighbourhood. Some few persons actually tried to pass them, and on being refused payment brought them back to me, upon which occasions I was obliged to put them off with the best excuses in my power; and my general answer was, 'I should follow the example of the bank, and pay in notes of my own.' Surely, if a public company could make their payments, for pounds, in this way, an individual might be allowed to make his, for pence, in like manner."

I am not aware if any of these notes issued in the name of Mendoza for the value of twopence has survived to our time. I have never seen or heard of any. If such do exist, it is clear from Mendoza's testimony that they would have a one in three chance of bearing an authentic signature of the great pugilist.

A little known fact concerning Daniel Mendoza is that at one time there were plans afoot to produce a motion picture based on his life. The main mover in this project was the well-known Hollywood director Herbert Kline (*The Kid from Cleveland, Heart of Spain, Five Were Chosen, The Fighter*, etc.) Kline described his project as a "British-Jewish Rocky." This description was written in 1983 and Kline proposed to use Mendoza's own memoirs as the major source for his screenplay. Kline is dead now and the project, apparently, never got too far, which is a pity. The background of Regency England and the colorful, teeming London Ghetto would have made a wonderful frame for the remarkable career of one of the greatest boxers that England and the Jewish people have ever produced.

MEMOIRS

OF

THE LIFE

OF

DANIEL MENDOZA;

CONTAINING

A FAITHFUL NARRATIVE

OF THE

VARIOUS VICISSITUDES OF HIS LIFE,

AND AN ACCOUNT OF THE

NUMEROUS CONTESTS

IN WHICH HE HAS BEEN ENGAGED, WITH OBSERVATIONS ON EACH;

COMPRISING ALSO

Genuine Anecdotes of many Distinguished Characters,

TO WHICH ARE ADDED,

OBSERVATIONS ON THE ART OF PUGILISM;

RULES

TO BE OBSERVED WITH REGARD TO TRAINING, &c.

A NEW EDITION.

London:

PRINTED FOR D. MENDOZA,

BY G. HAYDEN,

BRYDGES STREET, COVENT GARDEN.

1816.

JOE CHOYNSKI

Joe Choynski (pronounced koi-yen-sky) is the earliest of the great Jewish American boxers who did much to occupy, if not dominate, the sport in the late years of the nineteenth century and the early years of the twentieth. Joe would never hold a championship title, but his impact on the sport was greater than many that did.

He fought and, sometimes, defeated such heroes of the ring, all far heavier and larger than himself, as John L. Sullivan, "Gentleman" Jim Corbett, James Jeffries, Bob Fitsimmons, and Jack Johnson. Always he fought with a degree of skill, an indomitable courage, and a powerful punch that amazed his contemporaries.

It was in regard to Jack Johnson that, perhaps, Choynski made his greatest impact on American sport. On February 25, 1901, Choynski fought Jack Johnson, the future heavyweight champion, and the first African-American boxer to hold this title, indeed to hold any sport's title in America. The fight took place in Galveston, Texas and lasted just 3 rounds. The fight ended when Choynski knocked out the far larger future champ. But immediately after the fight both men were arrested and put in jail, for boxing was illegal in Texas at that time. For the next twenty-eight days Choynski and Johnson shared a cell. During that time Joe generously shared his hard won knowledge of the fine points of the art of boxing. The two men were allowed out of their cell to spar, much to the pleasure of their fellow inmates, but Johnson made the most of his time learning pugilistic fine points from the masterly Choynski. Johnson never forgot the skill or generosity of his cellmate and often talked of him with great affection and giving him much credit for his later success in the ring.

Joseph Bartlett Choynski's background was a strange one for a master of the most primitive and brutal of sports. His family background hardly seemed preparation for his achievements in the ring.

His father, Isadore Nathan Choynski, was born in Poland but came to

114. Joe Choyinski.

OGDEN'S CIGARETTES

the United States at a young age. He grew up in New Haven and was a graduate from Yale, where he received a teaching certificate. He settled in San Francisco, where he served as a correspondent for the American Israelite. He also ran a used bookstore, which catered to the likes of Mark Twain, Bret Harte, Joaquin Miller, and Robert Ingersoll. These and other West Coast intellectuals were often guests in young Choynski's house, where his father and equally cultured mother would entertain. Joe learned much at these soirees and much from the no-nonsense attitude his father took toward anti-Semitism. When the growing lad was faced with slurs and disdain in the streets of the pioneer city he found the most effective way to answer jeers was with blows. Soon the reputation of the "California Terror" and the "Chrysanthemum Kid" were known all over the city. The last name was a reference to Joe's long blonde locks.

In no time Joe had turned professional and was matched with the likes of the future champion James J. Corbett. Years later, Corbett would declare that he received more punishment from his

THE REAL McCOY

The term "the real McCoy," meaning the genuine article is of mysterious origins, with a number of contending theories. One theory attributes the phrase to the advertising campaign of a brand of Scotch whiskey. Another theory attributes it to the name of a clever inventor. But one of the soundest theories is that it stems from a newspaper article that appeared following the historic battle between Joe Choyinski and Charles "Kid" McCoy (born Norman Selby) on January 12, 1900, in New York City.

This fight was a most controversial one. The match had attracted heavy betting and there was a great deal of talk of dishonesty. Joe was knocked out in the fourth round of the battle with the reigning welter-weight champion. But contemporary descriptions of the fight seem to be of two absolutely different events. Those who favored Choyinski claimed that their hero actually should have won the contest. In the *New York Journal*, for instance, appeared this account, by Tad Dorgan:

"Joe Choyinski KO'd Kid McCoy last night by all that was fair and holy, but was a victim of a deploring plot. He had McCoy knocked out in the second round but the bell was rung one minute ahead of time, saving the Kid from being counted out. Then to make things even more unbearable, the minute's rest period was extended to two full minutes, giving McCoy plenty of time to clear.

"One man was robbed of a prize fight and 8,000 others, boiling with rage, were robbed of thousands of dollars. Fifty policemen saw the robbery committed-policemen in uniform sent to the ringside.

"According to the referee, Choyinski was KO'd at the end of the 3rd round—but a more pointed and fair description would have been—McCoy would have to drop dead in order to lose.

first combat with Choynski that in all his other fights put together. Nevertheless, it was Corbett who won this fight and the subsequent four other matches between them.

Joe had better luck with future champion Bob Fitzsimmons, who he knocked out in 1894. He managed a 20 round draw with Jim Jeffries in 1897. But in all his fights with future champions, Joe was always the lighter fighter, from 30 to 70 pounds lighter. If his career had been a few years later he would have fought in the light heavyweight category, but this category did not exist until 1903, just one year before the close of Joe's 20 year career.

After his retirement, Joe, who held a degree in chiropody, was often

called on to train or second other boxers. He also worked in Pittsburgh and Cincinnati as a boxing and athletic instructor. One of his last jobs was as a consultant for the Errol Flynn movie of the life of his old San Francisco rival, Jim Corbett. Joe died on January 25, 1943.

ALPHONSE HALIMI

Alphonse Halimi was born on January 18, 1932 in Constantine, Algeria. He was the youngest child of his parents' 18 children. The Halimi family, despite the father's position as a postal inspector, lived in great poverty. The only bed the children knew was the hard floor and often they went to bed hungry. Nevertheless, the family was strict in its religious observances. Like almost all Sephardic Jews, the Halimi family was strictly Orthodox.

At the age of 10 years Alphonse ran away from home and hitchhiked some 300 miles to the city of Algiers. There he lived in the back alleys of the casbah, the famous native quarter of the city. His life was a daily struggle for existence. He finally found that he could earn a meager subsistence by challenging other boys to fight, hoping that a passersby would provide a few coppers to the winner.

A short time latter, Alphonse was adopted by a French woman of the city, Mme. Marcelle Faty, a 19-year-old mother who needed a companion for her young son. Alphonse was well treated by this Catholic woman. She did attempt to convert the young boy to Catholicism, but he remained firm in his Jewish faith. After a few years, Alphonse was apprenticed to a tailor. When he had enough skill, he sewed for himself a pair of boxing trunks, marked with a Magen David and he began his career as an amateur boxer.

Through the early 1950's, Alphonse took part in 187 amateur bouts, of which he won 152. In 1953 he won the amateur bantamweight title of France. He repeated this feat in 1954 and 1955. In the latter year, he was also crowned All-Mediterranean champ. After that feat, in 1955, he turned professional.

Alphonse is a small man, only 5'3" and he fought at the 118 lbs. mark, but he fought with a determination and intelligence that won him the reputation as an all-round fighter, both a skilled boxer and a dangerous puncher. Twenty-one of Alphonse's 50 professional fights ended with knockout victories for him.

In his first professional fight, fought in Paris, Alphonse knocked out

George Lafage in the first round. His next three bouts also ended in the first round, all victories for Alphonse. His next bout, against Rino Stiaccini in Milan, lasted into the second round, before Alphonse won. After 12 more easy victories, Alphonse was drafted into the French army. Considering the need of his impoverished family back in Algeria, the Army released him after just two months of service.

On March 16, 1956, Alphonse first attracted international attention when he defeated Billy Peacock, a former North American champion. The fight was a 10-rounder held in Paris. Alphonse won the fight on points. This eventually led to Alphonse's fight for the championship against Mario D'Agata, of Italy. Alphonse was successful in this battle, which was memorable for an exploding light fixture and first aid applied to the fighters in the midst of the fight.

Alphonse, however, was not yet recognized for the bantamweight title by the NBA. The question was settled in Los Angeles in a fight against Mexico's Raton Macias. Alphonse won this fight on a split decision and was recognized as the World's undisputed bantamweight champion. But Alphonse was not to hold the title for long. On July 8, 1959, he fought with another

HALIMI

Mexican fighter, Jose Becerra. Alphonse was knocked out in the eighth round. On February 4, 1960, there was a rematch with Becerra, but again Alphonse was knocked out, this time in the ninth round.

Alphonse continued his career, taking the European bantamweight title in a fight with Fred Gilroy in London. On May 30, 1961, he lost this title to John Caldwell, in a fight that took place in Wembley. He also lost a rematch to Caldwell. But on June 26, 1962, Alphonse once again captured the European title in a bout fought against Pierro Rollo. This fight took place in Israel. This fight was the first professional boxing match ever staged in the Jewish state. Alphonse lost a rematch against Rollo, surrendering the last title of his career. He fought on for two more years before retiring from the ring.

Alphonse spent the years after his

retirement as a swimming instructor and as a fight promoter.

The career of Alphonse Halimi marks the end of the golden age of Jewish boxing, a period which began in the late 1880's and which stretched to Halimi's last fight. During this period, while Jewish boxers could never claim to dominate this sport, they were always well-respected and often held world titles. The names of the Jewish boxers of this period are a veritable roll call of legendary heroes, modern Maccabees and Bar Kochbas.

Jewish Players In The National Football League

- **Sid Abramowitz** 1983-85, 1987 Offensive tackle (22 games)
- **Nathan "Nate" Abrams** 1921 Offensive end (1 game)
- **George Abramson** 1925 Guard/Tackle (10 games)
- **John Alexander** 1922, 1926 Tackle (17 games)
- **Joseph "Doc" Alexander** 1921-27 Center/Guard/ Tackle/Offensive end (40 games)
- **Lyle Alzado** 1971-85 Defensive end/Tackle (196 games)— Jewish Mother
- **Robert "Bob" Barrabee** 1931 Offensive end (10 games)
- **John Barsha** 1920 Fullback (3 games)
- **Harris Barton** 1987-96 Center (138 games)

JOE ALEXANDER *Guard-Center*

- **Herman "Reds" Bassman** 1936 Tailback/Halfback/ Defensive back (8 games)
- **Edward Bell** 1947-49 Guard/Tackle (35 games)
- **Joseph Bernstein** 1921, 1923-24 Fullback/Guard/ Tackle (11 games)
- **Melvin "Mel" Bleeker** 1944-47 Halfback/Defensive back (28 games)
- **Morris "Maury" Bodenger** 1931-34 Halfback/Defensive back (48 games)

- **RONALD "RON" BOTCHAN** 1960-61 Linebacker (28 games)
- **LEO CANTOR** 1942, 1945 Defensive back/Halfback/Fullback (20 games)
- **ABRAHAM "ABE" COHEN** 1960 Offensive guard (14 games)
- **C. IRVING "IRV" CONSTANTINE** 1931 Halfback (1 game)
- **ALBERT "AL" CORNSWEET** 1931 Fullback (4 games)
- **LEO DISEND** 1938-40 Tackle (27 games)
- **ARTHUR "ART" DORFMAN** 1929 Center (9 games)
- **MAURICE "MAURY" DUBOFSKY** 1932 Guard (5 games)
- **DANIEL "DAN" DWORSKY** 1949 Linebacker/Blocking back (11 games)
- **WILLIAM "BILL" ELLENBOGEN** 1976-77 Offensive guard & tackle (23 games)
- **HAYDEN EPSTEIN** 2002-03 Kicker (15 games)
- **CARL ETELMAN** 1926 Blocking back/Wingback/Tailback (1 game)
- **BERNARD "BERNIE" FEIBISH** 1941 Center/Linebacker (3 games)
- **JAY FIEDLER** 1994-95, 1998-2004 Quarterback (74 games)
- **RICHARD "DICK" FISHEL** 1933 Blocking back/Linebacker/Defensive back/Wingback (8 games)
- **ALEXANDER "ALEC" FISHMAN** 1921 Guard/Fullback (5 games)
- **SAMUEL "SAM" FOX** 1945 Offensive & Defensive end (8 games)
- **JOHN FRANK** 1984-88 Tight end (66 games)
- **BENJAMIN "BENNY" FRIEDMAN** 1927-34 Tailback/Defensive back (81 games)
- **JACOB "JAKE" FRIEDMAN** 1926 Offensive end (3 games)
- **LENNIE FRIEDMAN** 1999-2004 Guard (54 games)
- **ROBERT "BOB" FRIEDMAN** 1944 Tackle (10 games)
- **MORRIS GLASSMAN** 1921-22 Offensive end (15 games)
- **MARSHALL GOLDBERG** 1939-43, 1946-48 Tailback/Defensiveback/Fullback/Halfback (77 games)
- **WILLIAM "BILL" GOLDBERG** 1992-94 Nose tackle/Defensive tackle (14 games)
- **CHARLES "BUCKETS" GOLDENBERG** 1933-1945 Guard/Linebacker/Blocking back/Defensive back (120 games)
- **SAMUEL "SAM" GOLDMAN** 1944, 1946-49 Offensive & Defensive end (46 games)
- **ALLAN "AL" GOLDSTEIN** 1960 Offensive end (14 games)

- **AUBREY GOODMAN** 1927 Tackle (1 game)
- **LOUIS "LOU" GORDON** 1930-38 Tackle/Guard/Offensive & Defensive end (83 games)
- **JEROME "JERRY" GREEN** 1960 Offensive end (2 games)
- **BENJAMIN "BEN" GREENBERG** 1930 Fullback/Tailback (2 games)
- **"CURT" RANDY GROSSMAN** 1974-81 Tight end (118 games)
- **JACK GROSSMAN** 1932, 1934-35 Defensive back/Tailback/Fullback/Wingback (34 games)
- **ROBERT "BUCK" HALPERIN** 1932 Tailback (2 games)
- **WILLIAM "WILLIE" HALPERN** 1930 Guard/Tackle (3 games)
- **PHILIP "MOTSY" HANDLER** 1930-36 Guard (53 games)
- **ARNOLD HORWEEN** (aka Arnold Horowitz) 1921-24 Blocking back/Fullback/Tailback (32 games)
- **RALPH HORWEEN** (aka MacMahon; Ralph Horowitz) 1921-23 Fullback/Wingback/Blocking back/Tailback (22 games)
- **ROY ILOWIT** 1937 Tackle (4 games)
- **DAVID "DAVE" JACOBS** 1979, 1981, 1987 Kicker (12 games)
- **MAX KADESKY** 1923 Offensive end (8 games)
- **EDWIN "EDDIE" KAHN** 1935-37 Guard (24 games)
- **BERNARD KAPITANSKY** 1942 Guard (7 games)
- **BERNARD KAPLAN** 1935-36, 1942 Guard (22 games)
- **KENNETH "KEN" KAPLAN** 1984-85, 1987 Offensive tackle (35 games)
- **SAMUEL KAPLAN** 1921 End (1 game)
- **ABRAHAM "ABE" KARNOFSKY** 1945-46 Halfback/Defensive back (19 games)
- **PERRY KLEIN** 1994 Quarterback (2 games)
- **MILTON "MICKEY" KOBROSKY** 1937 Quarterback/Defensive back (7 games)
- **IRVING "IRV" KUPCINET** 1935 Blocking back/Defensive back (2 games)
- **MORTIMER "MORT" LANDSBERG** 1941, 1947 Halfback/Defensive back (17 games)
- **JAMES "JIM" LEVEY** 1934-36 Halfback/Defensive back/Tailback (13 games)
- **CHAD LEVITT** 1997 Running back (10 games)

- **HARVEY LEVY** 1928 Tackle/Guard (12 games)
- **LEONARD "LEN" "BUTCH" LEVY** 1945-48 Guard/Tackle (42 games)
- **MICHAEL LONDON** 1966 Linebacker (3 games)
- **SIDNEY "SID" LUCKMAN** 1939-50 Quarterback/Defensive back/ Halfback (128 games)
- **"GERALD" BOOTH LUSTEG** 1966-69 Kicker (39 games)-Jewish Father
- **EDWARD MERLIN** 1938-39 Guard (16 games)
- **BRUCE MESNER** 1987 Nose tackle (11 games)
- **SAUL MIELZINER** 1929-1934 Center/Tackle/Guard/Linebacker (60 games)
- **ALFRED "AL" MILLER** 1929 Halfback/Fullback/Blocking back (7 games)
- **JOSH MILLER** 1996- 2005 Punter (137 games)
- **DAVID MISHEL** 1927, 1931 Tailback/Quarterback/Wingback/Fullback (10 games)
- **RONALD "RON" MIX** 1960-69, 1971 Offensive tackle & guard (142 games)
- **BRIAN NATKIN** 2001, 2003 Tight end/Fullback (3 games)—Jewish Father
- **EDWARD "ED" NEWMAN** 1973-84 Offensive guard (167 games)
- **HARRY NEWMAN** 1933-35 Tailback/Defensive back (32 games)
- **BRENT NOVOSELSKY** 1988-94 Tight end (98 games)
- **HENRY OBST** 1931, 1933 Guard (3 games)
- **MAX PADLOW** 1935-36 Offensive & Defensive end (5 games)
- **MAURICE "MAURY" PATT** 1938-42 Offensive & Defensive end (48 games)
- **ISADORE "RED" PEARLMAN** 1920-21, 1924 Guard/Tackle (18 games)
- **PHILIP PERLO** 1960 Linebacker (7 games)
- **GORDON POLOFSKY** 1952-54 Offensive guard/Linebacker (26 games)
- **MERVIN "MERV" PREGULMAN** 1946-49 Center/Linebacker (47 games)
- **WILLIAM "BILL" RAFFEL** 1932 End (4 games)
- **RICHARD HERBERT "HERB" RICH** 1950-56 Defensive back (64 games)
- **HARRY RICHMAN** 1929 Guard (1 game)
- **DONALD "DON" ROGERS** 1960-64 Center (68 games)
- **STANLEY ROSEN** 1929 Blocking back/Tailback (8 games)
- **SAGE ROSENFELS** 2001-04 Quarterback (8 games)—Jewish Father
- **MIKE ROSENTHAL** 1999-2004 Guard (58 games)
- **LARRY RUBENS** 1982-83, 1986 Center (41 games)
- **LEONARD "LENNY" SACHS** 1920-26 Offensive end (51 games)

- JACOB "JACK" SACK 1923, 1926 Guard (12 games)
- BERNARD "OLLIE" SATENSTEIN 1929-33 Guard/Offensive & Defensive end/Tackle (49 games)
- HERMAN "HERM" SAWYER 1922 Wingback/Blocking back (3 games)
- JOSEPH "JOE" SCHEIN 1931 Tackle (11 games)
- ABRAHAM "BABE" SCHEUER 1934 Tackle (1 game)
- HERMAN "HERM" SCHNEIDMAN 1935-40 Blocking & Defensive back/ Linebacker/Offensive end (46 games)
- ADAM SCHREIBER 1984-98 Offensive guard/Center (199 game)
- HARRY "RED" SEIDELSON 1925-26 Guard/Tackle (17 games)
- HARRY SELTZER 1942 Fullback/Linebacker (6 games)
- JACK SHAPIRO 1929 Blocking back (1 game)
- HARRY SHAUB 1935 Guard (1 game)
- ALEXANDER "ALLIE" SHERMAN 1943-47 Quarterback/Defensive back (93 games)
- SAUL "SOLLY" SHERMAN 1939-40 Quarterback/Defensive back (14 games)
- STEVEN "STEVE" SHULL 1980-1982 Linebacker (41 games)
- WALTER "WALT" SINGER 1935-36 Ofensive & Defensive end (22 games)
- HARRY DAVID "DAVE" SKUDIN 1929 Guard/End (6 games)
- PHILIP "PHIL" SLOSBURG 1948-49 Defensive back/Halfback/Tailback (15 games)
- SCOTT SLUTZKER 1996-2000 Wide receiver (41 games)
- DAVID SMUKLER 1936-39, 1944 Fullback/Linebacker (38 games)
- BEN "BENNY" SOHN 1934 Wingback/Defensive back/Fullback/ Linebacker (2 games)
- BENJAMIN "BEN" SOHN 1941 Guard (11 games)
- ARIEL SOLOMON 1991-96 Center/Offensive tackle & guard (61 games)
- MICHAEL "MIKE" SOMMER 1958-61, 1963 Halfback/Defensive back (22 games)
- ROBERT "BOB" STEIN 1969-75 Linebacker (89 games)
- SAMUEL "SAMMY" STEIN 1929-32 Offensive end/Tackle (31 games)
- ALAN "AL" STEINFELD 1982-83 Offensive guard/Center/Offensive tackle (20 games)

- **RICHARD STOTTER** 1968 Linebacker (3 games)
- **J. ARTHUR "DUTCH" STRAUSS** 1923-24 Fullback/Wing back (13 games)
- **MICHAEL "MIKE" STROMBERG** 1968 Linebacker (2 games)
- **KARL SWEETAN** 1966-70 Quarterback (36 games)
- **PHILIP "PHIL" SWIADON** 1943 Guard (3 games)
- **STEVEN "STEVE" TANNEN** 1970-74 Defensive back (61 games)—
    Jewish Father
- **JOSH TAVES** (aka Josh Heinrich) 2000-03 Defensive end (29 games)
- **ANDRE TIPPETT** 1982-88, 1990-93 Linebacker (151 games)—
    Convert to Judaism
- **ALAN VEINGRAD** 1986-87, 1989-92 Offensive tackle & guard (86 games)
- **HENRY WEINBERG** 1934 Guard/Tackle (8 games)
- **SOL WEINBERG** (aka Weinberger) 1923 Tailback (2 games)
- **ALBERT "REDS" WEINER** 1934 Fullback/Linebacker/Blocking &
    Defensive back (5 games)
- **BERNARD "BERNIE" WEINER** 1942 Tackle/Guard (10 games)
- **ISADORE "IZZY" WEINSTOCK** 1935, 1937-38 Linebacker/Fullback/
    Blocking back (24 games)
- **LAWRENCE "LARRY" WELTMAN** 1922 Blocking back/Tailback (4 games)
- **GARY WOOD** 1964-69 Quarterback (63
    games)—Convert to Judaism
- **JULIUS "IZZY" YABLOK** 1930-31 Blocking
    back/Tailback (20 games)
- **SIDNEY "SID" YOUNGELMAN** 1955-63
    Defensive tackle & end (107 games)

SID
YOUNGELMAN
DEFENSIVE TACKLE • NEW YORK TITANS

THE FOUNDER OF THE GREEN BAY PACKERS

History can be quite misleading. A glance at most encyclopedias would show that dirigibles were the invention of Count Zeppelin. But this is simply not true. A Jewish inventor name David Schwartz built the first rigid, lighter than air vehicle and his widow sold the idea to Count Zeppelin. It is not unusual in "history" to find that it is the Jew who is ignored or forgotten, while the more connected or colorful gentile who follows in his footsteps gets full credit for the innovation.

Such was the case with the Green Bay Packers. It was in 1918 that Nathan Abrams organized a football team for Green Bay, Wisconsin. The city had had an earlier football team, but this had dissolved during the First World War. Abrams, a successful cattle merchant, financed the team that first year, organized it, and even served as the team's captain. The following year, 1919, the team elected the talented Earl L. "Curly" Lambeau the team's player-coach. The Christian Lambeau was a long time friend of the Jewish Abrams and his neighbor. So by joining the team and taking charge of its on-field direction, he in no way was trying to steal Abrams's thunder. Nevertheless, latter historians have attributed the team's founding to Lambeau and mistakenly placed this event in the year 1919, when Lambeau joined. Others count the beginning of the team to 1921 and the founding of the NFL. Others still, point out that Lambeau received a revised charter to the team as a member of the NFL in 1922. (The team had lost its first charter for using college players in a game, a violation of the League rules. To reenter the NFL, the team had to put up $1,000 in cash to guarantee its solvency. It was Abrams who put up this money for Lambeau.)

Abrams never abandoned his creation. In fact, he continued to play as a member of the Packers through 1921. In that year he made his only appearance in an official NFL game. Through the following years, Abrams remained a close associate of Curly Lambeau. For instance, in 1922, he loaned the team $3,000. This debt was not repaid until 1925.

It was out of his enthusiasm for the game of football and his pleasure in playing it that Nate Abrams created the team that today is known as the Packers. Out of similar motives, as well as friendship, he supported Curly Lambeau's leadership of his creation. "History," not Lambeau, has robbed Nate of his true title as the "Father of the Green Bay Packers."

PIONEER JEWISH FOOTBALL PLAYERS IN THE IVY LEAGUE

BROWN:

- **JOSEPH GETTSTEIN** (1891-?) First game 1912

COLUMBIA:

- **MOSES HENRY EPSTEIN** First game November 12, 1870

CORNELL:

- **JOHN HAWLEY TAUSSIG** (1876-1925) First game 1893

DARTMOUTH:

- **GABRIEL "GAY" BROMBERG** First game 1928

HARVARD:

- **LUCIUS NATHAN LITTAUER** (1859-1944) First game October 23, 1875

PRINCETON:

- **PHILIP "PHIL" KING** (1872-1938) First game October 14, 1890

PHIL KING

UNIVERSITY OF PENNSYLVANIA:

- **RABBI EMIL HIRSCH** (1851-1923) First game December 9, 1871

YALE:

- **JOHN "DUTCH" LEVINE** (1881- 1944) First game 1905

BENNY FRIEDMAN

Benjamin Friedman was born on March 18, 1905 in Cleveland, Ohio, the son of a tailor who had come from Russia. He was blessed at birth with unusually large hands, hands that would later control the fat footballs of the 1920's. As a youth he began weightlifting to strengthen his forearms. This combination of large hands and mighty forearms made him one of the greatest passers of all time.

Benny had excelled at football in high school and he entered the University of Michigan in 1923. He played on the school's freshman team and there his performance so impressed the coaching staff that he was invited to try out for the varsity in 1924. Coach George Little kept Benny on the bench for the first half of the season, but during a game with Illinois, he was put in to relieve, after Red Grange had garnered so many points for Illinois that victory was out of reach. Benny's performance was so impressive that he was called on to start the next game at quarterback and he never was relieved, even for a minute, during the rest of his time at Michigan. Benny was chosen as an All-American in 1925 and 1926. His combination with receiver Bennie Oosterbaan was one of the finest passing combinations in collegiate history, from "Benny to Bennie." In 1926, Friedman received the Chicago Tribune's trophy for the Most Valuable Player in the Big Ten.

In 1927, he came back to his native Cleveland to join the newly formed NFL franchise Cleveland Indians. His advent was a triumph for the team and himself. His team had a record of 8-4-1 and finished in fourth place.

The following year, 1928, Benny played for the Detroit Wolverines. In this year, he led the NFL in both rushing touchdowns and touchdown passes, something that has never been done since. During the team's game with the Detroit Giants, Benny's cunning and skillful play led the Wolverines to a 19-19 tie, after having trailed the Giants 19-7 in the fourth quarter. This so impressed the Giants' owners that they decided they had to have Benny for their team. When all other negotiations failed, they bought out the Wolverine's entire franchise, just to get Benny.

The Giants' money was well invested, for Benny brought them from a 4-7-2 record in 1928 to a 12-1-1 record in 1929, scoring 318 point for the season, compared to their opponents' 77 points. In 1930, Benny led the Giants to a 13-4-0 record. In the meantime, he worked part time as a coach for the Yale football team.

In 1931, he decided to accept the better paying job as coach of Yale, rather than continuing with the Giants. But in the middle of the season, hearkening to the pleas of the Giants' owners, he returned to the team. At the end of the season, after having his offer to purchase a share of the Giants rejected, he moved to the Brooklyn Dodgers Football team for the 1932 and 1933 seasons. In Brooklyn he served both as quarterback and head coach. In 1933, he led the NFL in both rushing and passing rating.

After a brief return to Brooklyn, in 1934, he retired from play and took the job as head coach of the Football program at the City College of New York. He remained at CCNY until the War, when he joined the Navy, where he attained the rank of lieutenant commander aboard an aircraft carrier. He also would do some football coaching in the Navy.

After the War, he returned to CCNY, until 1949, when he became head football coach and athletic director at Brandeis University. When Brandeis decided to drop its football program, Benny continued as athletic director, until his retirement in 1963.

It had been clear since the founding of the Pro Football Hall of Fame in that same year, 1963, that Benny should be elected as a member. But year after year passed and he was not selected. He did what he could to advertise his own case and this offended some electors. So Benny was never properly honored in his lifetime.

Was anti-Semitism part of the reason for Benny's failure to enter the Hall during his life? Did this failure contribute to the depression that eventually would lead to his death?

It was depression that led to Benny's death. Benny's health began to decline in 1979. In that year he suffered a blood clot in his left leg, which had to be amputated. He developed a serious case of shingles, which tormented him. On November 24, 1982, at the age of 77, he retired to his East Side apartment in New York and took his own life by shooting himself in the head. He left behind a note indicating that he didn't wish to end up as "the old man on the park bench."

On February 5, 2005, Benny Friedman, at last, received his dearest wish. On that day his election to the Pro Football Hall of Fame was announced. Benny entered the hallowed Hall at Canton, Ohio along with Fritz Pollard, another long dead pioneer of the game, Dan Marino, and Steve Young.

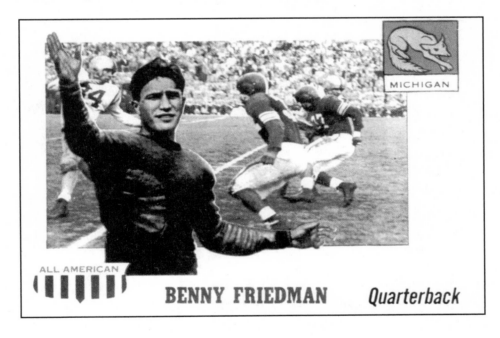

ALL AMERICAN **BENNY FRIEDMAN** *Quarterback*

CONCERNING BENNY FRIEDMAN

FIELDING YOST:

"In Benny Friedman I have one of the greatest passers and smartest quarterbacks in history. He never makes a mistake, and as for football brains, it's like having a coach on the field when Benny is out there calling signals."

GRANTLAND RICE:

"What about [Red] Grange and Friedman? These two were the best quarterbacks in the country. Grange was the better ball carrier, Friedman the better passer and in many respects the better all-round man."

And

"Friedman was a great quarterback, a marvelous passer, a good runner, a good kicker, and a brilliant field director who deserves equal rank with Grange."

And

"For all-around football smartness and football ability it is impossible to find a better man than Benny Friedman."

KNUTE ROCKNE:

"I had never seen Benny Friedman play [before]...It was an afternoon of thrills at the miraculous dexterity of his passing. Four-yards, 10-yards, 40-yards-harassed and pounded-he threw the ball from all angles, standing or running at terrific speed, hitting his target right on the button-never a miss."

And

"There are those who say Friedman is the greatest passer of all time. They are not far wrong."

PAUL GALLICO,

describing how easy it was to catch one of Friedman's passes:

"The receiver merely has to reach up to take hold of it, like picking a grapefruit from a tree."

RED GRANGE:

"Friedman was the man who first jolted the defense out of the stereo type, unimaginative line-and thus injected thinking into defensive strategy. He was the first quarterback to recognize the potentialities of the pass as a touchdown weapon on par with the running play."

RON POLLACK:

"The greatest oversight in NFL history continues…As far as I am concerned, professional football will shed tears of sorrow as long as Benny Friedman is not a member of its Hall of Fame."

Benny Friedman was finally inducted into the Hall of Fame in the class of 2005.

SID LUCKMAN

It has been more than 50 years since he played his last game, yet Sid Luckman's touch down pass percentage of 7.9 remains the best ever in professional football history. Furthermore, Sid's 8.42 yards-per-attempt mark is still the second best in football. Yet Sid did not even begin his remarkable football career as a quarterback.

Sidney Luckman was born in Brooklyn on November 21, 1916. When he was eight, his father's gift of a football sparked an interest in the game that would last throughout his lifetime. At New York's Erasmus High School, Sid's skill attracted the attention of universities all over the country. Sid was offered some 50 scholarships. Instead, he chose to attend Columbia, where he would have to work to pay for his tuition, as well as his room and board. Sid washed dishes in fraternity houses and took jobs painting, even when he was building his reputation as one of the finest players in Columbia's history.

On Columbia's team, Sid played as a halfback. Despite Sid's constantly outstanding play and the excellent coaching of Lou Little, Columbia won only 10 games during Sid's three years of eligibility, 1936-1938. This was due to the general weakness of the rest of the team. Sid showed remarkable ability throughout his college years in running, passing, punting, and placekicking.

When Sid was ready to graduate, he set aside the idea of becoming a professional football player. He planned to join his brother in the trucking business. But the owner of the Chicago Bears, George Halas, who had been following Sid's career since his high school days, contacted him and pleaded with him to reconsider his decision. Sid did. After some negotiations with the Pittsburgh Steelers, who had an earlier draft pick than the Bears, Sid joined the Chicago team on July 24, 1939 as the quarterback for their new T-formation.

The T-attack was new in 1939 and Sid did not immediately grasp all its complexities. But by 1940, Sid was recognized as master of the formation and one of the greatest and smartest quarterbacks of the game. His team's 73-0 trouncing of the Washington Redskins, led by the veteran star Sammy Baugh, in the 1940 championship game confirmed the world's impression of Luckman as the game's offensive master.

Under Sid Luckman's leadership, the Bears would win NFL championships in 1940, 1941, 1943, and 1946. They won their division title in 1942, with a perfect 11-0 record, but lost the championship game to Washington, 14-6. The team was second in its division in 1939, 1944, 1947, 1948, 1949, and 1950. Only in 1945 did the Bears fail to either win or contend in its division during Luckman's service. In the fifty years since, the Bears have appeared in only four league championship games.

In 1943, Sid was named the National Football League's Most Valuable Player. During a game that year in his native New York, a game during which he was honored, Sid threw seven touchdown passes, a league record. During the same game he completed 23 passes for 30 attempts for 443 yards, also a league record. The Bears defeated the Giants that "Sid Luckman Day" 21-7.

Sid was elected to the Pro Football Hall of Fame in 1965. He is also a member of the College Football Hall of Fame and the Jewish Sports Hall of Fame in Netanya, Israel.

After his retirement from the field, Sid continued his connections with the Bears, often acting as a coach for the team's quarterbacks. In the meantime he built up his own very successful business in cellophane packaging.

Sid died at the age of 81 on July 10, 1998.

MARV LEVY

Marv Levy served as head coach of the Buffalo Bills of the NFL during 12 seasons. During that time his record was 112-70 during regular season play and 11-8 for playoff games. He won more games than any other coach in Bills's history. He took his team to the Super Bowl four consecutive times. Starting in 1988, he led the Bills to the first of six AFC Eastern Division championships. He led the Bills to the playoffs in 8 of his 11 full seasons. During the period 1988 to 1997, his team was the first in the AFC in winning percentage. At the time of his retirement at the age of 72, he was the oldest man to have ever served as the head coach of an NFL team and he ranked 10th in overall wins in that position. In 2001 he was elected to the Pro Football Hall of Fame, a worthy recognition of one of the game's greatest coaches.

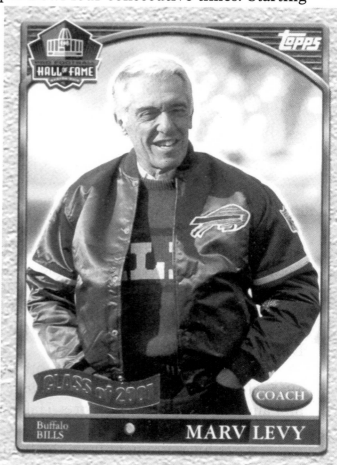

Marv was born on August 3, 1925 in Chicago, Illinois. After high school, he spent three years in the Air Force. Then he attended Coe College in Cedar Rapids, Iowa, where he earned eight letters in athletics, including football, basketball and track. On his graduation from Coe, he was elected to Phi Beta Kappa. Marv then earned a master's degree in English history at Harvard. He was accepted to Harvard Law School and had attended for two weeks when he was offered a job to coach football. He took the job, dropped out of law school and never looked back. Marv served as a football coach in a number of universities and colleges, even high schools. Starting in 1960, Marv was head coach at the University of California at Berkeley. Among his players at Berkeley was the future baseball great Mike "SuperJew" Epstein, who was outstanding in the full back position during the early 1960's.

In 1969, Marv made the transition to the NFL as kicking teams coach for the Philadelphia Eagles. In 1970 he was named as special teams coach of the Los Angeles Rams. Then, following the departure of the Los Angeles head coach George Allen, to take a similar position with the Washington Redskins, Marv also went to Washington to take over their special teams for 1971 and 1972. The next five seasons, Marv served as head coach for teams in the Canadian Football League. In 1978, he was back in the NFL, now as a head coach of the Kansas City Chiefs. His time there was not wasted and Marv continually saw improvement in his team, moving from a 4-12 record his first year to a 9-7 record in 1981.

After a two year coaching hiatus and one year as head coach of the Chicago Blitz of the United States Football League, Marv accepted the head coaching position at Buffalo. It was midway through the 1986 season and Marv was something new to his players. They were used to the standard model of coaching, but Marv was also a historian and a teacher. He often confused his players with his references to Hannibal and Caesar. But one thing soon became clear, if Marv knew his history, he also knew his football. Marv was chosen as NFL Coach of the Year in 1988 and AFC Coach of the Year in 1988, 1993, and 1995.

Following his retirement, Marv has been seen regularly as a football commentator on various television shows. His expertise and scholarly demeanor set him apart from the vast array of former jocks that often fill such positions.

ELVIS AS A JEWISH ATHLETE

Elvis Presley, the "King of Rock and Roll" and teen idol of the 1950's and 1960's, was a Jew according to Jewish law. Elvis's mother, Gladys Love Smith, was the daughter of Robert Smith and Octavia Mansell. Octavia was the daughter of the Jewess Martha Tacket (1852-1887). As a Jew is defined as the child of a Jewish mother and as Elvis's ancestry in the female line was uninterrupted from Martha Tacket, Elvis was a Jew. Elvis was aware of his Jewish background, though he did little to advertise it, nor was he known to participate in Jewish religious rituals. A statue of Elvis wearing a yarmulka, however, stands in Israel.

Elvis's favorite sport was football. He was dropped from his high school team when his coach insisted he shave his long sideburns and he refused. But throughout much of his tumultuous life he continued to play in amateur games. During his service with the army, he often participated. While stationed in Bad Neuheim, Germany, his Sunday Afternoon Football Association named him its MVP for 1959. Back in the States, he often played friendly games with local buddies and other rock 'n roll singing stars, including Pat Boone and Ricky Nelson.

Elvis supported his own amateur softball team as part of a local Memphis league. In 1962, Elvis was presented with a trophy from his team for his on-going financial support for both the team and the league.

In movies, Elvis several times portrayed sporting figures. These included a boxer in *Kid Galahad* (1962) and a race car driver in *Speedway* (1968). His most successful foray into sports, aside from amateur football, was as a participant in karate. He had his first experience with karate in the Army and eventually attained a black belt.

Elvis Presley is not the first person one thinks of when either the words Jew or athlete are mentioned. But, to a certain extent, Elvis was both.

Jewish Players In The National Hockey League

Michael Cammalleri
Championnat Mondial
de Hockey Pee-Wee Québec
Québec Pee-Wee Hockey
World Championship

- **ANDY BERENZWEIG** 1999-2003 Defenseman (37 games)—Jewish Father
- **HY BULLER** 1943-45, 1951-54 Defenseman (188 games)
- **MIKE CAMMALLERI** 2002-03 Center (28 games)—Jewish Mother
- **JUSTIN DUBERMAN** 1993-94 Right Wing (4 games)
- **STEVE DUBINSKY** 1993-2003 Center, Left Wing (376 games + 10 playoff games)
- **DOUG FRIEDMAN** 1997-99 Left Wing (18 games)
- **JEFF HALPERN** 1999-2004 Center (368 + 17 playoff games)
- **WILFRED "GIZZY" HART** 1924-28, 1932-33 Left Wing (104 games + 8 playoff games)
- **MIKE HARTMAN** 1988-1995 Left Wing (397 games)
- **PETER ING** 1989-1994 Goalie (74 games)—Jewish Mother
- **JOE IRONSTONE** 1924-1928 Goalie (2 games)
- **WALTER KALBFLEISH** 1933-37 Defenseman (36 games + 5 playoff games)
- **MAX KAMINSKY** 1933-37 Center (130 games + 4 playoff games)
- **MAX LABOVITCH** 1943-44 Right Wing (5 games)
- **ALEX "MINE BOY" LEVINSKY** 1930-39 Defenseman (367 games + 37 playoff games + 1934 NHL All-Star Game)
- **DAVID LITTMAN** 1989-1992 Goalie (3 games)

MAX KAMINSKY
St. Louis "Eagles"

- **DAVE NEMIROVSKY** 1995-1999 Right Wing (91 games + 3 playoff games)
- **BOB PLAGER** 1964-78 Defenseman (644 games + 74 playoff games)—Convert to Judaism
- **STEVE RICHMOND** 1984-89 Defenseman (159 games + 4 playoff games)
- **MAURICE "MOE" ROBERTS** 1925-26, 1931-34, 1951 Goalie (10 games)
- **SAM ROTHSCHILD** 1924-28 Left Wing (100 games + 6 playoff games)
- **MATHIEU SCHNEIDER** 1987-2004 Defenseman (992 games + 86 playoff games + 1996 NHL All-Star Game + 1998 US Olympic Hockey team)
- **TODD SIMON** 1993-94 Center, Right Wing (15 games + 5 playoff games)
- **RON STERN** 1987-2000 Right Wing (638 games + 43 playoff games)
- **MIKE VEISOR** 1973-84 Goalie (139 games + 4 playoff games)
- **BRIAN WILKS** 1984-89 Center (48 games)
- **BERNIE WOLFE** 1975-79 Goalie (120 games)
- **LARRY ZEIDEL** 1951-54, 1967-69 Defenseman (158 games + 12 playoff games)

ANTI-SEMITISM ON THE RINK:

LARRY ZEIDEL AND THE EVENTS OF MARCH 7, 1968

During a hockey match on March 7, 1968, Larry Zeidel of the Philadelphia Flyers and Eddie Shack of the opposing Boston Bruins fought a fencing-like duel using their hockey sticks as weapons. Just before the fight with Zeidel (who was the only Jewish player in the National Hockey League at the time), some of Shack's teammates chanted anti-Semitic epithets, including, "Jew Boy, we'll carry you out on a slab and send you to the gas chamber." The comments, which continued during the on-ice struggle, hit an emotional chord with Larry whose grandparents were killed in the concentration camps and cremated by the Nazis.

Larry struck first and opened a cut on the top of Shack's head. Boston's 6' 3" forward turned back on Larry with fury and began swinging away right and left. Larry raised up his stick to cover his face as Shack rained seven powerful blows, one after the other at his head. Larry suffered a cut on his neck. According to eyewitnesses, Larry got the best of the battle. The majority of the crowd was stunned by the violence of the struggle, terrifying in its brutality even within the context of a hockey game. The battle lasted for more than a minute.

On the day following the incident, Larry raised accusations of anti-Semitism. Zeidel claimed that tensions between him and "the Big Bad Bruins," (a term used to describe the unusually violent 1968 team) had existed for quite a while. Larry told a reporter "When I was a kid coming up with the Rangers 10 years or so ago, we had an exhibition at Niagara Falls with [Shack's] Hershey team. He came after me in the stands, but I took care of myself all right." Earlier in the season, during two games in early January, there had been ugly name-calling on the part of the Bruins. By the March 7th game, Larry was fed up.

Due to suspicions surrounding this particularly brutal fight, the NHL President, Clarence Campbell, ordered a hearing to be held on March 9, 1968.

There was a particular urgency in calling the meeting because of the extreme nature of the violence. Although the teams were both contenders in the late stage in the season, Campbell suspended Shack for three games and Larry for four. Campbell explained why there was a difference in the sentences. He claimed that Larry "was more at fault than Shack by reason of his initial cross-check and the first blood-letting blow to Shack's head." He later went on to contradict his decision, making the argument that, "Shack's particularly vicious attack on Zeidel in which he persisted even after he had subdued his opponent into a strictly defensive posture was completely unwarranted." Campbell described the event as "Undoubtedly the most vicious stick-swinging episode that the League had experienced in many years."

During the meeting, Campbell would not allow evidence of anti-Semitism to be presented by Larry as he never accused Shack of making any of the offensive remarks. He named Shack's teammates Ted Green, Don Awrey, Gerry Cheevers, and Tom Williams as the hecklers. Larry later explained Shack's role in the events to the press. "Eddie wasn't involved in anything verbally. He was just the one who did the dirty work, giving me that extra elbow and high stick while the rest of the Bruins egged him on."

The Bruins's coach Harry Sinden defended his players to the press and in the process, justified bigotry on the rink. "Name-calling including a man's nationality happens all the time in pro sports. Some of our guys get it too. But it's never malicious—simply a device that might psyche a player a bit." But Larry had found that the Boston Bruins alone used anti-Semitic language.

And, after all, who else could judge? Larry was the one and only Jewish player in the league.

Again Larry spoke to the press, "I don't want to sound like a crybaby. I've never been one and never will be one. It's part of the game, part of the psychological approach and warfare. But it went too far in this case. I couldn't have lived with myself if I tolerated this abuse and turned my cheek again."

This brought Sinden's own reply to the papers, "I didn't hear any of the remarks last Thursday, but it's possible somebody called him a 'Jew boy,' or something like that. Guys are always taunting each other. That doesn't mean they're bigots. You know, Zeidel has a reputation of being one of the all-time stick-men in hockey."

When A. Alan Borovy, director of the Canadian

LARRY ZEIDEL   PHILADELPHIA DEFENSE

Labor Committee for Human Rights read Sinden's remarks, he was enraged that the Bruin's coach effectively denied Larry his rights as a worker and as a human being. He stated, "Racist invective does not qualify as good-natured needling. It should be clearly stated, from the league president to the custodian of the locker room, that anti-Semitic, anti-ethnic insults have no place in the NHL. Any player who engages in them or any official who condones them should be disciplined by the league officialdom."

The allegations were quickly and quietly investigated by the NHL, as well as by the Anti-Defamation League of B'nai B'rith. The Director of Domestic Affairs at the American Jewish Committee, Nathan Perlmutter, made a statement defending Larry's rights, "We don't expect garden club language at a hockey game, however, the same sense of reality suggests to us that tormenting Larry Zeidel with 'You're next for the gas ovens,' is downright obscene-whether the hecklers knew or didn't know that Zeidel's grandparents were cremated by the Nazis. President Clarence Campbell of the National Hockey League has acted wisely in calling for a full report. A full apology to Zeidel and to millions of Jews who were brutally murdered by the Nazis is in order. Also, a clear-cut statement from Mr. Campbell that even competitive baiting has its limits, should be forthcoming. To do otherwise is tantamount to removing sportsmanship from the game and leaving it only with brutish competitiveness."

Campbell concurred with this statement, but added the bizarre constraint that, "However, every small town in the United States now has an Anti-Defamation League and it gains attention. I think it is curious that this has been going on since the 20th of January and Zeidel didn't say anything about it." This remark seems to imply that since the Anti-Defamation League is a nation-wide movement with great resources, that it would therefore have been impossible for any incidents of anti-Semitism to go unreported for two months.

Immediately, the accused players denied Larry's allegations. Don Awrey was quoted by the press as saying, "I never referred to Zeidel's religion in any way. I'm shocked that he made such an accusation...Sure, there's a lot of needling, a lot of taunting, but I never made any remarks about the 'gas chamber' or anything like that." Gerry Cheevers remarked that he "wasn't even near the guy," while Tom Williams claimed, that the story was a "lot of bull. I wasn't in the game or even on the bench. I have nothing else to say." Two other Boston players sided with their teammates. Bobby Orr and Ron Murphy claimed that they did not hear any anti-Semitic remarks.

League President Clarence Campbell reacted to the accusations by remarking, "According to Zeidel, the trouble started on January 20 in Boston, and no one from the Philadelphia club contacted me about it. How can you stop something like this if it isn't brought out?" By making this excuse, Campbell managed to wash his hands of the controversy by placing blame on Larry for not informing him sooner of the persecution that he felt. He also discussed the problem of discrimination in such a way that belittles its hateful nature and seems to recommend that Larry should have taken the abuse and remained silent, "We've had trouble like this before. Twenty years ago, the French-Canadian hockey players took a lot of abuse. By now, they're a vital part of the league. It's different, of course, with Zeidel. He's a man alone, and I do respect him for his restraint. But only to a point. It's up to anyone in society to put an immediate stop to prejudicial talk. Zeidel is no exception..."

Campbell claimed that "no one on the Philadelphia team complained to any of the officials." However, Larry clearly stated that when remarks were made during the workout proceeding the January 20 game, "he complained to Referee Bob Sloan and Eastern Supervisor of Officials Frank Udvari."

Soon after the allegations were made public, two letters were written to the NHL President's office by witnesses that supported Larry's claim. Mary Patterson and Mike Meade claimed to have heard the abuse shouted by the Boston players. Mary Patterson, who sat near the Boston bench, said that she clearly heard the abuse the Boston players hurled against Larry. She said, "The remarks were uncalled for and ignorant." Both witnesses corroborated Larry's story by naming the players and the remarks made.

The Board Chairman of the Philadelphia Flyers, Edward M. Snider, who also is Jewish, decided to close the case against the Bruins players. According to him, the fight was triggered not by anti-Semitic remarks, but by "rough, hard-hitting hockey play." It seems clear, however, that Snider acted less from conviction than from a desire to get the matter over with.

Clarence Campbell made a statement of the findings of his "investigation" after the end of the year's post-season. The statement recognized that the accused players had used the term "Jew" or "Jewish" as well as other terms of abuse to bait Larry. Campbell continued, "The use of abusive remarks or gestures as part of the baiting or needling of opposing players in sports is contemptible at any time. This is something which all sports can do without and recently some very heavy fines have been imposed against offenders in this League. We are prepared to take even more stringent measures to stamp it out. It contributes nothing to the playing of the game itself and is highly offensive to those who hear it whether they are opposing players or spectators. It can be stated with certainty that there is not anti-

racial or anti-religious feeling or other form of discrimination of any kind in this league at any level of participation—from players to the owners—and none will be tolerated. Anytime it appears, it will be dealt with severely."

The unfortunate result of this incident was that Larry was ridiculed within the hockey world. His decision to protest against the anti-Semitism of his fellow players found little sympathy among his peers. Throughout the 1968 season, Larry was ranked as the best player of the Philadelphia Flyers. When, after the incident, he was benched he knew that it was not because of his fighting, but because of his protest.

Larry spent all of the 1969 season on the bench as well. He realized that his tenure as a hockey player was over and retired at the end of 1969. He has stated that he believed that his career was brought to a premature end because of his courage in protesting the racism of the league.

When asked to comment on the incidents, Larry Zeidel told me that he could not possibly speak about his hockey career without stirring up too many strong emotions that would be detrimental to his health. Larry claimed that he was like an alcoholic or drug addict, in that one taste of his past would cause him to spiral into a long-lasting state of obsession.

(Adapted from a research project by Desiree Horvitz submitted to Brandeis University.)

OLYMPIC MEDAL WINNERS

[All are single medals except where noted in brackets.]

1896

GOLD

- **ALFRED FLATOW** (Germany) Gymnastics [3]
- **FELIX FLATOW** (Germany) Gymnastics [2]
- **ALFRED HAJOS-GUTTMAN** (Hungary) Swimming [2]
- **DR. PAUL NEUMANN** (Austria) Swimming

SILVER

- **ALFRED FLATOW** (Germany) Gymnastics

BRONZE

- **OTTO HERSCHMANN** (Austria) Swimming

1900

GOLD

- **MYER PRINSTEIN** (USA) Track

SILVER

- **MYER PRINSTEIN** (USA) Track
- **OTTO WAHLE** (Austria) Swimming [2]

BRONZE

- **SIEGFRIED FLESCH** (Austria) Fencing

1904

GOLD

- **SAMUEL BERGER** (USA) Boxing
- **MYER PRINSTEIN** (USA) Track [2]

SILVER

- **DANIEL FRANK** (USA) Track

BRONZE

- **OTTO WAHLE** (Austria) Swimming

1906

GOLD

- **HENRIK HAJOS-GUTTMAN** (Hungary) Swimming
- **MYER PRINSTEIN** (USA) Track
- **OTTO SCHEFF** (Austria) Swimming

SILVER

- **EDGAR SELIGMAN** (Great Britain) Fencing

BRONZE

- **HUGO FRIEND** (USA) Track
- **OTTO SCHEFF** (Austria) Swimming

1908

GOLD

- **DR. JENO FUCHS** (Hungary) Fencing [2]
- **DR. OSZKAR GERDE** (Hungary) Fencing
- **ALEXANDRE LIPPMANN** (France) Fencing
- **JEAN STERN** (France) Fencing
- **RICHARD WEISZ** (Hungary) Wrestling
- **LAJOS WERKNER** (Hungary) Fencing

SILVER

- **ALEXANDRE LIPPMANN** (France) Fencing
- **EDGAR SELIGMAN** (Great Britain) Fencing

BRONZE

- **PAUL ANSPACH** (Belgium) Fencing
- **ODON BODOR** (Hungary) Track
- **CLAIR S. JACOBS** (USA) Track
- **OTTO SCHEFF** (Austria) Swimming

1912

GOLD

- **HENRY ANSPACH** (Belgium) Fencing
- **PAUL ANSPACH** (Belgium) Fencing [2]
- **DR. JENO FUCHS** (Hungary) Fencing [2]
- **DR. OSZKAR GERDE** (Hungary) Fencing
- **JACQUES OCHS** (Belgium) Fencing
- **GASTON SALMON** (Belgium) Fencing
- **ZOLTAN SCHENKER** (Hungary) Fencing
- **LAJOS WERKNER** (Hungary) Fencing

SILVER

- **IMRE GELLERT** (Hungary) Gymnastics
- **DR. OTTO HERSCHMANN** (Austria) Fencing
- **ABEL KIVIAT** (USA) Track
- **ALVAH T. MEYER** (USA) Track
- **IVAN OSIIER** (Denmark) Fencing
- **EDGAR SELIGMAN** (Great Britain) Fencing

BRONZE

- **MARGARETE ADLER** (Austria) Swimming
- **MOR KOVACS** (Hungary) Track
- **KLARA MILCH** (Austria) Swimming
- **JOSEPHINE STICKER** (Austria) Swimming

1920

GOLD

- **SAMUEL MOSBERG** (USA) Boxing

SILVER

- **PAUL ANSPACH** (Belgium) Fencing
- **GERARD BLITZ** (Belgium) Waterpolo
- **MAURICE BLITZ** (Belgium) Waterpolo
- **SAMUEL GERSON** (USA) Wrestling
- **ALEXANDRE LIPPMANN** (France) Fencing

BRONZE

- **GERARD BLITZ** (Belgium) Swimming
- **MONTGOMERY "MOE" HERZOWITCH** (Canada) Boxing
- **ALEXANDRE LIPPMANN** (France) Fencing
- **FRED MEYER** (USA) Wrestling

1924

GOLD

- **HAROLD ABRAHAMS** (Great Britain) Track
- **LOUIS A. CLARKE** (USA) Track
- **JACKIE FIELDS** (USA) Boxing
- **ELIAS KATZ** (Finland) Track
- **ALEXANDRE LIPPMANN** (France) Fencing

SILVER

- **HAROLD ABRAHAMS** (Great Britain) Track
- **PAUL ANSPACH** (Belgium) Fencing
- **GERARD BLITZ** (Belgium) Waterpolo
- **MAURICE BLITZ** (Belgium) Waterpolo
- **JANOS GARAI** (Hungary) Fencing
- **ALFRED HAJOS-GUTTMAN** (Hungary) Architecture
- **ELIAS KATZ** (Finland) Track
- **ZOLTAN SCHENKER** (Hungary) Fencing

BRONZE

- **BARON H. L. DE MORPURGO** (Italy) Tennis
- **JANOS GARAI** (Hungary) Fencing
- **SYDNEY JELINEK** (USA) Crew
- **ZOLTAN SCHENKER** (Hungary) Fencing

H. M. ABRAHAMS

1928

GOLD

- **JANOS GARAI** (Hungary) Fencing
- **DR. SANDOR GOMBOS** (Hungary) Fencing
- **HANS HAAS** (Austria) Weightlifting
- **HELENE MAYER** (Germany) Fencing—Jewish Father

- **DR. FERENC MEZO** (Hungary) Literature
- **ATTILA PETSCHAUER** (Hungary) Fencing
- **FANNY ROSENFELD** (Canada) Track

SILVER

- **ISTVAN BARTA** (Hungary) Waterpolo
- **FRITZIE BURGER** (Austria) Figure Skating
- **LILLIAN COPELAND** (USA) Track
- **ATTILA PETSCHAUER** (Hungary) Fencing
- **FANNY ROSENFELD** (Canada) Track

BRONZE

- **HARRY DEVINE** (USA) Boxing
- **HARRY ISAACS** (South Africa) Boxing
- **S. RABIN** (Great Britain) Wrestling
- **ELLIS R. SMOUHA** (Great Britain) Track

FANNY ROSENFELD

1932

GOLD

- **ISTVAN BARTA** (Hungary) Waterpolo
- **GYORGY BRODY** (Hungary) Waterpolo
- **LILLIAN COPELAND** (USA) Track
- **GEORGE GULACK** (USA) Gymnastics
- **IRVING JAFFEE** (USA) Speed-skating [2]
- **ENDRE KABOS** (Hungary) Fencing
- **ATTILA PETSCHAUER** (Hungary) Fencing

SILVER

- **FRITZIE BURGER** (Austria) Figure Skating
- **DR. PHILIP ERENBERG** (USA) Gymnastics
- **HANS HAAS** (Austria) Weightlifting
- **KAROLY KARPATI** (Hungary) Wrestling
- **ABRAHAM KURLAND** (Denmark) Wrestling

LILLIAN COPELAND

BRONZE

- **RUDOLPH BALL** (Germany) Ice Hockey
- **NIKOLAUS HIRSCHI** (Austria) Wrestling [2]
- **ENDRE KABOS** (Hungary) Fencing
- **ALBERT SCHWARTZ** (USA) Swimming
- **JADWIGA WAJSOWNA** [Weiss] (Poland) Track
- **PAUL WINTER** (France) Track
- **EMILIA ROTTER** (Hungary) Figure Skating
- **LASLO SZOLAS** (Hungary) Figure Skating

IBOLYA CSAK

1936

GOLD

- **SAMUEL BALTER** (USA) Basketball
- **GYORGY BRODY** (Hungary) Waterpolo
- **IBOLYA K. CSAK** (Hungary) Track
- **ENDRE KABOS** (Hungary) Fencing [2]
- **KAROLY KARPATI** (Hungary) Wrestling
- **ILONA SCHACHERER-ELEK** (Hungary) Fencing—Jewish Father

EMILIA ROTTER & LASLO SZOLAS (1936)

SILVER

- **HELENE MAYER** (Germany) Fencing— Jewish Father
- **JADWIGA WAJSOWNA** [Weiss] (Poland) Track

BRONZE

- **GERARD BLITZ** (Belgium) Waterpolo
- **EMILIA ROTTER** (Hungary) Figure Skating
- **LASLO SZOLAS** (Hungary) Figure Skating

1948

GOLD

- **FRANK SPELLMAN** (USA) Weightlifting
- **ILONA SCHACHERER-ELEK** (Hungary) Fencing—Jewish Father
- **HENRY WITTENBERG** (USA) Wrestling

SILVER

- **DEZSO GYARMATI** (Hungary) Waterpolo
- **AGNES KELETI** (Hungary) Gymnastics
- **DR. STEVE SEYMOUR** (USA) Track

BRONZE

- **NORMAN C. ARMITAGE** (USA) Fencing
- **JAMES FUCHS** (USA) Track

1952

GOLD

- **SANDOR GELLER** (Hungary) Soccer
- **MARIA GOROKHOVSKAYA** (USSR) Gymnastics [2]

- BORIS GUREVICH (USSR) Wrestling
- DEZSO GYARMATI (Hungary) Waterpolo
- DR. GYORGY KARPATI (Hungary) Waterpolo
- AGNES KELETI (Hungary) Gymnastics
- CLAUDE NETTER (France) Fencing
- MIKHAIL PERELMAN (USSR) Gymnastics
- EVA SZEKELY (Hungary) Swimming
- JUDIT TEMES (Hungary) Swimming

SILVER

- MARIA GOROKHOVSKAYA (USSR) Gymnastics [5]
- AGNES KELETI (Hungary) Gymnastics
- GRIGORI NOVAK (USSR) Weightlifting
- ILONA SCHACHERER-ELEK (Hungary) Fencing—Jewish Father
- HENRY WITTENBERG (USA) Wrestling

BRONZE

- JAMES FUCHS (USA) Track
- AGNES KELETI (Hungary) Gymnastics [2]
- JUDIT TEMES (Hungary) Swimming
- LEV VAINSHTEIN (USSR) Shooting

1956

GOLD

- ISAAC BERGER (USA) Weightlifting
- LASZLO FABIAN (Hungary) Canoeing
- DEZSO GYARMATI (Hungary) Waterpolo
- DR. GYORGY KARPATI (Hungary) Waterpolo
- AGNES KELETI (Hungary) Gymnastics [4]
- ALICE KERTESZ (Hungary) Gymnastics
- BORIS RAZINSKY (USSR) Soccer
- LEON ROTTMAN (Romania) Canoeing [2]

SILVER

- **ALLAN ERDMAN** (USSR) Shooting
- **RAFAEL GRACH** (USSR) Speed-skating
- **AGNES KELETI** (Hungary) Gymnastics [2]
- **ALICE KERTESZ** (Hungary) Gymnastics
- **EVA SZEKELY** (Hungary) Swimming

BRONZE

- **YVES DREYFUS** (France) Fencing
- **IMRE FARKAS** (Hungary) Canoeing
- **BORIS GOIKHMAN** (USSR) Waterpolo
- **ANDRE MOUYAL** (France) Fencing
- **YAKOV RYLSKY** (USSR) Fencing
- **DAVID TYSHLER** (USSR) Fencing

1960

GOLD

- **VERA KREPKINA** (USSR) Track
- **MARK MIDLER** (USSR) Fencing

SILVER

- **ISAAC BERGER** (USA) Weightlifting
- **BORIS GOIKHMAN** (USSR) Waterpolo
- **ALLAN JAY** (Great Britain) Fencing [2]
- **VLADIMIR PORTNOI** (USSR) Gymnastics
- **ILDIKO USLAKY-REJTO** (Hungary) Fencing

BRONZE

- **ALBERT AXELROD** (USA) Fencing
- **MOSES BLASS** (Brazil) Basketball
- **IMRE FARKAS** (Hungary) Canoeing

- **KLARA FRIED** (Hungary) Canoeing
- **RAFAEL GRACH** (USSR) Speed-skating
- **DEZSO GYARMATI** (Hungary) Waterpolo
- **ROBERT HALPERIN** (USA) Yachting
- **DR. GYORGY KARPATI** (Hungary) Waterpolo
- **VLADIMIR PORTNOI** (USSR) Gymnastics
- **LEON ROTTMAN** (Romania) Canoeing
- **DAVID SEGAL** (Great Britain) Track

1964

GOLD

- **GERALD ASHWORTH** (USA) Track
- **LARRY BROWN** (USA) Basketball
- **TAMAS GABOR** (Hungary) Fencing
- **DEZSO GYARMATI** (Hungary) Waterpolo
- **DR. GYORGY KARPATI** (Hungary) Waterpolo
- **IRENA KIRSZENSTEIN** (Poland) Track
- **MARK MIDLER** (USSR) Fencing
- **ARPAD ORBAN** (Hungary) Soccer
- **RUDOLF PLYUKFELDER** (USSR) Weightlifting
- **YAKOV RYLSKY** (USSR) Fencing
- **ILDIKO USLAKY-REJTO** (Hungary) Fencing

SILVER

- **ISAAC BERGER** (USA) Weightlifting
- **IRENA KIRSZENSTEIN** (Poland) Track [2]
- **MARILYN RAMENOFSKY** (USA) Swimming

BRONZE

- **JAMES BREGMAN** (USA) Judo
- **YVES DREYFUS** (France) Fencing

1968

GOLD

- **BORIS GUREVITCH** (USSR) Wrestling
- **IRINA KIRZENSTEIN-SZEWINSKA** (Poland) Track and Field
- **WALENTIN MANKIN** (USSR) Yachting
- **GREGORY MONDZOLESKY** (USSR) Volleyball
- **MARK RAKITA** (USSR) Fencing
- **MARK SPITZ** (USA) Swimming [2]
- **EDUARD VINOKAROV** (USSR) Fencing
- **VICTOR ZINGER** (USSR) Hockey

SILVER

- **SEMYON BELITS-GEIMAN** (USSR) Swimming
- **ALAN CALMET** (France) Figure Skating
- **ALEKSANDR GORELIK** (USSR) Figure Skating
- **MARK RAKITA** (USSR) Fencing
- **MARK SPITZ** (USA) Swimming

BRONZE

- **SEMYON BELITS-GEIMAN** (USSR) Swimming
- **IRINA KIRZENSTEIN-SZEWINSKA** (Poland) Track and Field
- **GRIGORY KRISS** (USSR) Fencing [2]
- **NAUM PROKUPETS** (USSR) Canoeing
- **MARK RAKITA** (USSR) Fencing
- **MARK SPITZ** (USA) Swimming

MARK SPITZ

1972

GOLD

- **GYORGY GEDO** (Hungary) Boxing
- **WALENTIN MANKIN** (USSR) Yachting
- **FAINA MELNIK** (USSR) Track and Field
- **MARK SPITZ** (USA) Swimming [7]
- **SANDOR ERDOS** (Hungary) Fencing

SILVER

- **ANDREA GYARMATI** (Hungary) Swimming
- **NEAL SHAPIRO** (USA) Equestrian

BRONZE

- **PETER ASCH** (USA) Waterpolo
- **DONALD COHAN** (USA) Yachting
- **ANDREA GYARMATI** (Hungary) Swimming
- **IRINA KIRZENSTEIN-SZEWINSKA** (Poland) Track and Field
- **GRIGORY KRISS** (USSR) Fencing
- **NEAL SHAPIRO** (USA) Equestrian
- **EFIM CHULAK** (USSR) Volleyball

1976

GOLD

- **ERNIE GRUNFELD** (USA) Basketball
- **IRINA KIRZENSTEIN-SZEWINSKA** (Poland) Track and Field
- **VALERY SCHARY** (USSR) Weightlifting

SILVER

- **NATALIA KUSHNIR** (USSR) Volleyball
- **WALENTIN MANKIN** (USSR) Yachting

BRONZE

- **NANCY LIEBERMAN** (USA) Basketball
- **EDITH MASTERS** (USA) Equestrian
- **WENDY WEINBERG** (USA) Swimming
- **VICTOR ZILBERMANN** (Romania) Boxing

1980

GOLD

- **JOHAN HARMENBERG** (Sweden) Fencing
- **GENNEDY KARPONOSOV** (USSR) Ice Dancing
- **WALENTIN MANKIN** (USSR) Yachting

SILVER

- **SVETLANA KRACHEVSKAIA** (USSR) Track and Field

1984

GOLD

- **CARINA BENNINGA** (Netherlands) Field Hockey
- **MITCH GAYLORD** (USA) Gymnastics
- **DARA TORRES** (USA) Swimming—Jewish Father

SILVER

- **DANIEL ADLER** (Brazil) Yachting
- **ROBERT BERLAND** (USA) Judo
- **MITCH GAYLORD** (USA) Gymnastics
- **BERNARD ROJZMAN** (Brazil) Volleyball

BRONZE

- **MARK BERGER** (Canada) Judo
- **MITCH GAYLORD** (USA) Gymnastics

1988

GOLD

- **MIKE MILCHIN** (USA) Baseball—Jewish Father
- **ELENA SHUSHUNOVA** (USSR) Gymnastics

SILVER

- **DARA TORRES** (USA) Swimming—Jewish Father
- **ELENA SHUSHUNOVA** (USSR) Gymnastics

BRONZE

- **SETH BAUER** (USA) Rowing
- **CARINA BENNINGA** (Netherlands) Field Hockey
- **MARC BENNINGA** (Netherlands) Field Hockey
- **BRAD GILBERT** (USA) Tennis
- **DARA TORRES** (USA) Swimming—Jewish Father
- **ELENA SHUSHUNOVA** (USSR) Gymnastics

1992

GOLD

- **VALERY BELENKI** (Azerbaijan) Gymnastics—Jewish Father
- **JOE JACOBI** (USA) Canoeing
- **TATIANA LYSENKO** (Ukraine) Gymnastics [2]—Jewish Mother
- **ELENA SHUSHUNOVA** (Russia) Gymnastics [2]
- **DARA TORRES** (USA) Swimming—Jewish Father

SILVER

- **YAEL ARAD** (Israel) Judo
- **AVITAL SELINGER** (Netherlands) Volleyball
- **ELENA SHUSHUNOVA** (Russia) Gymnastics

BRONZE

- **VALERY BELENKI** (Azerbaijan) Gymnastics—Jewish Father
- **DAN GREENBAUM** (USA) Volleyball
- **TATIANA LYSENKO** (Ukraine) Gymnastics—Jewish Mother
- **PHOBE MILLS** (USA) Gymnastics—Jewish Mother
- **ELENA SHUSHUNOVA** (Russia) Gymnastics
- **SHAY OREN SMADGA** (Israel) Judo
- **KERRI STRUG** (USA) Gymnastics
- **ROBERT DOVER** (USA) Equestrian

1994

GOLD

- **OKSANA BAIUL** (Ukraine) Figure Skating—Jewish Paternal Grandmother

---

1996

GOLD

- **KERRI STRUG** (USA) Gymnastics
- **SERGEI CHARIKOV** (Russia) Fencing

SILVER

- **YANINA BATRICHINA** (Russia) Rhythmic Gymnastics
- **SERGEI CHARIKOV** (Russia) Fencing

BRONZE

- **MIRIAM FOX-JERUSALMI** (France) Kayak
- **GAL FRIDMAN** (Israel) Windsurfing
- **ROBERT DOVER** (USA) Equestrian
- **JULIA GARAEVA** (Russia) Fencing
- **MARIA MAZINA** (Russia) Fencing

1998

SARA DeCOSTA

GOLD

- **SARA DeCOSTA** (USA) Ice Hockey—Jewish Mother

SILVER

- **GORDY SHEER** (USA) Luge

2000

GOLD

- **SERGEI CHARIKOV** (Russia) Fencing
- **ADRIANA BEHAR** (Brazil) Beach Volleyball
- **ANTHONY ERVIN** (USA) Swimming—Jewish Mother
- **LENNY KRAYZELBURG** (USA) Swimming [3]
- **MARIA MAZINA** (Russia) Fencing
- **DARA TORRES** (USA) Swimming [2]—Jewish Father

SILVER

- **ANTHONY ERVIN** (USA) Swimming—Jewish Mother
- **SCOTT GOLDBLATT** (USA) Swimming
- **JASON LEZAK** (USA) Swimming
- **YULIA RASKINA** (Belarus) Rhythmic Gymnastics
- **SARA WHELAN** (USA) Soccer

BRONZE

- **ROBERT DOVER** (USA) Equestrian
- **MICHAEL KALGANOV** (Israel) Kayak
- **DARA TORRES** (USA) Swimming [3]—Jewish Father

2002

GOLD

- **SARAH HUGHES** (USA) Figure Skating—Jewish Mother

SILVER

- **ILYA AVERBUKH** (Russia) Ice Dancing
- **SARAH DECOSTA** (USA) Ice Hockey—Jewish Mother
- **DANNY KASS** (USA) Half-Pipe Snow Boarding—Jewish Father
- **IRINA SLUTSKAYA** (Russia) Figure Skating—Jewish Father

2004

GOLD

- **SUE BIRD** (USA) Basketball—Jewish Father
- **GAL FRIDMAN** (Israel) Windsurfing [Gal's is the first ever gold medal for Israel]
- **SCOTT GOLDBLATT** (USA) Swimming
- **LENNY KRAYZELBURG** (USA) Swimming
- **JASON LEZAK** (USA) Swimming
- **NICHOLAS MASSU** (Chile) Tennis [2]—Jewish Mother

SILVER

- **ADRIANA BEHAR** (Brazil) Beach Volleyball
- **GAVIN FINGLESON** (Australia) Baseball

BRONZE

- **LARRY BROWN** (USA) Basketball Coach
- **SERGEI CHARIKOV** (Russia) Fencing
- **ROBERT DOVER** (USA) Equestrian
- **SADA JACOBSON** (USA) Fencing
- **DEENA DROSSIN KASTOR** (USA) Marathon
- **JASON LEZAK** (USA) Swimming
- **SARAH POEWE** (Germany) Swimming—Jewish Mother
- **ARIK ZEEVI** (Israel) Judo

GAL FRIDMAN and 2004 ISRAELI OLYMPIC COIN

LON MYERS

Lawrence Eugene Myers was born on February 16, 1858 in Richmond, Virginia. His mother died of consumption when he was just a baby. He spent his childhood during the Civil War, along with his father, Solomon A. Myers, in the very heart of the South. In 1875, the pair moved to the North. Lon, as he was known to his friends and family, often wrote of his experiences for publication in magazines and newspapers. Speaking of the beginning of his running career: "Just when I started to run I don't know. I guess it must have been when I was about two years old. Ever since I can remember I have been noted for my fleetness of foot. In early childhood my companions would pit me against the champion of some other 'crowd,' and I never failed to defeat my opponent. When about thirteen or fourteen years of age, I was a member of a baseball nine, all of the other members being grown men. Not that I was such an extraordinary ball-player, but, if you remember, it was a common thing in those days for players to run for each other. This was what I was kept on the nine for; and many a game I've pulled out of the fire through my ability to run the bases in good style."

The Myers first settled in Jersey City and there Lon joined another baseball team. Shortly after, however, he put aside this pursuit to follow a career as a bookkeeper. After three years, his health began to fail. His doctor encouraged his to seek more outdoor activity to strengthen his weak pulmonary system. He took up running. Though he was only 5' 7 ¾" tall and weighed 109 pounds, his legs was disproportionately long compared to his body. He was described by some of his contemporaries as a perfect running machine. He began his career as a runner in 1878.

Running, at that time, was new as an organized competition, but Lon soon was recognized as a man of remarkable ability. By 1879 he already set the first of his many records, for the 440 yards, in 49 seconds. Eventually Lon would compete in 22 different distances between 50 yards and 1 mile. He held 15 United States titles, 10 Canadian, and 3 British. He held, at one time or another, every American record for the distances he ran. He was recognized far and wide as the greatest runner of his time. Today most scholars agree in regarding him as the greatest runner of the nineteenth century.

After defeating much of the competition in this country, while representing the Manhattan Athletic Club and wearing its cherry diamond symbol on his chest, he went abroad, to Canada, England, and Australia, to show the rest of the world the quality of American racers.

Here is Lon's account of one of his races in England: "There were about 6,000 people present, and it was raining all the time...It was as bad a day as could be picked for me, and if they couldn't beat me then, they have a poor show to do it now. When the pistol fired, I started off 'like a shot' and kept the lead for about 40 yards. Baker here ran right in front of me and cut me short, when Muspratt came up on the outside and I was pocketed. Muspratt stopped short, almost, at about 170 yards out, and I came near to running on top of him, but pulled out to the outside of the track and went for Baker. At 250 yards I was leading on the outside of the upper corner, and at 300 yards the race was over. Philips put on a wonderful finish, but it was no use, as I was watching him over my shoulder, and had just a few Yankee yards up my sleeve."

One of the strangest races in Lon's career took place on January 22, 1885. The track of the Manhattan Athletic Club was frozen over and Lon was asked to test his speed against an ice skater. The skater was Charles Pfaff, Jr. Lon was equipped with special spiked shoes. Lon was to run 120 yards, including a 5-yard handicap, while Pfaff was to skate 115 yards. By the 20-yard mark, Lon had already caught up with the skater. By the 80-yard mark Lon was well ahead. The wind was to Lon's back and he sailed along. At the finish, he was 6 feet ahead of Pfaff and had set a new amateur record for the distance of 11¾ seconds.

Lon's health continued to be troublesome throughout his life. He would have terrible attacks of various cold-like disorders time after time. After returning from his tour of Australia, at the age of 30, Lon Myers retired from running. He started a new career as a bookmaker for horse races, at that time a legal occupation. He had some success in this, even owning several racehorses. One of his horses was named in honor of the great Jewish author and British Prime Minister, Benjamin Disraeli. It was called Lord Beaconsfield, after the title that had been awarded Disraeli by Queen Victoria. At the age of 41, after a bout of pneumonia, Lon Myers died at his home in New York. This was on February 15, 1899. Many of Lon's records stood long after his death. For instance, his world record for 1000 yards stood until 1910. His American record for 60 yards stood until 1923.

LON MYERS PLAYS A PRACTICAL JOKE

Lon E. Myers, the great 19th century racer, traveled a number of times to England to compete against his British competitors. During such absences from home he often wrote letters to his friends back in America. This is from such a letter written from London on June 21, 1884:

There is a gymnasium on the grounds, back of the grandstand, and in this place the [racing] surface was put down. We went in this morning, and I broke off a piece of the surface, which I enclose, and which may be of use one of these days. I fooled Uncle Avery with it. When I got back from the grounds I asked him if he would have a piece of butterscotch, at the same time laying a small piece on the table where he was writing. Before I could stop him he put a piece in his mouth and began chewing on it. It didn't kill him.

ZIMMY

Charles Zibelman was born in New York in 1891. When he was nine, he was playing in the streets of the city when he was struck by a trolley. His life was feared for but he survived the catastrophic accident with the complete loss of his legs, leaving no more than two stumps. Many near to him felt that he would have been better off dead. What was a poor Jewish boy with no legs going to do in the world?

But this was not the attitude of Charles Zibelman himself. Charles, who called himself Zimmy, taught himself to swim and he began to put on exhibitions of his remarkable prowess in that sport. Through this means he was able to earn a living and live a normal life. He married and had two children. He drove a specially constructed car. He played golf. He smoked cigars. He walked about on his hands at great speed. Zimmy traveled around the world to display his amazing swimming talents and his amazing buoyancy, which he attributed to his legless condition. Those who saw him said that Zimmy bounced on the water like a cork. Zimmy could go for hours in the water without coming out and even slept there with his hands clasped behind his head.

It was on the stage of Oscar Hammerstein's old theatre in New York that in 1914 Zimmy thrilled an audience by keeping his head beneath water for 4 minutes and 17 seconds. He was always on the go, and it was in San Francisco's frigid and turgid bay that he swam across the Golden Gate in 52 minutes. This was long before the great bridge was built.

In 1927, a contest was held to swim from the coast of California to Catalina Island. Zimmy, who had settled in Long Beach, California,

ZIMMY   Worlds Champion Legless Swimmer

entered the contest, but he did not win, nor did he complete the swim. In November of the same year he planned to swim the widest part of Hell Gate in the East River in New York City. Zimmy also announced that year that he would swim down the Hudson River from Albany to New York. This last feat he would complete, probably the greatest achievement of his career, but not until 1937.

In 1931, Charles was more successful with a challenge of another sort. At that time the record for continuous swimming was 42 hours, held by Otto Kemmerich, who set it swimming around in a Berlin pool. Charles broke Kemmerich's record and set a new mark of 100 hours. This he did in a pool in Honolulu.

During the period of 1931-33, Charles Zimmy made a number of attempts to cross the English Channel. He was not successful, but he came very close. On his last attempt, he was in sight of his goal when he was stung by a jellyfish and had to be pulled from the water.

Charles Zimmy, in 1936, decided to swim across the Atlantic. Not swim from shore to shore, for this would be an impossibility for any swimmer, but swim continuously while crossing the ocean aboard the cruise ship the Queen Mary. This he did in the liner's swimming pool. Like any other passenger on the luxurious ship, Zimmy relaxed on the way across, smoking between 100 and 125 cigars and enjoying the ship's cuisine, all while constantly in the water.

It was in 1937 that Zimmy set off for his greatest challenge, to swim down the Hudson River from Albany, the state capital, to New York City, 147 miles away. No one would be paying him for this effort. It was designed to provide publicity for his performances. The story was covered step by step by the newspapers of the day. Zimmy left Albany on August 23 by diving off a pier. By the second day he had reached Coxsackie, New York. He floated for several hours off Old Rattlesnake Island while he waited for the tide to turn. He kibitzed with people in passing boats while he floated on his back and smoked cigars. When the tide changed, around 7:00 p.m., using his powerful overhand strokes, he continued downstream.

On the third day, August 25, he reached Saugerties early in the morning. But then the incoming tide caught him and carried him back six miles, back passed the village. He would not recover his ground until 9:00 p.m. that evening. Later in the evening he was spotted near Kingston, five miles further on. At 8:21 the next evening he reached the Mid-Hudson Bridge, the halfway point of his swim. A reporter in a motor launch went out to interview him. Zimmy used the opportunity to send a message to President Roosevelt, who was staying at nearby Hyde Park stating, "I salute you from the waters of the Hudson."

At 4:00 P.M. of August 28, it was announced that Zimmy had been in the water a constant 118 hours, surpassing his old record of 100 hours. The tide was against him so he just held his place, ate sandwiches that were brought to him and smoked cigars. Crowds lined the bank of the river and several hardy souls dived in and joined him for a brief visit.

By the evening Zimmy had reached Rockland Landing, some 30 miles from New York. When questioned, Zimmy insisted that he would stay in the water for the entire journey. This was despite the fact that the swimmer was covered with sores caused by the constant action of the water against his skin. After all his years of planning, he was not going to quit now, with the goal in sight. He told those who spoke to him that he expected to reach the George Washington Bridge the next day. One thing Zimmy did do at Rockland Landing was to apply a fresh layer of grease to his body.

At 11:00 am, Zimmy passed Alpine Boat Basin, but then the tide turned against him again and he had to spend the afternoon swimming and floating in the marina. His deep tan and his six days of beard struck those who saw him. Barnacles had attached themselves to his legless body. Zimmy's manager told a reporter when he was asked if his client swam as well as a sea lion, "Pooh! A sea lion, a sea lion is nothing. A fish, yes, but Zimmy might even outswim a fish."

Again, Zimmy socialized while he rested for the changing tide with the thousands of people on the shore and the hardier souls who swam out to him. The boat that accompanied him fed Zimmy some more sandwiches. Again, after eating he lit up a cigar and relaxed on the water with his hands across his chest. To someone who asked him what his plans were, he said, "When I finish this, my next big swim will be from Key West to Havana," indicating that his current swim made him long for sunny days to separate his cold nights in the water.

At about 10:00 P.M., Zimmy reached his planned destination, the 125th Street Ferry Dock, but the strong tide washed him a mile further down the river. A rowboat had to tow him back. Before completely ending his swim, he executed several dives back into the water, to show off to the crowd that had gathered. He was then rushed to an ambulance, which was waiting on the shore to take him to Harlem Hospital for observation and a checkup. Before he was driven away, he told a reporter that, "I feel kind of funny being out of water."

The next day, Charles Zimmy checked out of the hospital, despite having a 100 degrees fever. A few days later an interview with Mrs. Lottie Moore Schoemmel, another marathon swimmer, was published in which she warned Zimmy against making his proposed Key West to Havana swim because of the barracudas and other dangerous fish. Zimmy boldly responded, "I've got a grease I use that I think will keep those fish away."

DARA TORRES

Dara Torres is known for her beauty, her success in driving racecars, and her winning nine Olympic medals in swimming, the most of any Jewish female Olympian. [Mark Spitz is tied for the most of any athlete with 11.] Dara's total of nine Olympic medals, four gold, four bronze, and one silver, ranks second among all women in U.S. Olympic history. At the 2000 Sydney Olympics, Dara had one of the most remarkable comebacks in Olympic history, she returned successfully to the games after a seven-year retirement.

Dara Torres was born on April 15, 1967 in Beverly Hills, California to a Jewish father and a non-Jewish mother. She has always identified with the Jewish religion and later in her life, conforming with religious law, she went through the conversion ceremony. She was the first American to swim in four different Olympiads, 1984, 1988, 1992, and 2000. When Dara competed in 1984, she impressed the world with her height (5'11"), her athleticism, and her beauty. In the 1984 Olympics, she won gold in the 400-meter freestyle. For this achievement alone she was inducted into the Jewish Sports Hall of Fame at the Hebrew University of Jerusalem in 1984. But her Hall of Fame career was far from over. In 1988, she won the silver in the 400-meter medley relay and bronze in the 400-meter freestyle.

After this Olympics, Dara took her first retirement from international competition, a departure that turned out to be brief. She used this time to complete her education at the University of Florida, where she won 28 All-America honors (the maximum possible in the NCAA). In 1989, Dara began her career in television sports research at NBC.

In January 1991, after two years respite from competition, Dara put her TV career on hold in order to train for the 1992 Olympics. At the games, Dara was the captain of the U.S. Olympic team, where she won the gold in the 400-meter freestyle. She decided to retire from swimming following the 1992 Barcelona Olympics. This retirement would be far longer than her first.

During this departure, Dara spent her time participating in such varied activities as modeling, serving as a spokeswoman for Tae-Bo, working in journalism, and competing in extreme sports. Because of her renowned beauty, she became, in 1994, the first real athlete to appear among the models in *Sports Illustrated's* swimsuit issue. In 2000, she participated in the inaugural ceremonies for President George W. Bush as a speaker and host. She made numerous television appearances, including working on-air for *ESPN*, *TNT* and *Fox News*, and hosting *Extreme Step*, a segment of the Discovery Channel's show, *The Next Stop*. On this show, she reported on and participated in scuba-diving with sharks, skiing uphill, climbing up frozen waterfalls, windsurfing, hang-gliding, and sky-surfing.

When Dara decided to return to the Olympics in 1999, she studied for 15 months with Coach Richard Quick at Stanford University. The training was difficult, but Dara was soon back in racing form. After seven years of retirement, Dara made an unprecedented comeback and competed at the 2000 Games in Sydney. Her success was even greater than her previous achievements. She won gold medals in the 400-meter freestyle and the 400-meter medley relay; and bronze medals in the 50-meter freestyle, the 100-meter freestyle, and the 100-meter butterfly.

Prior to the 2000 Olympics, Dara was one of only 10 American swimmers to have participated in three Olympics. With her comeback, she became the only American swimmer and one of only nine swimmers in the world to have competed in four Olympiads. At the age of 33, her two gold medals in Sydney made her the oldest woman swimmer to ever win a gold medal.

Dara is the American record-holder in 50-meter freestyle and the 100-meter butterfly. She was at one time the world record-holder in 50-meter freestyle and the American record-holder in 100-meter freestyle. She holds the second-fastest 100-meter free relay split in history and the fastest in America.

In 2002, Dara became the first woman to win the Toyota Pro/Celebrity automobile race in the event's 26-year history. She attributes her success at Long Beach in this completely different sport to her intensely competitive spirit.

In recent years, given the climate of violence and terrorism present in Israel, most athletes invited there have refused to come. This was not the case with Dara Torres, who on September 26, 2002 held a one-day swim clinic, as part of the High Holidays Sports Clinic at Wingate Institute. She guided Israel's elite youth swimmers by teaching them the butterfly and the freestyle, drilling them, discussing her career with them, showing them her medals, and encouraging their success. Dara Torres currently lives in New York City.

SWORDS OF HUNGARY

The Jewish people have had more success in the Olympic Games as citizens of Hungary than as citizens of any other nation of the world. One-third of all medals awarded to Jews have gone to Hungarians. Almost half of all the Jewish gold medals have gone to Magyar contestants. And considering the history of anti-Semitism in Hungary and the habit many Jews have taken over the years of changing their names or hiding their ethnic identity, these numbers may actually be higher. Indeed, the number of gold medals awarded to Hungarian Jews is only slightly less than the number awarded to American and Russian Jews combined, including all members of the former Soviet Union.

In no field has Hungarian Jewish Olympic success been more spectacular than in the area of fencing. The swordsmanship of the finest of these Jewish contestants set a mark that awed the entire world.

Dr. Jeno Fuchs (1882-1955), the doyen of this generation of fencing heroes and heroines, was as unspectacular a figure as could be imagined. He was a short man, of slender build, bald, with a quiet and unassuming demeanor, neither Cyrano nor D'Artagnan. But once Fuchs had a saber in his hand, his cool, fierce and technically perfect methodology turned him into a competitor to be greatly feared. When Fuchs went to London in 1908 for that year's Olympic Games, the gravel surfaced outdoor field suited him and he was unbeatable. After taking the individual gold medal in saber, Fuchs joined four of his countrymen to also capture the team gold medal. Of the five members of the team, only one was not Jewish. Besides Fuchs, the other Jewish members of the team were Dezso Foldes (1880-1950), Oszkar Gerde (1883-1944), and Lajos Werkner (1883-1943).

The Stockholm Olympics of 1912 was another venue to display the excellence of Fuchs's technique. The official report of the Olympics said of him, "Dr. Fuchs awakened general admiration by the skill and strength he displayed during the course of the competition. Although of slight build and rather low stature, he succeeded by means of well-calculated sabre play, in repelling the attacks of and defeating the most powerfully built and vigorous opponents. One saw the results of good schooling and methodical training; there was no attempt at artificial surprises, nothing left to chance; determination and strength were not spared, on the other hand, whenever an attack was made it was from some well chosen position." Again Fuchs won individual saber and team saber gold medals. Fuchs was the first Jewish athlete to win four Olympic gold medals.

As in the 1908 Olympics, four of the members of the Hungarian team were Jewish. Repeating their efforts of 1908, alongside Fuchs, were Foldes, Gerde, and Werkner.

Noted for the coolness of his defensive style of fencing, outside of sports Fuchs's personality was quite the opposite. He was quick tempered and known to start an argument over nothing. In a country where most sporting competition was through clubs, he refused to join any club. (Except for a brief period in 1908, when he served as a coach in one of the leading clubs.) Eventually, he gave up fencing and took up rowing, but being a loner, only in singles competition. When he attempted a comeback in fencing in 1928, he was matched with Ervin Meszaros, a Christian teammate from the 1912 Olympics. Like Fuchs, Meszaros was a specialist in defense. The two elderly experts faced each other before a large, but hushed audience. The bout began and the two fencers faced each other, each waiting for the other to start. The minutes ticked by, but neither man moved. Finally Meszaros pulled off his helmet and addressed his opponent, as old as himself, "My dear Jeno, I really don't think this is for us anymore." Fuchs agreed and both men walked away, neither to ever fence again.

The Olympic Games held in Amsterdam in 1928 were the first time the attention of the world was directed to Attila Petschauer (1904-1943). Before this he was already well known throughout Hungary as the winner of the Heroes' Memorial Tournament and the bearer of the title of Hungary's Best Fencer. As Fuchs was a master of defense, Petschauer was a master of attack. Yet his attacks were not wild, spur of the moment improvisations, but technically perfect forays. As he lunged forward he would shout out "Hollalah-oplah-allalah." This call became soon recognized as his personal trademark. Just as the two men differed in their style of fencing, so too their personalities were markedly different. Fuchs was moody and unsociable; Petschauer was warm and charming. His optimism was irrepressible. In the 1928 Games, Petschauer won a gold medal in team fencing and took the silver in individual saber. In the 1932 Games he was again a member of the gold winning fencing team, along with Endre Kabos.

During the Holocaust, Attila Petschauer was sent to Davidovka, Ukraine as part of a labor service unit. Among the prisoners he was known for his good spirits. One day, from among the Hungarian officers guarding his unit, Attila recognized a lieutenant colonel as an old friend from the Amsterdam Olympics, Kalman Cseh, who had participated as an equestrian. Attila called out to Cseh, who recognized him. The Hungarian officer turned to one of his ordinates and said, "Make things hot for the Jew!" The great

Olympian who had brought honor to Hungary was ordered to undress in the frigid weather and climb a tree. Then he was ordered to sing like a rooster. He was then sprayed with water, which froze to his naked flesh. He died shortly thereafter on January 20, 1943. These tragic events were witnessed by Karoly Karpati, a Jewish wrestler from Hungary who in 1936, before Hitler's own eyes, defeated the German National Champion to capture the gold medal of the Berlin Olympics.

Endre Kabos (1906-1944), besides his Olympic titles, was World Individual Saber Champion in 1933, 1934, and 1936. Endre was a tall man, unassuming, sensitive and quietly witty. Where Petshauer was always the life of any party, Kabos was by himself in a dark corner. In 1930, Endre was part of the national championship saber team. In the Olympics of 1932, he was part of the gold winning team and individually took the bronze, when Petshauer took the gold. Yet despite these accomplishments and the World Individual Championships, by 1935 he was ready to quit fencing altogether. He had become a grocer and the time and effort needed for this was simply too much for him. A benefactor had promised an appointment that would allow him the flexibility he needed to earn a living and practice his sport. But this promise fell through and Endre announced his retirement from competition. He even gave away his saber. But another patron came forward with just the right job for Endre that would allow him time to practice. Endre then withdrew his retirement and prepared for the 1936 Berlin Olympics.

Endre Kabos came out of the 1936 Olympics as a true national hero, with gold medals in both individual saber and as part of the Hungarian team. His style seemed to combine the best of the styles of Fuchs and Petschauer, a mastery of both defense and offense. Like his countrymen he was technically perfect with his own manner of extreme patience mixed with unbounded energy and lightning speed when the right moment should appear. The Hungarian team defeated both the German team and the Italian team, much of the credit for these victories being attributed to its Jewish members, Kabos and Petschauer.

Following the start of the Second World War, Endre, like thousands of other Jews, was arrested by the Nazis and Hungary's home grown Nazis, the Arrow Cross. Endre was sent to a forced labor camp. On November 4, 1944, he was sent with a detachment to transport armaments. As the truck he was riding in drove across the Margit Bridge, one of the bridges that spanned the Danube to connect the two cities of Buda and Pest, a pipe bomb was thrown by someone. The bridge had been mined to greet the oncoming Russian Army. The combination of the small pipe bomb, striking the large quantity of explosives attached to the bridge and the armaments on the truck on which Endre was riding created a terrible explosion which destroyed the bridge and killed hundreds of people on the busy span, casting the victims, living and dead, into the churning waters of the Danube. Endre Kabos was one of these victims.

Ilona Schacherer-Elek (1907-1988), or just Ilona Elek, as she is often known, is often considered the greatest female fencer of all time. She was the daughter of a Jewish father and a Catholic mother, but was raised as a Catholic. Nevertheless, in pre-war Hungary, most people considered her a Jew. Ilona first came to world attention in 1934 when, as a 27-year-old who played classical piano with the same expertise as she fenced, won the World Woman's Foil Championship. She captured the same title again in 1935.

A great deal of attention was placed on Ilona in 1936 when she was matched in the Berlin Olympics against the German contestant Helene Mayer (1911-1953). Helene, like Ilona, was the child of a Jewish father and a Catholic mother. Helene had won the gold medal in women's foils in 1928. Her inclusion in the German team had been a great "compromise" on the part of the German government, which had been threatened with losing the Olympics if they could not put on a more liberal appearance. Helene had been a resident in the United States and great pressure was put on her to return to her native Germany to take part in the Olympics. Ilona took the gold medal for Hungary, with Helene taking the silver. After the Olympics, Helene returned to the United States.

In 1936, Ilona also won the Hungarian national championship. But the following year she lost this title. But there was some consolation as she lost it to her own younger sister, Margit Elek. In 1934 and 1935, Ilona had won the European championship, coming in second in 1936. Margit had placed second in the 1934 competition and fourth in 1935. If this were the end of the careers of the Elek sisters, this would be most impressive, for the sisters had no opportunity to compete during the terrible years of the Second World War and their very survival was a triumph in itself. But their story does not end there.

In 1946, Ilona Elek was 39 years old. But she entered the competition for the Hungarian national championship, a title she had first held 12 years before. And she won it. She won it again in 1947. Then she won it again in 1949 and in 1950. Her last national title came in 1952 at the age of 45.

But it was Ilona's victories in the Olympics after the war that has won her the unofficial title as the world's greatest swordswoman. In the London Olympics of 1948, Ilona won the gold medal. She seemed destined to repeat this in the Helsinki games of 1952. She had won her first 5 matches, which tied her for first with the Italian Irene Camber. Then she lost the play-off match with Camber by a single point, 4-3.

Ilona was equally successful in the Women's World Fencing championships, taking the gold, as I have already mentioned, in 1934 and 1935. Then she came back and won this title again in 1951. She took the silver in 1937 and 1954 and the bronze in 1955, at the age of 48. In the 1934 contest, Margit placed second to her sister.

While Margit Elek is somewhat overshadowed by her sister, she had her own share of victories, including membership in Hungary's world championship teams of 1933-35, 1937, and 1952-1955. While she never matched the Olympic success of her sister, she did participate in both the 1948 and 1952 Olympiads.

Because of the tradition of hot tempers and military training, Hungary has been described as the "nation of fencers." The first fencer to ever bring Hungary an Olympic gold medal was Dr. Fuchs, a Jew. As late as the 1950's, despite the deprivations of the Holocaust, the Jewish excellence in fencing was still a part of Hungarian tradition.

THE MIGHTY ATOM

$E = MC^2$. No, it was not the scientists working beneath the stadium of the University of Chicago who first unleashed the power that Einstein had proposed was hidden within the atom. It was Joseph L. Greenstein, the Mighty Atom, a 5' 4½" wrestler, weightlifter and strongman who showed the world the potential of that small, but mighty object.

Joe Greenstein was an athlete of both the body and the spirit and his accomplishments have served as an inspiration to many who have followed after him. Among his pioneering efforts were his interest in Japanese martial arts long before any other Western athlete, his concern about proper nutrition as an overall approach to healthy living, and his precedent setting feats of strength, like pulling trucks and holding an airplane by his hair.

Joseph Lewis Greenstein was born on July 15, 1893 in Suvalk, Poland. He was born premature and was barely alive. However, against all odds, he survived. When Joseph was five, his father died from asthma. At 14, doctors told Joseph's mother that he too would soon expire from respiratory disease.

With this news ringing in his ears, Joseph ran away from home and apprenticed himself to a circus strongman, Volanko. Volanko, a Jew like young Joseph, began a training process for him that involved a vegetarian, whole grain diet, weight lifting, and rigorous exercise. The circus took young Joseph as far as India, where he studied strength training. After a year and a half, Joseph returned home. His mother fainted and his siblings thought he had risen from the grave. But now Joseph was no longer an asthmatic weakling, but perfectly healthy.

After marrying his childhood sweetheart, Joseph set off for America to found a decent life for himself and his family. Joe had relatives in Texas, so it was there that he headed. He soon found work in some of the toughest areas imaginable. He was an oilfield hand and a stevedore. Among the toughest of the tough, this little Jew, just 5' 4 ½", was soon recognized as a powerhouse in everything he did. Whether in wrestling or in racing with heavy carts, Joe Greenstein distinguished himself as the champion.

It was while racing such carts filled with 500 pound bales of cotton, that Joe first met Jack Johnson, the heavyweight boxing champion of the world and the first African-American champion in that sport or any other. Johnson was visiting Galveston, the scene of some of his first triumphs and was there introduced to Joe, who was now the champion of the cart race, a title that Johnson once held. The two men raced, the 6' 1" boxing champion against the diminutive Jew. The result was a dead heat. The two men became fast friends. They would remain friends until Johnson's death.

Under Johnson's encouragement, Joe tried his hand at boxing. The flowing blood of his opponent, after Joe had knocked him out, made Joe faint and Joe's one professional fight was declared a draw.

Joe had better luck at wrestling, but his inherent honesty and refusal to "throw" bouts limited any possibility of longterm success in that field. This, despite the fact that he was never defeated in any wrestling match.

Joe eventually found his profession as a strongman in vaudeville. He soon became a major star of the stage as "the Mighty Atom." He would pull trains and stop moving cars. He used his hair to hold still a moving airplane. His feats were incredible and made him famous throughout the nation.

With the Depression and the decline of vaudeville, Joe, or "Atom" as his friends often called him, became a salesman for his own line of healthcare products. He sold soap, shampoo, laxatives, and other products. He continued during his sales pitches to demonstrate his remarkable strength. He would straighten horseshoes with his hands and bend nails with his teeth. He would talk of his experiences and philosophize on healthy living. His devotees were legion, whether in New York, Coney Island, or in the Pennsylvania Dutch country. Everywhere he went he was advertised as "the World's Strongest Man." No one was ever able to dispute this claim, no matter what difficulty they might propose to him.

In his old age, he took pleasure in wandering the most dangerous parts of New York City. The little old Jewish man with the long beard would appear to be the perfect mark for muggers and thieves. Whether they came at him with guns or knives, no such attacker ever escaped unscathed from their meeting with the Mighty Atom. He was a one man Vigilance Committee.

In 1974, Joe's wife, Leah, died. He was disconsolate without his lifetime companion. After a period of grave difficulties, he remarried and found a brief period of equilibrium. In 1976, at the age of 83, he gave a performance of his skills and strength at Madison Square Garden that amazed the audience.

On October 8, 1977, Joseph L. Greenstein died of cancer at Kingsbrook Hospital in Brooklyn. Students and disciples around the world mourned his passing.

In 1977, a competition was established to determine the World's Strongest Man. This is a competition that is held every year to this day and one viewed with great popularity. Even as the arrangements were taking place for the first competition, Joe Greenstein was coming to the close of his great act. He had been the recognized master of many of the tasks that would become part of the competition, including the truck pull. The old posters declare the Mighty Atom as the World's Strongest Man, the Modern Hercules, and the Ancient Samson. The title now would be the subject of competition, rather than declaration. But there is no doubt that at his prime Joe Greenstein, the Mighty Atom, was in bodily strength and mental toughness, the World's Strongest Man.

JOE AND NAZIS

Joseph L. Greenstein, the "Mighty Atom," the "World's Strongest Man," known as the second "Samson," was strolling down a street in New York in February of 1939. He was outraged when he saw a sign hammered onto the second floor of a building reading "No dogs or Jews allowed." Inquiries made by Joe in that predominantly German section indicated that the sign decorated the meeting place of the pro-Nazi group, the German-American Bund. Joe was furious and went to a nearby paint store to rent a ladder. Then he went into a nearby sporting goods store and bought a Louisville Slugger, the Hank Greenberg model.

Joe planted the bat at the foot of the ladder and then climbed up and ripped the offending sign from the wall, which quickly crashed to the gutter. This was observed by the Bund members meeting in their hall and they ran out of the building. Joe was not yet down from the ladder when he was surrounded by a crowd of angry Hitler-sympathizers. They shook the ladder and Joe was soon on the ground, but with his Hank Greenberg model bat in his hand. First one large Bund member charged and he went down. Then a group approached, arms swinging, they too went down. One after another, the whole gang of Aryan Obermenschen attacked the 5' 4½" strongman and every one fell back with a broken nose or arm or leg or worse. Joe was truly a second Samson, but with a bat instead of the jawbone of an ass. By the time the police arrived, eighteen Bund members had to be rushed to the hospital.

Police arrived to quell the riot and Joe was arrested. Soon, Joe was in a courtroom and before a judge being arraigned on charges of assault, battery, mayhem, aggravated assault, and numerous other crimes. The room was filled with the wounded and maimed to stand as witnesses to the veracity of the charges. On the other side, Joe had one black eye. Before the wounded masses there stood a Bund lawyer. Joe stood all by himself.

The white haired judge was completely bewildered by the whole thing. He turned to the bearded and mild mannered doctor of Naturopathy, the president of the International Health Product Company. He asked him if he had done all these things to these hulking men, each a head taller than himself and each half his age. Joe admitted that he had. Then the judge turned to the police sergeant who had brought Joe in. He asked him too if Joe alone had done all this damage to so many men. The sergeant told the judge that he had, as well as to the other men that were still in the hospital.

But, the sergeant pointed out to the judge that the men had attacked Joe, not the other way around. The judge asked the sergeant why in the world they would do that. The sergeant replied that they were Nazis. The judge immediately declared Joe innocent and dismissed the case. The Bund lawyer tried to object, but the judge reiterated that the case was dismissed and walked out of the courtroom.

Joe's comment on the incident was the following:

"Every time I swung the bat it was a home run!"

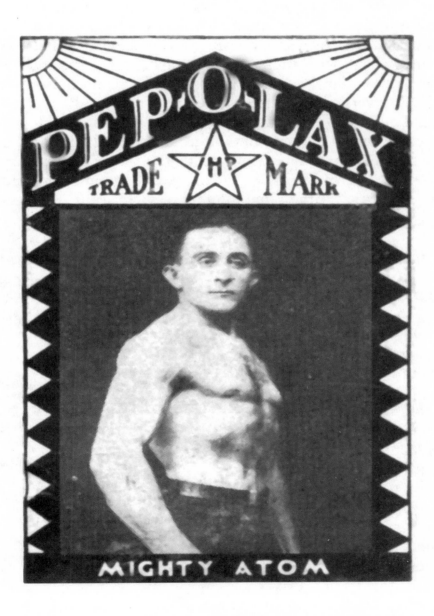

GEORGES STERN

Two Jewish jockeys dominated the sport of horse racing in the early years of the twentieth century, Walter Miller in America and Georges Stern in Europe. Georges, born in France in 1882, was known as the "the King of the Jockeys" and the "King of the Derbies." His more than one thousand victories and his 1908 victories in the French, Austrian, and German Derbies more than qualify him for such titles.

On April 30, 1898, in Colombes (a small town near Paris), a small seventeen year old boy won, after a ferocious competition, his first victory riding Finlas, a horse owned and trained by his father. Finlas won by a head over Chateau-d'Eau, with Indien a close third. Seeing the style of the young rider, many a spectator thought, "This boy will go places in life." But the most optimistic observers were modest in their predictions. The career of Georges Stern would be a road of triumph.

The year by year account of Georges's victories is amazing. In 1898, the year he debuted, he rode four winners. In 1899, the number increased to 33. By 1900, he was already ranked as the world's number one rider with 91 victories. He achieved the same number of victories in 1901. 1902 was the

first year that a large number of American riders began to compete in Europe. Facing this stiff competition for the first time, Georges's position slipped to third, behind J. Reiff and M. Henry. Some doubters began to predict Georges's imminent decline. But in 1903, he began to rebound. He ranked in second place, behind only Ransch. Then, starting in 1904, his triumphs increased. He reclaimed the premier position on the list and held on to it for many years to come. In 1904, he went from victory to victory: the Poules of Longchamp, the Prix de Diane, the Derbies of Germany, Austria, and France, the Grand Prix of Vichy, Baden, and Paris, and

the Prix of the President de la Republique. He won them all. Georges was a fine linguist and he spoke English as well as he did French. In 1905 he traveled to England to race in the famous Epsom Derby. He came in first runner-up. In 1909, he again placed second in the Derby. But in 1911, he was at last triumphant, winning the race riding Sunstar. In the same year and riding the same horse, he won the English 2000 Guineas Race.

In 1908, Georges rode Quintette to a dead-heat tie for first in the French Derby. He would be the victor in this same race in 1913 aboard Dagor, in 1914 aboard Sardanaple, and in 1922 aboard Ramus.

Georges's first great victory was capturing the Grand Prix de Deauville, riding Monsieur Amedée in 1900. He won Deauville again in 1901 with Jacobite and in 1902 with Maximum. In 1909, Georges reprised his earlier victories in Deauville on Biniou.

Georges garnered great admiration in his career and it became a preferred system for gamblers in his time to simply bet on the horse he was racing, a system that proved far more successful than any other that was contrived. Stern's contemporary jockey O'Connor stated in an interview: "The one thing that struck me the most in France was the skill of your jockey, Stern. I have ridden in many countries—the United States, France, England, and Germany—but nowhere have I seen such a jockey, so complete and perfect as Georges Stern." Ten years after his debut, Georges was in the same fine condition he was at his first race. His success continued despite thousands of races, often against opponents who were determined to stop him. Among these other jockeys were Tom Lane, Watkins, Dodge, Bowers, Dodd, Reiff, Milton Henry, Rausch, and O'Connor himself. Georges was equally successful against English and American jockeys, as well as his own countrymen.

During his career Georges was always able to adapt his techniques to the changing styles of his competitors. But Georges never completely adopted either of the two outstanding styles of riding popular during his time, the English style and the American style. His particular style was a combination of the two, a unique style all his own. His style was so unique, indeed, that seen through binoculars or on a photograph, the knowledgeable viewer could recognize Stern's silhouette out of thousands of riders.

Stern wore his stirrups shortened and tight and he sat well balanced on the saddle. His seat cleared the rear-hand of the mount without over-crowding the neck. And as far as tactics were concerned, he knew how to use a false trail, as well as how to hold back just enough to dash forward at the finish. His most important qualities lay in his sang-froid and his tact, as well as his ability to make split-second decisions. Few jockeys indeed possessed Georges's energy and vigor when he was making his ultimate push to the finish line.

GEORGES STERN LEADS THE RACE.

Georges retired from racing in 1926, after a career of 29 years of excellence. He died in his native France in November of 1928 at the age of 48.

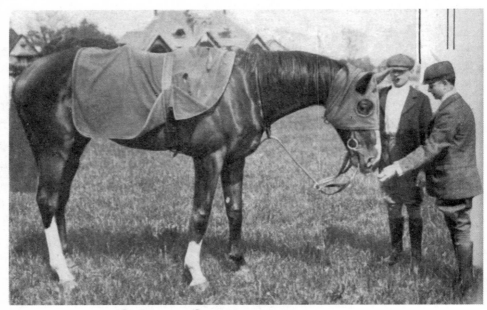

GEORGES STERN FEEDS HIS HORSE.

DAMON RUNYON REMEMBERED

WALTER MILLER

Damon Runyon, the "Guys and Dolls" guy, remembered with fondness the skill of jockey Walter Miller. On August 12, 1922, he wrote a poem lauding the skill of Earl Sande, an outstanding jockey of the '20's and '30's. The poem concludes with a reflection back to an earlier time, including his reflections on Walter Miller, whose career was at its peek between 1904 and 1909:

> Spencer was sure a wonder,
> And Miller was worth his hire.
> Seldom he made a blunder
> As he rode 'em down to the wire.
> Them was the old-time jockeys;
> Now when I want to win
> Gimme a handy
> Guy like Sande
> Bootin' them hosses in!

ALEX BROMBERG

The front pages of the Egyptian newspapers for Monday, January 26, 1948 were discussing on one column a battle near the city of Jerusalem between Arabs and Jews that had taken place the day before. The State of Israel would not be declared until May 13, but intense attacks by Arab "volunteers" had been going on since November. On another column of those same papers they were proclaiming the triumphant victory on that same Sunday, January 25 of Jewish-Egyptian bicyclist, Alexandre Bromberg, in the race for the Grand Prize of Cairo.

Alexandre Bromberg was a native of Egypt, born in Cairo on December 12, 1926. His father had been a Russian Jew who had settled in Egypt and had married a Swedish émigré, who was not Jewish. Alex's father had his son converted to Judaism at birth. When Alex was 3½, his father remarried. His stepmother, Fortunee Bromberg was Jewish and Alex always thought of her and spoke of her as being his actual mother. Alex was an enthusiastic member of both the Maccabi Club and the Egyptian Club of Cyclists.

Here is one of the newspaper accounts of Bromberg's victory in the Tour d'Caire:

"The bicycle racers wearing multi-colored tee-shirts and bicycle shorts, their caps over their eyes, were thronged at the departure point to compete in the great race. At exactly 8:30 am the competitors started racing at the signal given at the level of the tunnel of Ghizah. From the start, Metwally and Tallarico, both from Alexandria led a rather sustained pace, but the leading peloton (group) remained compact until the 18 kilometer mark. It was then that Tallarico proceeded by repeated attacks to drop the pelaton; only Alexandre Bromberg (of Maccabi Club) responded to all his attacks and stayed on his wheel.

"Behind them Erfan Sobhi, El Sami and Levy followed on them less than 100 meters behind, trying to shorten the distance separating them from the leaders. Tallarico and Bromberg were riding together up to the 50 kilometer mark, when the latter, feeling threatened by his pursuers, accelerated suddenly. He redoubled his efforts, began to advance on all his competitors and paid himself the luxury of arriving at the finish line amid the cheers of an enthusiastic crowd. His advance took him to the finish line seven minutes before the arrival of the second fastest racer. The winner finished the 100-kilometer race in 3 hours 22 minutes, an average of 30 kilometers an hour, which constitutes a beautiful performance...

"Erfan Sobhi (Ararat Club) had several problems with his chain on the way back. He joined Victor Levy (Maccabi Club) at 18 kilometers from the finish line and followed behind him until the end of the race, which he finished in third position, behind Bromberg and Levy...

"This competition was followed from beginning to end by Mr. A. Marziah, director of the race, Julien Hannier and Freddie Ward, commissioners, as well as Mr. Sidaoui... At the end of the meeting, the president of the Cairo Section, Max Steinauer presented to the winners two beautiful silver trophies given by S. Romoli Motors, as well as medals.

"The police and Public Assistance generously helped and contributed largely to the success of the race. This demonstration constitutes an important step in cycling history and owes its creation to the dynamic organizer, Mr. Carlo Romoli, Commissioner of the section."

It is interesting to note that both the first and second place winners in this race were Jews. The man who placed third was an Arab, as were the three first place winners of the second division of the race (50 kilometers only.)

Following his victory, Bromberg continued his connections with the cycling fraternity. He often acted in his native land as an official of races, often following the bicyclists on a motorcycle. This included one occasion in 1955, a famous race of Lower Egypt, and during races held in Egypt of Soviet bloc nations, when his knowledge of Russian came in very handy.

In 1959, reacting to the now unfriendly atmosphere in Egypt, Alex emigrated with his family to San Paulo, Brazil. In 1969, Alex changed his residence again, moving to Philadelphia. But throughout his travels, Alex's interest in bicycling never waned. In June of 1990, he was observing Philadelphia's famous CoreStates USPRO (Bicycle) Championship. During the excitement of the race, he suddenly felt himself growing short of breath. He had suffered a heart attack. He died ten days later.

Alexandre Bromberg, after his victory in the 100 kilometer race for the Grand Prix du Caire, hungrily biting a "well deserved" sandwich.

KENNY BERSTEIN

Kenny Bernstein has excelled in a sport where Jews have rarely participated and has, indeed, become recognized as one of the greatest in the history of the sport, automobile drag racing. Kenny's interest in drag racing, driving at remarkable speeds over a short course, has seen him do the mile in 4.477 seconds, the quickest run in the history of the sport, and set the speed record of 332.18 mph (miles per hour). Kenny has earned six NHRA World Championships. He is the first and only driver to win championships in both divisions of the sport, Funny Car (1985-1988) and Top Fuel (1996 and 2001).

Kenny was born on September 6, 1944. He was raised in Lubbock, Texas, where his father managed a department store. Kenny played for the Lubbock High School football team as a first string player. By 1966, Kenny was an amateur drag racer with ambitions towards a professional career. But it was not until 1978 that he earned his first career number one qualifying award, in a race in Seattle. The following year, 1979, saw his first career victory, in a race at Baton Rouge.

In 1984, Kenny became the first driver in the Funny Car division to exceed 260 mph. The next year, when he won his first Funny Car Championship, he had six first place victories to his credit. In 1986 he won the championship again and became the first Funny Car driver to surpass 270 mph. He also became the first driver to do the mile in less than 5.50 seconds. The next year, another championship season, he set a new record of seven victories. In 1990, Kenny moved from Funny Car to Top Fuel. The following year he had a record six-victory season.

In 1992, Kenny became the first driver to break the 300-mph mark with a speed of 301.70 mph on March 20, 1992 at Gainesville. During a race at Pomona, in 1993,

Kenny escaped without injury from a fiery crash, when his car went out of control and flipped over a retaining wall. The following years saw Kenny at the top of his form. But in May 2001, Kenny announced his retirement at the end of the end of the 2002 season.

Kenny retired with 65 career wins and 114 career final rounds. But Kenny was not through with drag racing, despite his honest intentions. He planned to act as advisor and assistant to his son Brandon, who was to do the actual driving. Brandon was born to Kenny and his wife Sheryl on August 2, 1972. Sheryl is not Jewish and Brandon was not raised as a Jew. On May 18, 2003, Brandon crashed his car and fractured a vertebra. Kenny stepped into the breach and completed the entire season as driver for his team in both Top Fuel and Funny Car divisions. Kenny was 59 years old.

Kenny is known among dragsters as the "King of Speed." It is a title that he has won with some 40 years of outstanding competition and dedication to a most taxing, difficult, and dangerous pursuit.

RONNIE ROSENTHAL
AND OTHER ISRAELI SOCCER PLAYERS IN ENGLAND

Ronnie Rosenthal was born in Haifa, Israel on November 10, 1963 and began his sports career with his hometown team of Maccabi Haifa. But it was as a football (soccer) player in England that he was to achieve his greatest acclaim. From his home town, Ronnie first moved his base of operations to Belgium. Ronnie played for both Bruges and Standard Liege.

In 1990 a deal was struck for Ronnie's contract between Standard Liege and the club of the Italian city of Udine, near the border with Yugoslavia. Before the papers could be signed, massive protests sponsored by neo-fascist fans of the Udinese club broke out. Anti-Semitic slogans were daubed on the walls of the team's stadium and office. The team folded under the pressure and withdrew their offer to Ronnie. A timely offer, to borrow Ronnie from Liege for the Liverpool team, then sent Ronnie to England.

In England, Ronnie started his career with Luton Town. He then had an opportunity to appear briefly as a replacement on the Liverpool team and he made an assist. He was impressive enough that he was called on to start for Liverpool at the very next game. On March 31, 1990, he made his full debut with Liverpool. It was a spectacular one, with Liverpool winning over Charlton Athletic 4-0. The amazing thing was that Ronnie scored three of those four goals, a hat-trick, a far rarer feat in soccer than hockey. To make his only Liverpool hat-trick even more unique, he scored one of his goals with his left foot, one with his right, and the third with his head.

Liverpool's very next game was against Nottingham Forest and again Ronnie scored. His contributions to the team helped it clinch that season's championship. However, when the medals were distributed to the players, Ronnie was left out, as he did not have enough games under his belt. The team's manager, Kenny Dalglish summed up his contributions for the season, "Ronnie gave us momentum. He had five starts, three appearances as sub and seven goals. That was a very good return which helped us to win the championship."

During 1989/90 season, Ronnie had been on loan to Liverpool from Standard Liege, but they began the following season by purchasing Ronnie's contract for 1.1 million pounds. Ronnie was used mostly as a substitute during this year and he did not start until December 22. But the wait was worth it and Ronnie scored two goals in a 3-2 victory. In his next game, against Leed United, he scored one goal and created the other two goals in a 3-0 win. Though he spent much of the year on the sidelines, he finished the season as the top scorer for Liverpool reserves, with 18 goals in just 25 appearances.

During 1991-2, Ronnie's role was somewhat expanded, but he still did not make the teams final 13. One of Ronnie's most memorable moments of this season was his contribution to the 3-2 victory over Ipswich Town in the fifth round of the FA Cup.

The following year, Ronnie was better remembered for a miss than a goal. During a 4-2 loss at Aston Villa, Ronnie had a clear shot at the goal, but his mighty blast hit the crossbar of the goal and went out. Later in the game, Ronnie did score, but the legend of Ronnie is still haunted by "that miss." Ronnie did have 6 goals for 27 appearances in 1992-3.

Ronnie began the season of 1993-4 with Liverpool, but after just 3 appearances he was traded to Totenham. With the latter team he had 15 appearances and 2 goals.

Ronnie continued with Totenham for the remainder of his career, until 1997. Since his retirement from playing, Ronnie has become a football agent. His reputation as a great striker is secure.

Since Ronnie's entrance into English soccer, two other Israelis have gained places on English teams, Eyal Berkovic and Idan Tal. Eyal was born on February 4, 1972 in Haifa. Like Ronnie, he began his career

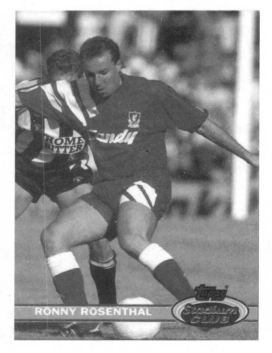

RONNY ROSENTHAL

with Maccabi Haifa. In 1996 he played midfield with Southampton. The following year he was traded to West Ham United. Then Celtic purchased him for 5.75 million pounds. After a fine opening season with Celtic, he was loaned out to Blackburn Rovers. In 2001, Eyal was sold to Manchester City for 1.5 million pounds, his value diminished by his numerous injuries since he began to play in England. But Eyal has made a fine showing with City and, despite some further injuries, his future looks bright.

Idan Tal was born on September 13, 1975 in Petach Tikva. He started his career in Israel and soon was a star with Hapoel Petach Tikva. Idan played 39 games with his hometown team and scored 13 goals for them. This won him the attention of Everton, which purchased his contract for seven hundred thousand pounds. Idan traveled with the team during the summer of 2000 to Italy, for a pre season exhibition tour. He impressed the coach. During the 2000/2001 season, Idan made 12 appearances and scored two goals. But during the next season, Idan suffered a series of injuries that minimized his appearances and effectiveness. On September 7, 2002, Idan was traded to the Madrid based Spanish club Rayo Vallecano.

Eyal Berkovic

Idan Tal

DANIEL PRENN

From 1928 to 1932, Daniel Prenn was ranked as the number one tennis player in Germany. But with the coming of the Nazis to power in 1933, he was banned from competition. The German Tennis Federation published in April of 1933 the following resolutions:

1. No Jew may be selected for a national team or the Davis Cup.

2. No Jewish (or Marxist) club or association may be affiliated with the German Tennis Federation.

3. No Jew may hold an official position in the Federation.

And, in case Daniel Prenn did not get the point, they added, "The player Dr. Prenn (a Jew) will not be selected for the Davis Cup team in 1933."

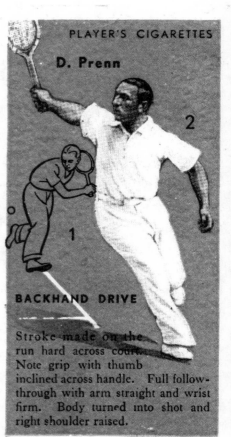

PLAYER'S CIGARETTES

D. Prenn

BACKHAND DRIVE

Stroke made on the run hard across court. Note grip with thumb inclined across handle. Full follow-through with arm straight and wrist firm. Body turned into shot and right shoulder raised.

Daniel Prenn was born on September 7, 1904 in Poland. He held a doctorate in engineering. He first attracted attention as a tennis player in 1926 with a number 10 ranking in Germany. In 1929, Prenn was ranked as the number 8 player in the world, with Bill Tilden as number 1. In 1932, he was ranked as number 6 in the world and selected by American Lawn Tennis Magazine as Europe's number 1.

With Prenn's ban from German tennis, the English champions Fred Perry and Bunny Austin issued a protest. The king of Sweden, Gustav V was in the midst of a state visit. After his reception by the German President and Chancellor, the king announced that he was going to have a friendly game of tennis with Daniel Prenn.

Shortly after this, Prenn fled Germany and took refuge in England. He took British citizenship and continued his career in tennis. In 1934 he was rated as the world's number 7 player. Following this his career declined. Prenn's son Oliver, born in England in 1938, achieved some success as a tennis player, winning the Boy's National Junior Lawn

Tennis Championship (Wimbledon) in 1955.
Daniel Prenn died on September 3, 1991, just short of his 87th birthday.

TROUBLE AT WIMBLEDON

During the Wimbledon contests of 2002, a pair of tennis players, one a 22 year old Muslim from Pakistan and one a 24 year old Jew from Israel, decided to combine their talents as a doubles team. Aisam-ul-Haq Qureshi from Pakistan and Amir Hadad of Israel had met on the tennis circuit some three years before and they had become good friends. They enjoyed sharing their concerns about religion, parents, and health. And most of all they enjoyed talking about tennis. The results of their first pairing were promising. They made it to the third round at Wimbledon. This was better than any player from Pakistan had ever finished in a Grand Slam event. But then Qureshi is ranked as his nation's best player. Hadad was also pleased with the results, even when the pair was eliminated by Czechs Martin Damm and Cyril Suk.

But then the storm burst. Qureshi was soundly denounced by the Pakistan Sports Board. In those days following September 11, 2001 and the Israeli conflict with Palestinian suicide bombers, there seemed little sympathy in Pakistan for individual alliances or freedom of association. The Board threatened to suspend Qureshi and ban him from Davis Cup competition.

The International Tennis Federation, in reply, threatened to ban Pakistan from competition altogether if it did any such thing. "ITF understands the political sensitivity of this issue," their statement said, "but, as Davis Cup was founded with the aim of furthering international understanding through sport, we hope the Pakistan Tennis Federation will choose Mr. Qureshi to participate in Davis Cup so long as his abilities warrant selection."

Quershi and Hadad

Qureshi accepted the situation with good humor. "That's their own loss," he said of the proposed ban. "If I believe I could do well with Amir in the big event's Grand Slams I'll stay and play with him. Why not? I know all the Israelis on the tour."

Hadad said of Qureshi, "We all like him, we have no problem with him."

Unlike the Pakistanis, the Israelis had no difficulties with the Qureshi-Hadad pairing. David Harnik, the president of Israel's tennis federation, defended the two players and hoped that their personal amity might be a foreshadowing of future political situations. "It's a natural thing. There's no animosity between players." He cited other instances where "sport came before diplomatic relations. We like the idea. We think there's nothing like sports to bridge the gap between nations and to be the start of solving problems."

During the U.S. Open, held in New York in September of 2002, Hadad and Quershi, appeared again together. They lost a second-round match to fifth-seeded Wayne Black and Kevin Ullyet of Zimbabwe. During 2003, they played together at Copenhagen and Wimbledon, in both tournaments being eliminated in the first round. Nevertheless, their commitment to their partnership remains a single light in the grim darkness of this period.

On February 6, 2003, the world took notice once again of this remarkable pair. On that date it was announced that they would receive the prestigious Arthur Ashe Humanitarian Award. Hadad said of this recognition, "It's an honor, we didn't expect this. We do something we love, playing tennis, and then we get an award, it's great....I hope people can learn from this and take a positive attitude."

Qureshi added, "This means a lot for me, I think it's the first sports award for a Pakistani athelete. I feel very honored for my country....Sport can change people's life. I hope people can learn something from us and live peacefully together."

BORIS SCHAPIRO

As America had Charles H. Goren, a great Jewish bridge player and author, so Britain had Boris Schapiro. The game of bridge, like all card games, it could be argued, is not a sport, as there is no physical component. I have chosen to take the opposite point of view and include cards, as well as checkers and chess, in this book. However, I have made one compromise, more to make my own job easier than to in any way diminish the accomplishments of great game players. I have created a separate list for the giants of games. This allows for a much greater scope, as both physical sports and pure games deserve the full breadth of their accomplishments to be recorded.

Boris Schapiro was born in Riga, Latvia on August 22, 1909. The Russian Revolution was the signal to the Schapiro family to leave and they immigrated to Britain. Very early on Boris showed an aptitude for bridge and he was already playing for money by the age of 10. At 20, Boris entered his first major Bridge tournament, the 1929 World Auction Bridge Pairs, with his partner Oswald Jacoby. In 1932, he won his first world title, the World Pairs, with Jacoby again as his partner. In 1945, he won the first of his 11 Great Britain's Gold Cups; the last would be in 1998. He won the European championships of 1948, 1949, 1954, and 1963. In 1955, he won the Bermuda Bowl and, in 1962, the World Mixed Teams. Boris placed second in the first World Team Olympiad in 1960 and in the Mixed Pairs in 1962. In 1964, he was again back on top as the winner of the Sunday Times Invitational Pairs.

But in 1965, Boris became involved in a scandal that would cast a shadow over his career that would take years to be removed. In that year, during the Bermuda Bowl World Championships in Buenos Aires, Argentina, Boris and his partner, Terence Reese, were accused of cheating by using illegal hand signals. John Gerber, captain of the American team, brought this accusation. The World Bridge Federation peremptorily found them guilty and they withdrew from the tournament. The case was then referred to the British Bridge League. The League, after a year's long investigation, concluded that there was not sufficient evidence to sustain the charge. The case against Schapiro and Reese was further weakened by Sam Kehela, the vice-captain of the American team, who testified that he considered the men innocent. Nevertheless, the World Federation suspended both players from international competition. In protest against this decision, the British team withdrew from the 1968 World Bridge Olympiad. Three years later, the suspensions of Schapiro and Reese were lifted, with the proviso that the two men not play together in international competition. Reese, considered one of the greatest players of all time, never again participated in international competition; Schapiro did, but not for many years.

Meanwhile, the rulings did not stop all collaboration between the two men. They published a book together, *Bridge Card by Card*, in 1969. Meanwhile Boris had become the bridge correspondent for London's *Sunday Times*, a job he held from 1968 until his death.

Allan Truscott came out with a book that purported to explain how the two men had cheated, detail by detail. Reese replied with his own book, which again defended himself and his friend Boris. In the long run, world opinion finally seemed to settle for the accused, bolstered by the simple argument that players of such phenomenal ability as Schapiro and Reese did not need to cheat.

Boris wrote another book, *Bridge Analysis*, in 1976. As the years passed, his abilities seemed to improve. His weekly columns continued to appear. He advocated the playing of bridge for the elderly as a preventative against Alzheimer's Disease. Then, in 1998, Boris again startled the world. At the age of 89, partnered with Irving Gordon, he won the World Senior Championship at the World Championships in Lille, France. As the press was quick to point out, no person had ever won a world title in any sport whatsoever at that age. Boris was the world's oldest world champion!

Boris continued writing and playing right up to his death on December 4, 2002, at the age of 93. The English Bridge Union lauded him for all his many achievements and also said of him that he was one of Britain's "most colorful, irreverent and irrepressible bridge players."

EMMANUEL LASKER, BOBBY FISCHER, AND OTHER JEWISH WORLD CHESS CHAMPIONS

Emanuel Lasker was one of the greatest figures in the history of chess. From 1894 until 1921 he was the world champion of the game. His texts on chess are still recognized as standard works on the subject. His games are still studied as among the most brilliant and instructive in chess history.

Lasker was born in Berlinchen, Prussia on December 24, 1868. His father was a cantor and his grandfather had been a rabbi. Young Emanuel's interests lay in the direction of mathematics. His mathmatical studies led to a doctorate from the University of Berlin. His original contributions to mathematics were noted in the field and his name is still current in mathematics through the "Neother-Lasker decomposition." Around this time he formed a friendship with Albert Einstein. Lasker also showed early talent in the field of philosophy and he wrote a number of original works in that discipline. Throughout his life, Lasker would teach at various universities courses in advanced mathematics.

However, it was in the field of chess that Lasker quickly rose to world prominence. By 1890, he was regarded as the leading contender for the world title. In 1894, he got his opportunity to compete for the title against the reigning champion Wilhelm Steinitz (1836-1900), who had held the title since 1866, when he defeated Adolf Anderssen. Steinitz was the first Jew to hold the world championship and held the title longer than any other figure in history. Steinitz, unlike Lasker, had converted to Christianity.

Following his victory against Steinitz, Lasker often defended his title, including a return match against Steinitz in 1896-7. His tournaments took him around the world and he competed in London, New York, St. Petersburg, and Paris. Lasker's *Common Sense in Chess* appeared in 1896. In 1902 he settled in New York and edited *Lasker's Chess Journal*, as well as wrote chess columns for *The New York Evening Post*. In 1907 he returned to Germany. During the First World War, he served as a soldier and was captured by the British. He was brought to London and won his freedom by winning the London chess championship.

In 1921, Lasker placed his world title on the line in Havana, Cuba against the Cuban master Jose Capablanca. After 14 games played in torrid tropical heat, and having failed to win a single game (there were 10 draws and 4 losses), Lasker conceded his title to the much younger Cuban.

This hardly marked any real decline in Lasker's abilities. He continued to triumph in most tournaments in which he participated, including one held in New York a few years after he had lost the world title. He won this tournament, despite the participation of Capablanca and Richard Reti, leader of the "hypermodern" school of chess.

In 1927, Lasker published his *Manual of Chess*. This work is famous not only for its handling of its subject, but also for its psychological insights. The following is a typical and often quoted example of how Lasker used the chessboard as a window to deeper understanding of the world around him. "On the chessboard lies and hypocrisy do not survive long. The creative combination lays bare the presumption of a lie; the merciless fact, culminating in a checkmate, contradicts the hypocrite. Our little chess is one of the sanctuaries where the principle of justice has occasionally had to hide to gain sustenance and respite, after the army of mediocrities had driven it from the market place. And many a man, struck by injustice as, say, Socrates and Shakespeare were struck, has found justice realized on the chess-board and has thereby recovered his courage and his vitality to continue to play the game of life."

During the 1920's, Lasker took an interest in the Japanese board game of go. Go, like chess, is played with black and white pieces and strategy is used to control the board and capture one's opponent's pieces. In 1927, Lasker became a founding member of the New York Go Club, which still exists today.

Following the advent of Nazi government in Germany, Lasker fled his native land. He accepted an invitation from the Soviet Union to organize a chess academy, which he did in 1935. Many credit Lasker's chess academy

1968 medal in honor of the 100th anniversary of the
birth of Emanuel Lasker

with being the fountainhead of Russian chess superiority, a distinction that exists to this day. In 1937, having seized his German property, the German government officially expelled Lasker from the Berlin Chess Club. In the same year, Lasker left the Soviet Union and returned to New York City. Emanuel Lasker died in New York on January 11, 1941.

One question that the career of Emanuel Lasker and other chess stars forces us to ask is whether an expert in a board game like chess can be considered as an athlete? His very appearance in these pages expresses the positive opinion of this book's author. The vast majority of standard references on sports include chess, checkers, pool, and billiards as athletic endeavors. There is not a single sport, no matter how physical, which does not have a mental component necessary for mastery of the game. If the physical side of chess is minimal, its competition is made cutthroat and thrilling through the amazingly high level of its mental aspects.

Following Lasker's loss of the World Championship title to Capablanca in 1921, that title was held by non-Jewish titleholders until 1948. In that year the Russian Jew, Mikhail Botvinnik, captured it. Botvinnik would hold the title until 1957, when he lost the title to another Russian Jew, Vassily Smyslov. Botvinnik regained the title from Smyslov in 1958. Botvinnik lost the title again in 1960 to another Russian Jew, Mikhail Tal. But Tal only held the title until 1961, when Botvinnik again regained it. He lost it finally in 1963 to the non-Jewish Tigran Petrosian.

In 1969, Petrosian lost the title to Borris Spassky, the son of a Jewish mother. Spassky has never shown any interest in his Jewish heritage and resists being identified as a Jew. Spassky held the title until 1972, when he lost it during a match in Iceland that caught the whole world's attention. The winner of this match was the American Robert ("Bobby") Fischer. Fischer is one of the most controversial and strangest figures in the history of this sport.

It was longed believed that Bobby Fischer was the son of his Jewish mother and her non-Jewish, German husband. However, FBI documents obtained through the Freedom of Information Act, published in November 2002, show that Mr. and Mrs. Fischer had been separated for six years at the time of Bobby's birth. These documents indicate that Bobby's real father was Paul Nemenyi, a Hungarian Jew who came to the United States in the 1930's and taught college mathematics. Nemenyi, a specialist in fluid mechanics, was a brilliant man, but difficult to get along with. He was one of many Jewish scientists to work on the Manhattan Project during WWII. As a youth, Bobby Fischer had taken Judaism seriously and he refused to compete on the Sabbath. Later in his life he would become a member of a radical Christian group, then later he would abandon that affiliation as well.

While in Iceland, during his matches with Spassky, Fischer made strange anti-Semitic remarks. In the years that have followed, Fischer has become a ranting anti-Semitic, anti-American recluse and man of mystery. He roams about the world, disguised and fleeing from the CIA, which may or may not be following him. He broke American laws in 1992 when he participated in a tournament in Yugoslavia against his old opponent and friend Boris Spassky and the State Department has threatened to arrest him on sight.

In the aftermath of the September 11, 2001 attacks on New York and Washington, Fischer launched an amazing tirade over Philippine radio denouncing the Jews and hailing the attack as a victory over the imperialist United States. Tigran Petrosian, the former world chess champion, when he heard of Fischer's virulent diatribes, made this statement, "It is scary to think that a great man like Fischer has lost his mental faculties. I pray that he will recover his senses and live a normal life". Fischer is universally regarded as one of the greatest geniuses to have ever participated in the game of chess. It seems equally clear that today he is as mad as a hatter.

Following his victory in Iceland, Fischer refused to defend his title and he was stripped of it in favor of the leading contender, the non-Jewish Russian Anatoly Karpov in 1975. Karpov lost the title in 1985 to Garry Kasparov, the son of a Jewish father and an Armenian mother. Garry was born Garry Weinstein on April 13, 1963, so he was only 22 years old when he won the championship, making him the youngest man ever to hold the title. Garry changed his name in 1975 under advice from Mikhail Botvinnik, the former world champion and Garry's chess coach. Botvinnik argued that the Soviet authorities would never allow a citizen with a Jewish name to compete for the world title. Whether this was true or not, it was as Kasparov that Garry held the world title until 2000, when he lost it to the Russian Vladimir Kramnik.

On July 13, 2004 Bobby Fischer was recognized at the airport at Narita, Japan trying to board a flight to Manila. He was using a revoked U.S. passport and was detained by the Japanese police.

Fischer was held in a detention center in Ushiku, Japan. His deportation was ordered, but for almost a year no country would accept him. Finally Iceland, the seat of his greatest triumph and the one land where he was still fondly remembered, stepped forward and offered him honorary citizenship. Fischer, accompanied by his fiance Miyoko Watai, president of the Japanese Chess Association, left for exile in Iceland on March 24, 2005, denunciations of both Japan and America on his lips.

THE BOX SCORE

At the start of this book I presented my views on who were the greatest 150 Jewish athletes of all time. Certainly there will be some who will challenge individual selections. Should I have included Moe Berg, a third string catcher, but with genius and a life of mystery and adventure? Where is Gabe Kapler, who wears a World Series Ring? Does Benny Leonard deserve a higher position than Barney Ross? To answer every question of this sort that will arise, it would take a work the size of The Talmud. I only hope that my work can serve a basis for the start of dialogue.

What should be clear to all readers is that each of these athletes has achieved amazing feats. They have succeeded in the face of history's most horrendous oppression. Some have been martyred in the very places of competition. And even while facing their staunchest enemies, they have succeeded and succeeded in a way that identified them for all the world as the very best at what they did.

Lastly, you will find a Jewish Sports Trivia section in the following pages which I have included for readers as a source of amusement. This section is not an attempt to quiz the reader on previous chapters, so some questions will require a wider knowledge than the information contained in this work. For other questions, you will just have to take my word for it, the answers are not published anywhere else!

I can only hope you will find whatever you are looking for in these pages. If not, my dear publisher, Ian Shapolsky, has promised to publish as soon as possible *The Big Book of Jewish Athletes,* a sequel that will supplement the thrilling story of Jewish sports.

JEWISH SPORTS TRIVIA
QUESTIONS
(Answers begin on page 262)

1. The life of the Jewish fencer Endre Kabos, who won 4 Olympic medals (including 3 gold) for Hungary in 1932 and 1936, inspired what motion picture?

2. Where does swimmer Dara Torres keep her nine Olympic medals?

3. Who scored the goal that won for South Africa the 1995 World Rugby Cup?

4. What Israeli volleyball player was appointed coach of the U.S. Women's National Volleyball team in 1975?

5. Who caught Kevin Millwood's no-hitter on April 27, 2003?

6. Who was the winner of the 1932 Douglas Fairbanks Award, the first award given to the nation's best college football player, the ancestor of the Heisman Trophy?

Dara Torres

7. What Jewish boxer is the subject of a forth coming grand opera?

8. What is Major League Baseball catcher Brad Ausmus's favorite pastime outside of baseball?

9. What baseball player was the first ever to be elected unanimously MVP?

10. What American minor league player and major league coach had a distinguished career in Japan, including 2 batting titles, 1962 and 1963?

11. Who was the first All-American football player who was Jewish?

12. What left-handed Jewish pitcher defeated Sandy Koufax in his rookie year, the last year of Koufax's career?

13. What Jewish boxing champ was a hero at the Battle of Guadalcanal?

14. Which baseball player, in a minor league game in Memphis, stole a home run by climbing a flag pole and grabbing the ball before it could go over the wall?

15. What college did Marchmont Schwartz play football for?

16. What Jewish founder of a rental car company owned three Kentucky Derby winners?

17. What Jewish pitcher became a punk rock star when he joined Ten Foot Pole and later started the band Pulley?

18. Who was the welterweight champion of the world from 1925 to 1927?

19. How old was Mark Spitz when he set his first world record?

Mark Spitz

20. Who was the NFL's first great passing quarterback and first athletic director of Brandeis University?

21. What quarterback spent 3 years on the bench of the Miami Dolphins, but was never given a chance to play in a game?

22. At what university did Jeff Halpern play ice hockey?

23.   What basketball coach has coached in both the NBA and the WNBA?

24.   Who was the first Jewish World Champion chess player?

25.   Who is Russian figure skating star Irina Slutskaya's favorite author?

26.   What Major League baseball owner holds the record for hiring and firing the most field managers?

27.   What Jewish swimmer helped to popularize the butterfly stroke in the early 1930's?

28.   What drag racer set a speed record of one mile in 4.477 seconds?

29.   Which Jewish pitcher did baseball great Wade Boggs say gave him the most trouble as a batter?

30.   What world champion boxer fought three matches in a single day?

31.   What famous early basketball player became the youngest college coach in the country when he was appointed head coach at CCNY?

32.   What is the only Major League ballpark that serves glatt kosher hot-dogs?

33.   What position did collegiate football star Aaron Rosenberg play?

34.   What boxing champion was involved in the infamous "Black Sox" scandal?

35.   What basketball player served on the NBA championship winning Rochester Royals of 1951?

36.   What American Jew won the gold medals for the 5,000 meters and 10,000 meters speed skating contests in the 1932 winter Olympics at Lake Placid?

37.   What Jewish pitcher was the star of the Saint Louis Browns from 1903 to 1912?

38.   What English boxer is credited with introducing the upper cut?

39.   Who was the first Jewish tennis player to win the Wimbledon championship?

40.   Collegiate football star Fred Sington made his mark in what professional sport at the major league level?

Fred Sington

41.   Which Jewish basketball player was responsible for organizing and coaching the team that won the Inter-Allied Games championships, which took place in Paris in 1919?

42.   What Russian born American jumper brought home gold medals for the U.S. in three different Olympics, including the unofficial one of 1906?

43.   Who is considered the first Jewish boxer to fight for the Heavyweight Championship of the World title under the modern rules of the Marquis of Queensberry?

44.   What Jewish pitcher was born with two club feet?

45.   What Jewish hockey player was a member of three Stanley Cup winning teams?

46.   What baseball player was known as "SuperJew?"

47.   Swimmer Lenny Krayzelburg brought home gold medals with what stroke?

48.   How did Jack "Kid" Berg start as a boxer?

49.   What Jewish player was part of England's only team to win the Soccer World Cup?

50. What Jewish baseball player acted the part of Pete in John Wayne's 1960 western epic, *The Alamo*?

51. What team did tackle Harris Barton play for?

52. In what weight division did Maxie Rosenbloom fight?

53. How old was Olympic runner Abel Kiviat at the time of his death?

54. What Jewish baseball player holds the record of 9 homeruns in one week?

55. What cricket player scored over 175 centuries in his career, the latest scored at the age of 76?

56. What was remarkable about the birth of Mark Spitz, on February 10, 1950, that might have signaled to his parents his future achievements in swimming?

57. Which Jewish basketball player's father is a famous African-American author?

58. What hand did Sandy Koufax pitch with?

59. What golfer won the 1995 U.S. Open?

60. What Jewish boxer won the Olympic gold medal in the featherweight category in 1924?

61. Who was the youngest tennis player ever to win a Grand Prix title?

62. What Jewish jockey won 388 races in 1906, a record that stood until 1950?

63. What Jewish baseball player has the reputation as the greatest fungo batter of all time?

64. What Jewish speed skater won 2 gold medals in the 1932 Winter Olympics held in Lake Placid, NY?

65. Hitler passed special laws to prevent a particular German tennis player from representing Germany in the Stanley Cup Competition. Who was this tennis player?

66. What Jewish pitcher was a pioneer in the early year's of softball and helped to popularize the game at the Chicago World's Fair of 1933?

67. The racing career of what Jewish Olympic track star from England inspired the 1981 movie *Chariots of Fire*, directed by Hugh Hudson, with memorable music by Vangelis?

68. What Jewish boxer holds the record for the most boxing matches fought in a lifetime?

69. What Jewish NFL player had a concurrent career as professional wrestler during the off season?

70. Name 4 outstanding Jewish U.S. bowlers.

71. What quarterback appeared in 4 games for the Miami Dolphins in 2001-03 and shared the quarterback responsibilities with Jay Fiedler?

72. What Jewish woman fencer is sometimes regarded as the greatest woman fencer of all time and what country did she represent at the Olympics?

73. What Jewish boxer had a second career as a dentist?

74. Who was the star of the women's gymnastics team of the 1996 Olympics?

75. What Jewish NBA player retired with 19,249 points scored during his career, at that time the all-time record?

76. Who was the first Jewish manager of a Major League baseball team?

77. What two Jewish athletes represented Germany in the 1936 ("Hitler") Olympics?

78. Name a kicker on four different NFL teams over four years with a kicking percentage of 96%.

79. What position did Barry Latman play in Major League baseball?

80. What Jewish Hockey coach and team manager led the Montreal Canadiens to the Stanley Cup in 1930 and 1931?

81. What Jewish boxer was matched against featherweight Babe Herman in an epic series of 6 matches?

82. What Jewish hockey player was known as "Mine Boy?"

83. How many world records did Mark Spitz set or match in his swimming career?

84. Who was the first NFL quarterback to throw 7 touchdown passes in one game?

85. Boxer Joe Choynkski fought a series of famous bouts with a fellow San Franciscan and future heavyweight champion. Who was that champ?

86. Who was the latest Jewish pitcher to win the Cy Young Award?

87. What jockey from the early part of the twentieth century was known as the "King of the Derbies"?

88. What Jewish fullback-line backer played with the Detroit Lions in 1942?

89. What Jewish billiard player was the champion of England from 1931 to 1934?

90. How many Super Bowls did the Pittsburgh Steelers win during Randy Grossman's eight years with the team?

Randy Grossman

91. What Jewish Major League baseball player also had a career in the NFL?

92. Who were the earliest known Jewish boxers?

93. What athlete won 9 national titles in women's 8-pound shot put?

94. What future rabbi participated in the first football game ever played at the University of Pennsylvania?

95. What race car driver was heir to the Revlon Cosmetics Company?

96. Who was the first Jewish boxing champion born in North Africa?

97. Who was the only Jewish member of the 1969 "Miracle" Mets?

98. Which race of the famous Triple Crown of horse racing is named in honor of a Jewish financier and horseman?

99. What football coach of Stanford University resigned in1950, "because of his disgust over the practices used to recruit high school kids?"

KID BERG

100. Victor Hershkowitz is considered perhaps the greatest player ever to participate in what sport?

101. Why did gangster "Legs" Diamond try to have Jack "Kid" Berg bumped off?

102. What all-Jewish soccer team were the Austrian national champions?

103. What former Jewish cricket player from South Africa currently head's the Cricket World Cup organization?

104. What Jewish player has played more and scored more goals than any other Jewish player in the NHL?

105. Which college football star was named for a racehorse?

106. Who was the first Jewish baseball player to be inducted into Baseball's Hall of Fame?

107. For how many years did Abe Attell hold the featherweight title?

108. Who came to fame as a member and coach of the Philadelphia Sphas, the all-Jewish basketball team that would win four national titles, then later became one of the founders of the NBA. He also owned and coached the Philadelphia Warriors, now the San Francisco Warriors.

109. Who was the first Jew to ever play football (the American game)?

110. What Phillies outfielder batted .324 in 1939?

111. What Jewish runner at one time or another held every American distance record from 50 yards to 1 mile?

112. What was the last brother battery in baseball history and when did they last appear together?

113. Who was the only full-blooded Jewish boxer to compete for the Heavyweight title in modern times?

114. What Jewish athlete has the most Olympic medals?

115. Who was the first Jewish player in the National Hockey League?

116. Who pitched the first Major League no-hitter on the West Coast?

ABE ATTELL

117. What Jewish woman won more Olympic medals than any other?

118. What three Jewish coaches are members of the Pro Football Hall of Fame in Canton, Ohio?

119. What Jewish boxer once acted as a bodyguard for English fascist Oswald Mosley?

120. Name a notable Jewish matador?

121. What Jewish boxer was known as "the Ghetto Wizard?"

122. What long time Jewish catcher had a second career as a spy for the OSS (the predecessor of the CIA)?

123. Name three greatest Jewish male fencers from Hungary from the period before the First World War.

124. The goal-tending rule in basketball was created to thwart the style of play of what Jewish player?

125. The movie *Monkey on My Back* purports to tell the life story of what Jewish boxer?

126. Who first proposed using Jackie Robinson to break baseball's color line?

127. What football tackle won the nickname of the "intellectual assassin"?

128. Who was the last Jewish world champion boxer to capture the title from another Jewish boxer?

129. What is the athlete born with the name Sandford Braun most famous for?

130. What Jewish boxing champion from England was known as the "Aldgate Sphinx" from his place of birth and his calm demeanor in the ring?

131. Who was the youngest tennis player ever to win at Wimbledon?

132. What Jewish baseball player had the longest career in the entire history of organized baseball?

133. What Light-Heavyweight champion of the world was born Beryl Lebrowitz?

134. What athlete was named as "Canada's Female Athlete of the Half Century" in 1950?

135. Who was the first Jewish umpire?

136. Who are the earliest known Jewish basketball players?

137. Ben Cohen, nephew of George Cohen, star of England's 1966 World Cup winning team, is himself a star in another sport. What sport is it?

138. What was welterweight boxer Harry Lewis's favorite defensive trick?

139. Who was the first Jewish baseball player to hit four home runs in four consecutive at-bats, over 2 days?

140. What Jewish basketball player appeared in the most NBA games?

141. What Israeli was the first to become a sports star at the highest level of league play in another country?

142. What coach won the most games in the history of the Buffalo Bills Football team?

143. What Russian gymnast won 7 medals at the 1952 Helsinki Olympics?

144. Name two well known "Irish" boxers who were really Jewish.

145. Who was the Jewish owner of the 2002 Super Bowl-winning New England Patriots?

146. What leader of the 1960's Peace Movement was the captain of the Brandeis University tennis team?

147. What Jewish catcher hit for "the Cycle" in a Giant's victory over the Pirates on June 15, 1940?

148.   What was basketball player Max Zaslofsky's signature move?

149.   How did Jewish female figure skaters fare in the individual program in the 2002 Winter Olympics?

150.   What was Israel's first soccer victory in international competition?

151.   What was the nickname of Jewish football star Marshall Goldberg?

152.   Who was the only quarterback to have lead the NFL in both rushing touchdowns and touchdown passes in the same year and what year did this take place?

153.   What Jewish professional boxer with 30 matches to his credit became famous as an associate and sometimes bodyguard of gangster Benjamin "Bugsy" Siegel?

154.   What baseball manager popularized the "Ted William Shift"?

155.   Who are the three Jewish baseball players who had heart attacks while participating on the diamond and died shortly thereafter?

Marshall Goldberg

156.   When the Israel soccer team was still known as the Palestine Football Association, what was their first game in World Cup Competition?

157.   Who was the first Jewish baseball player to hit four home runs in the same game?

158.   What Jewish baseball player was known as "the Rabbi of Swat?"

159.   What Jewish pitcher was known in his lifetime as "the Yiddish Curver?"

160. What university did Harris Barton, National Football League tackle, attend?

161. What ice skater is credited with popularizing the sport in North America?

162. Who were the two finest Jewish jockeys in the period following the Second World War?

163. What Jewish Formula One racecar driver from South Africa won the World Championship in 1979?

164. What three Jewish baseball players refused to play on Yom Kippur?

165. What Jewish quarterback was the first great master of the "T" formation in the NFL?

166. What famous songwriter appeared in four Pacific Coast League baseball games during the 1950's?

167. What African American linebacker for the New England Patriots converted to Judaism?

168. What team did Sandy Koufax defeat in his one perfect game?

169. What Jewish football player threw the first touchdown pass in an NFL championship game?

170. What was the birthplace of Jack "Kid" Berg?

171. What is right fielder Shawn Green's favorite book?

172. How many Jewish athletes won medals in the first modern Olympics held at Athens in 1896?

173. Who was the last Jewish world champion boxing champion of the "Golden Age of Jewish Boxing?"

174. What is outfielder Gabe Kapler's favorite breakfast?

175. Who was the first Jewish Olympian to win a gold medal in boxing?

176. What Major League pitcher was once arrested and imprisoned on the request of the manager of his own team for giving up four consecutive walks?

177. What was football player Joseph Alexander's second career?

178. What is the favorite dish of Chinese food enthusiast Arnold "Red" Auerbach?

179. Who was the first person ever to swim across the 30½ mile wide Lake Baikal in Siberia?

Shawn Green (# 171)

180. How long was Benny Leonard lightweight champion of the world?

181. What Jewish quarterback led the University of Michigan team that featured future president Gerald Ford?

182. What was the oldest Jewish sports club in Western Europe?

183. What was the oldest Jewish sports club in Eastern Europe?

184. What town in Texas was the home of baseball player Andy Cohen?

185. Who was the first woman bowler to bowl 3 sanctioned 300 (perfect) games?

Benny Leonard

186. What American born basketball player was the captain of Maccabi Tel Aviv in 1977 and led the team to victory for the European Champions' Cup?

187. What golfer won the 1980 U.S. Woman's Open?

188. What world record did Jewish boxer Nick Antonelli set on July 26, 1926?

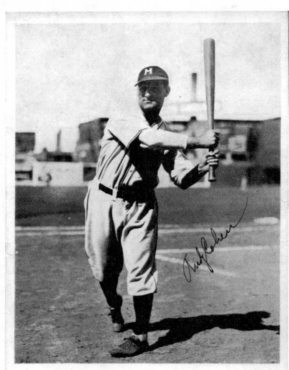
Andy Cohen (#184)

189. What two Jewish sluggers tied the Major League record by hitting 4 grand slam home runs in a single season and did it in consecutive years?

190. What two basketball players were known as the "Heavenly Twins"?

191. What Jewish football player holds the NFL record for highest average yardage in a season (for a qualified player)?

192. What Jewish boxing world champion would never fight on any Jewish holiday?

193. What Jewish basketball player was chosen second overall in the 1969 NBA draft?

194. What Jewish baseball player set a new Major League record of 7 home runs in three games?

195. In 1955, Topps Card Co. honored the 100 greatest collegiate football players of alltime with their All-American set. How many of these players were Jewish? (See question # 197)

196. What former Jewish boxer served as referee in the Rocky Marciano-Joe Louis fight?

197. Football great Aaron Rosenberg became a Hollywood producer. Can you name one of the films he produced?

198. What is the international competition for Jewish athletes that started in 1932 and is held every four years in Israel?

199. What outstanding woman basketball player came out of retirement to play for the WNBA during its debut year?

200. What Jewish boxer was known as the "Jewel of the Ghetto?"

201. What Jewish statistician is a full-fledged member of one of the major sports halls of fame and what sport does he represent?

AARON ROSENBERG Guard

202. What longtime catcher was awarded the Medal of Freedom?

203. What boxer starred in the 1933 English feature film *Money Talks*?

204. What Jewish baseball player was the first designated hitter (DH) in the Major Leagues (American League)?

205. What Jewish NBA player was married to Olympic diver Wendy Lucero?

206. Who was the first Jewish boxing champion, and, indeed, the first Jewish champion of any sport?

207. What Jewish baseball player and club executive first proposed inter-league play?

208. What Polish runner won medals in 4 consecutive Olympic games?

209. What Jewish NBA player has been wheelchair bound since 1987, when he underwent surgery for a spinal tumor?

210. What weight class is boxer "Dangerous" Dana Rosenblatt?

211. What former Jewish football player for its varsity team was named as Harvard's first official football coach?

212. What Jewish high school basketball player became known as the "Jewish Michael Jordan?"

213. In March, 1891, what weightlifter won the first World Championship ever in this sport?

214. What Jewish baseball player is tied for fourth on the list of the most home runs for a rookie with Albert Pujols?

215. Who was the first non-Jewish heavyweight boxing champion of the world who had a Jewish wife?

216. What Jewish ice hockey player led the Russian Hockey League in scoring in the 1990-91 season?

217. What Jewish baseball player tied the minor league record of reaching base in consecutive games?

218. Who was the shortest man ever to play in the National Football League?

219. What Jewish tennis player from Hungary won the French Women's Singles title in 1958?

220. What Jewish basketball star scored the first basket ever in the history of the National Basketball Association?

221. Who was the Hungarian ice hockey star who became the Swedish national tennis champion in 1942?

222. Who was the last man to ever pitch at Philadelphia's Veteran Stadium on September 28, 2003, the second day of Rosh Hashanah, 5764?

223. Who is the only Jewish athlete who was a known survivor of a Nazi concentration camp to participate in the Olympic games?

224. What college basketball player still holds the record of 34 rebounds in a single game during the NCAA playoffs, a record set in the late 1950's?

225. What does catcher Mike Lieberthal eat for lunch during the playing season?

226. What basketball coach is immortalized in a life-sized statue of himself sitting on a bench near Boston's Faneuil Hall Marketplace?

227. What was the first important book in English on the subject of the present volume, Jewish athletes?

ANSWERS

1. *Sunshine*. This Hungarian film (1999) was directed and co-written by Istvan Szabo. The other author was Israel Horovitz. The film also borrowed details from the life of the Jewish Olympic medallist Attila Petschauer, who brought two gold medals and one silver home to Hungary. Both Kabos and Petschauer died in the Holocaust, as did Adam Sors, the character in Sunshine who they inspired.

2. Under her mattress.

3. Joel Stransky.

4. Arie Selinger.

5. Longtime Phillies catcher Mike Lieberthal.

6. Harry Newman of the University of Michigan.

7. Jack "Kid" Berg. The opera is being composed by Howard Frederics, with a libretto by Paul Bentley. Frederics is a distant cousin of the late boxer, their grandfathers having been brothers.

Mike Lieberthal

8. Surfing. Brad often surfs with fellow baseball players Ryan Klesko and Trevor Hoffman.

9. Al Rosen.

10. Gordon "Jack" Bloomfield.

11. Phil King, of Princeton University, who was picked in 1890 for only the second All-American team chosen.

Kid Berg

Jack Bloomfield

12. Ken Holtzman. When Holtzman was hailed by the press as a "New Koufax," Koufax replied that he was "the first Kenny Holtzman."

13. Barney Ross, who was awarded the Silver Star for "Conspicuous Gallantry." However, poor medical treatment of Barney's wounds led him to become addicted to drugs. Only after the collapse of his marriage and self-commitment to an Army medical facility, did Barney overcome his habit.

BARNEY ROSS

14. Sam Mayer, brother of pitcher Erskine Mayer.

15. Notre Dame.

16. John Hertz, founder of the Yellow Cab Company and Hertz Rent-a-Car, owned Reigh Count, the 1928 winner, Count Fleet, which won not only the Derby, but took the entire Triple Crown in 1943, and Count Turf, the 1951 winner.

17. Scott Radinsky.

18. Charlie Phil Rosenberg.

19. Mark was 17 when in June, 1967 he set a record for the 400 meter freestyle of 4 minutes, 10 and 6/10 seconds. This meet was held in California.

20. Benny Friedman.

21. Pete Woods.

22. Princeton.

23. Ron Rothstein.

Charlie "Phil" Rosenberg
99   Bantam Champion

24. Wilhelm Steinitz who won the title in 1866 by defeating Adolf Anderssen. Steinitz held the title until 1894 when he was defeated by Emanuel Lasker, another great Jewish champion.

25. Russian novelist Mikhail Bulgakov (1891-1940). Her favorite book by Bulgakov is *The Master and Margarita*.

26. Between 1895 and 1902, Andrew Freedman, the Jewish owner of the New York Giants, hired and fired sixteen managers, a record never matched--even by George Steinbrenner.

27. Paul B. Friesel, whose friend invented this style of breaststroke. Friesel claimed to have coined the name.

28. Kenny Bernstein.

29. Scott Radinsky, along with Randy Johnson and Tony Fossas, gave Wade the most trouble.

30. "Battling" Levinsky.

31. Nat Holman.

32. Baltimore's Camden Yards.

33. Running guard.

34. Abe Attell.

35. Red Holzman.

36. Irving Jaffee.

37. Barney Pelty.

Barney Pelty

38. "Dutch" Sam Elias.

39. Richard "Dick" Savitt, of the United States, won the Men's singles title in 1951.

40. Baseball.

41. Marty Friedman, who is credited with helping to introduce the game overseas.

42. Myer Prinstein.

43. Joseph "Jewey" Smith, who challenged Tommy Burns on April 18, 1908 in Paris and was knocked out in five rounds.

44. Larry Sherry.

45. Alex Levinsky played on the 1931-32 and 1932-33 Toronto Maple Leafs and on the 1937-38 Chicago Black Hawks.

46. Mike Epstein.

47. The back stroke.

48. Jack, as a kid, was the doorkeeper at a gym in London. When a promising contender failed to give young Jack his expected tip for opening the door, Jack knocked him out. Jack was immediately taken under the wing of one of the trainers there and began his climb.

49. George Cohen was part of England's 1966 World Cup team.

50. Cy Malis.

51. The San Francisco 49'ers.

52. Maxie was a light heavyweight and held the world title in that division from 1930 to 1934.

53. 99.

54. Shawn Green.

55. Jack Hyams.

George Cohen

56.　　Mark was born with webbed feet.

57.　　Jamila Wideman of the WNBA is the daughter of John Edgar Wideman. Her mother is Jewish.

58.　　The left.

59.　　Corey Pavin.

60.　　Jackie Fields, who was only 16 at the time.

61.　　Aaron Krickstein, who at 16 years, 2 months, won the Tel Aviv Grand Prix in 1983.

62.　　Walter Miller.

63.　　Jimmie Reese, longtime coach (for fielding practice) of the California Angels.

64.　　Irving Jaffe (1906-1981).

65.　　Daniel Prenn.

66.　　Harry "Coon" Rosen.

67.　　Harold M. Abrahams (1899-1978).

Jimmie Reese

68.　　Abe "the Newsboy" Hollandersky (1887-1966), who fought 1309 times between 1905 and 1918.

69.　　Sid Youngelman. Bill Goldberg's career as wrestler was not concurrent, but occurred after his retirement from football.

70.　　The most notable are Barry Asher, Marshall Holman, Mark Roth, and Sylvia Wene Martin.

71.　　Sage Rosenfels.

72. Ilona Schacherer-Elek (1907-1988) won the gold medal for Hungary in the 1936 Olympics in individual foils. Then, 12 years later, she repeated this accomplishment in the 1948 Olympics. Four years later, in 1952, she almost repeated again, but had to settle for the silver, after losing a play-off, following a tie for first. Ilona was world foil champion in 1934, 1935, and 1951.

73. Lightweight Leach Cross (1886-1957), known as a dentist under his real name, Dr. Louis C. Wallach.

Leach Cross

74. Kerri Strug.

75. Dolph Schayes.

76. Lipman Pike in 1871.

77. Helene Mayer (1910-1953) and Margarethe ("Gretel") Bergmann (born 1914). Helene took the silver medal in individual foils. Gretel, though invited by the German government to participate in the Olympics, to avoid an American boycott, was, at the last minute, refused permission to participate in the broad jump. Both girls left Germany and settled in the U.S. In 1937, Gretel took the American women's national titles in broad jump and shot put. In the U.S., she married a German-Jewish runner, Bruno Lambert.

78. Booth Lusteg.

79. Right-handed pitcher.

80. Cecil Hart. Cecil was a direct descendant of Aaron Hart, the first Jew to settle in Canada. Cecil's father, Dr. David Hart, donated the NHL MVP award, the Hart Trophy.

81. Louis "Kid" Kaplan.

82. Alex Levinsky, who played with the NHL from 1930 to 1939.

83. 32.

84. Sid Luckman, in 1943.

85. "Gentleman" Jim Corbett.

86. Steve Stone in 1980.

87. Georges Stern.

88. Harry Seltzer (1919-1990). Harry's widow provided me with this information. Harry had attended and played for Charleston College, Charleston, WV.

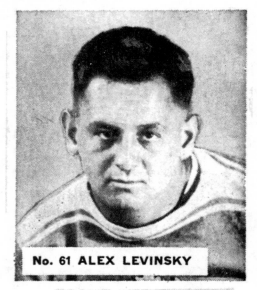

No. 61 ALEX LEVINSKY

89. Sydney Lee. Lee was also world's amateur champion in 1933.

90. Four.

91. Jim Levey. After his time with the St. Louis Browns, Jim played with the Pittsburgh Pirates Football Team from 1935 to 1936.

92. In 1768, according to Pierce Egan, Bill Darts, an English boxer, defeated a Jewish boxer named Tom Jachau. Nothing else is known about Jachau. In 1769, the English boxer Jack Lamb, beat "two Jews, Abraham da Costa in Moorfields, and Mousha at Stepney," according to the 1812 *Pancratia*. Other sources indicate that Mousha was a Turkish Jew. Daniel Mendoza, the first Jewish boxer to hold a title, was declared champion of the British Isles in 1792.

93. Lillian Copeland.

94. Emil G. Hirsch played in the first game at Penn on December 9, 1871. He went on to become one of the best known Reformed rabbis of his generation. His father had been Grand Rabbi of Luxembourg.

95. Peter Revson.

96.   Robert Cohen.

97.   Art Shamsky.

98.   The Belmont Stakes is named in honor of August Belmont Sr. Belmont Park was built by August Jr. and was also named in honor of the senior Belmont.

99.   "Marchy" Schwartz

100.   Handball (American). Jewish players have often dominated this sport. The European Handball is a completely different sport.

101.   Jack tried romancing Legs' girlfriend Kiki Roberts. That evening Legs sent gunmen to the Kid's hotel suit. They found the Kid's brother and some friends playing cards in the front room. While they were busy roughing up this party, the Kid escaped out the window and down the fire escape.

102.   Hakoah-Vienna, in 1924 to 1926 and 1928 to 1929. The Hakoah team had a worldwide reputation and paid visits to the United States in 1926-27 and Palestine in 1923-24.

103.   Ali Bacher.

104.   Mathieu Schneider.

105.   Marchmont Schwartz, who was generally known by his nickname "Marchy."

Mathieu Schneider

106.   Hank Greenberg.

107.   For more than eleven years, from October 20, 1901 to February 22, 1912. Abe held his world title longer than any other Jewish world champion did.

108.   Eddie Gottlieb (1898-1979).

109. Moses Henry Epstein played in the third ever football game on November 12, 1870. This game was between Columbia and Rutgers Universities, with Rutgers winning 6-3. Moses Epstein played for Columbia and graduated from the university in 1871. Rutgers had played against Princeton in the first ever football game in 1869.

110. Morrie Arnovich.

111. Lawrence E. Myers (1858-1889). Myers is considered by most critics to have been the greatest runner of the nineteenth century.

112. Larry and Norm Sherry, who last appeared together in 1962.

113. Abe Simon challenged Joe Louis on two occasions in the early 1940's. Simon was knocked out in both matches. Heavyweight champion Max Baer, although he fought with a Magen David on his trunks, had only a single Jewish grandparent, his paternal grandmother.

114. Mark Spitz, with 9 gold, 1 silver, and 1 bronze.

115. Sam Rothschild with the Montreal Maroons, starting in 1924.

116. Bo Belinsky, pitching for the Los Angeles Angels against the Baltimore Orioles on May 5, 1962.

117. Agnes Keleti, of Hungary, who won 10 Olympic medals, including 5 gold.

118. Al Davis, Sid Gillman, and Marv Levy.

119. Ted "Kid" Lewis. According to Lewis's son, Ted was naïve about Mosley's anti-Semitism. When he did become aware of Mosley's program, he confronted the want-to-be dictator and knocked him down and then beat up a group of other bodyguards. Ted's son was a witness to and participant in this fray.

Sammy Rothschild   19

120. Sidney Franklin is the only correct answer to this question.

121. Benny Leonard.

122. Moe Berg. However, some might argue this was hardly Moe's second profession, as he already had careers before joining the OSS as a businessman, lawyer, linguist, coach, radio personality, author, raconteur, and diplomat.

123. Dr. Jeno Fuchs, Endre Kabos, and Attila Petschauer.

124. Harry Boykoff.

125. Barney Ross. Ross felt the movie misrepresented his life and sued the production company, which settled the case out of court.

126. Isadore Muchnick, a Jewish Boston City Councilman. It was Muchnick's suggestion that ultimately inspired Branch Rickey.

127. Ron Mix.

128. Bob Olin, who took the light-heavy weight title from Max Rosenbloom in 1934.

129. Pitching. Sandford Braun is the birth name of Sandy Koufax.

130. Ted "Kid" Lewis.

131. Boris Becker, who won Wimbledon in 1985 at the age of 17. Boris also won Wimbledon in 1986 and 1989.

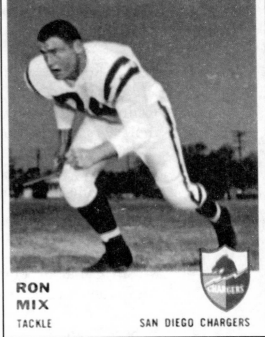

RON MIX
TACKLE   SAN DIEGO CHARGERS

132. Jimmie Reese, whose career spanned 77 years, from 1917, when he started as a minor league batboy, to 1994, when, at the time of his death, he was still serving as a coach for the California Angels. Jimmie spent only three years as a Major League player, but his playing career in the Pacific Coast League was a long and productive one.

133. Battling Levinsky.

134. Fanny "Bobbie" Rosenfeld.

135. Jacob Pike, who first served as a National Association umpire in 1875. Jacob's more famous brother, Lip, also served as an umpire.

136. F. P. Weil and Max Hess played for the Eastern District YMCA team of Brooklyn during the 1896-97 season.

137. Rugby.

138. He would allow his opponents to wear themselves out by punching him.

139. Shawn Green, on June 14 and 15, 2002. This tied a Major League record held by 21 other players. Remember, this was just a few weeks after Shawn had set a new Major League record of 7 home runs in three days.

140. Danny Schayes, with 1138 games.

141. Ronnie Rosenthal, who became a soccer star in Great Britain during the 1990's, playing for Liverpool and Totenham.

142. Marv Levy, with a record of 112-70 in the regular season and 11-8 in playoff games, during his more than 11 years with the Bills.

143. Maria Gorokhovskaya, who won 2 gold and 5 silver.

144. Mushy Callahan (born Vincent Morris Scheer) and Al McCoy (born Alexander Rudolph).

145. Robert Kraft.

146. Abbie Hoffman.

147. Harry Danning.

148. The one-handed push-shot.

149. Sarah Hughes (Jewish Mother) took the Gold Medal for the U.S.; Ilya Slutskaya (Jewish Father) took the Silver for Russia; and Sasha Cohen of the U.S. placed fourth.

150. A 5-1 victory over Turkey in 1950.

151. Biggie.

152. Benny Friedman in 1928.

153. Mickey Cohen.

154. Lou Boudreau.

155. Harry "Klondike" Kane suffered a heart attack in 1932, while serving as an umpire in a Pacific Coast League game in Portland, Oregon and died two days later. Herb Gorman collapsed on the field from a heart attack during a Pacific Coast League game in San Diego in 1952 and died shortly after. Sid Gordon died in 1975, after suffering a heart attack while playing in a softball game in New York's Central Park.

156. The Palestine team lost to Egypt 7-1 in 1934.

157. Shawn Green on May 23, 2002.

158. Mose Solomon.

159. Barney Pelty.

160. University of North Carolina, where Harris excelled both in football and academics.

161. Louis Rubinstein.

162. Walter Blum and Willie Harmatz.

Mose Solomon

163. Jody Sheckter.

164. Hank Greenberg in 1934, Sandy Koufax in 1965, and Shawn Green in 2001. These cases were well publicized. There may have been other instances where Jewish players quietly observed the holiday.

165. Sid Luckman.

166. Harry Ruby.

167. Andre Tippett.

Sandy Koufax

168. The Chicago Cubs, on September 9, 1965. This was Sandy's fourth and last no-hitter.

169. Harry Newman, whose 29 yard pass to Red Badgro in the 1933 NFL title game gave the Giants a temporary lead. However, they lost the game to the Bears, 23-21.

170. London.

171. *The Sirens of Titan* by Kurt Vonnegut.

172. Five. Alfred Flatow of Germany won three gold medals and one silver medal in gymnastics; his brother, Felix, won two gold medals in gymnastics; Alfred Hajos-Guttmann of Hungary won two gold medals in swimming; Dr. Paul Neumann of Austria won a gold medal in swimming; and Otto Herschmann of Austria won a bronze medal in swimming.

173. Alphonse Halimi.

174. A large array of fresh vegetables. Gabe has a reputation as a health food fanatic and body builder.

175. Samuel Berger (1884-1925) of the USA in the 1904 games. This was the first year that boxing was included as an Olympic event.

176. Sol Rogovin was arrested on November 17, 1947 while playing for Caracas in the Venezuelan Winter League.

177. Physician.

178. Shrimp and lobster sauce.

179. Ted Epstein, a lawyer from Denver, CO, who accomplished the deed in 15 hours, 59 minutes. Amazingly, Ted, at the time, in 1991, was 55 years of age. At about the same period, Ted completed a double iron-man triathlon (a 4.8 mile swim, a 224 mile bike ride, and a 52.4 mile run) in just 30 hours, 20 minutes.

180. Nine years, from 1917 to 1925.

181. Harry Newman.

Sol Rogovin

182. The Attila Jewish Gymnastics and Athletics Club of Groningen, Netherlands, founded on April 16, 1898. This club came into existence when a particularly talented Jewish athlete was refused membership in the local athletic club because the membership committee expressed fears that the club was becoming too Jewish. All the existing Jewish members resigned from the club and formed the Attila Club. The club was probably named for a famous Jewish strongman of the time, rather than for the Hunnish leader. This club continued to exist until November 1941, when the occupying German forces prohibited all Jewish sports clubs in the Netherlands. The second oldest Jewish sports club in Western Europe was the earliest such club in Germany, Bar Kochba of Berlin founded on October 22, 1898.

183. Technically, the first would be the Israelitischer Turnverein, for German and Austrian Jews only, founded in Istambul on January 7, 1895. However, Turkey is an Asian country, even if Istanbul is on the European side of the Bosporus. With no ambiguity, the first such club may be counted as the Club for Physical Education-Shimshon of Bulgaria, founded in 1897.

184. El Paso.

185. Sylvia Wene Martin.

186. Tal Brody.

187. Amy Alcott.

188. Nick set a new record for the fastest knockout ever, just 5 seconds into the first round.

189. Sid Gordon did it in 1950 and Al Rosen did it in 1951.

190. Barney Sedran and Marty Friedman.

191. Herb Rich, who set the record in 1950 with 23 yards per game (total of 276 yards in 12 games.) As 1950 was Herb's rookie season, this is also the yardage record for a rookie player. Herb, a defensive back who played with Baltimore that year, played a total of 7 years with the NFL, including championship teams in 1951 (Los Angeles Rams) and 1956 (New York Giants). Herb had played college football with Vanderbilt.

192. Benny Leonard.

193. Neal Walk, who was chosen by the Phoenix Suns. The number one pick was Lew Alcindor (later Kareem Abdul-Jebber) who was taken by the Milwaukee Bucks. The rights to the number one pick had been decided by a coin toss.

HERB RICH
Ace Halfback
VANDERBILT U.

194. Shawn Green during the games of May 23, 24, and 25, 2002.

195. Six: Joe Alexander, Benny Friedman, Marshall Goldberg, Sid Luckman, Harry Newman, and Aaron Rosenberg.

196. Ruby Goldstein.

197. Among Rosenberg's best known films were *Tony Rome, Mutiny on the Bounty* (the 1962 Marlon Brando version,) *The Benny Goodman Story, To Hell and Back, All American*, and *The Glen Miller Story*.

198. The Macabbiah Games.

199. Nancy Lieberman-Cline.

200. Ruby Goldstein.

201. Harvey Pollack, of the 76ers, is a member of the Basketball Hall of Fame. Harvey is a pioneer in the field of basketball statistics.

202. Moe Berg was given this great honor for his espionage work during the Second World War.

203. Jack "Kid" Berg.

204. Ron Blomberg.

205. Dan Schayes.

206. Daniel Mendoza, recognized as the champion of the world from 1792 to 1795.

JACK (KID) BERG

207. Hank Greenberg.

208. Irina Kirszenstein-Szewinska. She is the only Olympic runner, male or female, to accomplish this.

209. Neal Walk, who has been an outstanding motivational speaker since his surgery.

210. Middleweight.

211. Lucius Littauer(1859-1944), who had played for Harvard as a lineman in 1875 and 1877. Before 1881, the Harvard football team was self-coached, with the team captain taking the greatest role. Littauer became the team's coach for the 1881 season and then retired to join his father's glove business. He became a millionaire in that business and eventually a great benefactor to his alma mater, endowing the Harvard Graduate School of Public Administration and the Professorship of Jewish Literature and Philosophy.

 # 209

212. Tamir Goodman, of Baltimore's Talmudical Academy averaged 35 points a game. After failing to find a modus vivendi within American colleges, the deeply religious Tamir, a member of Chabad Lubavitch, moved to Israel to play professional basketball there. He currently plays with Maccabi Givat Shmuel.

213. Edward Lawrence Levy (1851-1932) of England, who compet ed against weightlifters from Austria, Belgium, England, Germany, and Italy in a three day contest.

214. Al Rosen, who in 1950 knocked 37 homers.

Tamir Goodman

215. John C. "the Benicia Boy" Heenan, who claimed the American championship from 1859, fought the English champ, Tom Sayers, in 1860. The results of this fight were indecisive, but Sayers' subsequent retirement left the world title (which at that time consisted of the combined English and American titles) clear for Heenan until 1861. On September 3, 1859, Heenan had married the Jewish actress Adah Isaacs Menken. The details of Menken's birth are not clear, but she claimed to have had a Jewish father. In any case, on her second marriage, to musician Alexander Isaacs Menken, she converted to Judaism. Despite a number of subsequent marriages, she remained a faithful Jew until her death, in 1868.

216. Ramil Yuldashev, right winger for the Sokol Kiev team led the league in both points, 56, and goals, 36. He also was eighth in the league in assists, with 20. Ramil, who was born on May 9, 1961, started playing for Sokol Kiev in 1984. As of 2002, he was playing with the same team, which now plays within the Ukrainian and East European Leagues.

217. Kevin Youkilis, third baseman of the Pawtucket Red Sox, reached base in 71 consecutive games from May 19 to August 4, 2003.

218. Jack Shapiro, at 5"1' for the Staten Island Stapletons in 1929. Jack, a blocking back weighing only 119 pounds, played in only a single NFL game.

219. Susi Kormoczi.

220. Ossie Schectman of the New York Knicks scored the first basket in the very first official NBA game on November 1, 1946, between the Knicks and the Toronto Huskies. New York won the game, 68-66. Oscar "Ossie" Schectman had been a member of the Philadelphia Sphas from 1942 to 1946.

221. Laszlo Rona (born 1913), who played with the Hungarian ice hockey team in the 1936 Olympics. He left Hungary and played hockey in Switzerland, Finland, and Sweden. After the Second World War, he played hockey for the Paris Lions team, 1949-50.

222. Jason Marquis of the Atlanta Braves, who recorded the first save ever of his career.

223. Ben Helfgott (born 1929), originally of Poland, was captain of the English weightlifting teams in both the 1956 and 1960 Olympics.

224. Fred Cohen of Temple University.

225. A tuna fish sandwich. When questioned about the lack of variety in his diet, Mike insisted that he had a great deal of variety. Some days he had tuna with tomato, some days with lettuce, and some days with melted cheese. Some days Mike has white bread, some days he has rye, and other days whole wheat. Every day Mike has the same gallon of fruit shake (that includes a power bar) for dinner.

226. Arnold "Red" Auerbach, who sits holding his cigar and ready to jump up in the statue by sculpture Lloyd Lillie. The statue of the eternally vigilant and victorious Red has become a favorite tourist stop in Boston and his bronze knee is worn shiny by the rubs of visitors sitting down next to him.

#226. Red Auerbach

227. *The Jew in Sports* by Stanley B. Frank 1936. The other important early work is *The Jew in American Sports* by Harold U. Ribalow, which was first published in 1948 and has been reprinted and revised many times since. After that there appeared *Encyclopedia of Jews in Sports* by Bernard Postal, Jesse Silver, and Roy Silver, the most thorough study of the subject, published in 1965. Other important works include *Great Jews in Sports* by Robert Slater, first appearing in 1983; *The International Jewish Sport Hall of Fame* (later editions *Jewish Sports Legends*) by Joseph Siegman, first in 1992; and *Ellis Island to Ebbets Field* by Peter Levine of 1992, the most scholarly approach to the subject. Since 1997 there has appeared a regular journal on the topic, *Jewish Sports Review*, published by Shel Wallman and Ephraim Moxson.

Postscript

It was recently brought to my attention that the English soccer star, David Beckham (born 1975), has a Jewish grandparent. Joseph West, the father of David's mother, Sandra, was Jewish. David talks about his Jewish background in his autobiography *My World* (2001): "I've probably had more contact with Judaism than with any other religion...I used to wear the traditional Jewish skullcaps when I was younger, and I also went along to some Jewish weddings with my grandfather." David also describes going to synagogue on a number of occasions.

David's specialty is the free-kick. He developed one known around the world as the "Beckham," that appears to bend around the goal post. Sir Alex Ferguson, the manager of Manchester United, said of him, "David Beckham is Britain's finest striker of a football not because of God-given talent but because he practises with a relentless application that the vast majority of less gifted players wouldn't contemplate." Given David's achievements in soccer with Manchester United, the English National Team, which he captains, and Real Madrid, it is clear that he deserves to be included on my list of the greatest Jewish Sports Stars.

(Note: **Team Index** is on page 293 and **General Index** is on page 295.)

TEAM INDEX

INDEX

Recent Releases
(Order Form on last page)

S.P.i. BOOKS

"The Small Publishers...with BIG Books!"

SPI BOOKS JUDAICA–SPORTS / GIFT TITLES

Retail Price

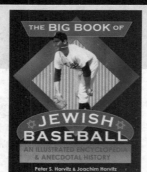

Amazon.com's #2 Selling Book in category: *"Jews In America"*!

THE BIG BOOK OF JEWISH BASEBALL:
An Anecdotal Encyclopedia
by Peter Horvitz & Joachim Horvitz

$19.95

The Baseball Bible Is Here! A lively and complete reference of the topic with comprehensive coverage of literally every Jew who has played in the Major Leagues—from Hall of Famers **Sandy Koufax**, **Hank Greenberg** and **Moe Berg** to players who spent only a day or two in the big leagues, to owners and managers. It's generously illustrated with baseball memorabilia & cards as well as many previously unpublished photos. For Ages 8 to Adult.

Soft • 8.5"x 11" • 200 B&W photos • 308 pgs • ISBN: 1-56171-973-0

THE JEWISH BASEBALL CARD SET:
8 Full Color Jewish Baseball Cards
by Joachim Horvitz & Peter Horvitz

$3.95

The first collection of Jewish Baseball Cards ever created! These collector's items feature the 8 top Jewish players, including: **Harry Danning, Jake Atz, Barney Pelty, Hank Greenberg, Lipman Pike, Jesse Levis, Andy Cohen** and **Moe Berg**

This is a limited edition of 1,000 sheets (with cards that are not cut out).
Coated Card Stock (printed on both sides) • 8.5"x 11" • 8 Color cards/per sheet

1 sheet = Retail Value: $3.95 • ISBN: 1-56171-905-6

THE INTERNATIONAL JEWISH SPORTS HALL OF FAME
by Joseph Siegman

$19.95

Details the accomplishments of "Jewish Sports Hall of Fame" members, packed with large action photos and little known Jewish Sports history from around the world, with the main focus on the U.S. This work covers all major Olympic Sports, even the Macabbiah Games held each year in Israel.

For ages 8 to Adult.

Hard • 8.5"x 11" • 100 B&W photos • 250 pgs • ISBN: 1-56171-028-8

THE JEWISH BOXERS' HALL OF FAME
by Ken Blady

$14.95

This one-of-a-kind Jewish sports book includes rare interviews, anecdotes, photos and records of past and current Jewish boxers. From the 1800's to the present, biographies of the great Jewish Boxers are featured here along with unique memorabilia of the sport.

For ages 8 to Adult.

Hard • 6"x 9" • Rare photos throughout • 336 pgs • ISBN: 0-93503-87-3

S.P.I Books • 99 Spring Street, 3rd FL • New York, NY 10012
Tel: (212) 431-5011 • Fax: (212) 431-8646 • E-mail: publicity@spibooks.com